Critical Responses to Kiran Desai

Edited by

Sunita Sinha
Bryan Reynolds

ATLANTIC
PUBLISHERS & DISTRIBUTORS (P) LTD

Published by

ATLANTIC

PUBLISHERS & DISTRIBUTORS (P) LTD

7/22, Ansari Road, Darya Ganj,
New Delhi-110002
Phones : +91-11-40775252, 23273880, 23275880, 23280451
Fax : +91-11-23285873
Web : www.atlanticbooks.com
E-mail : orders@atlanticbooks.com

Branch Office
5, Nallathambi Street, Wallajah Road,
Chennai-600002
Phones : +91-44-64611085, 32413319
E-mail : chennai@atlanticbooks.com

Printed in India at Glorious Printers, A-13, D.S.I.D.C.,
Jhilmil Industrial Area, Delhi-110095

For my mother, Dr. Manju Rani Sinha,
Ex-Principal, Head, Department of English,
Magadh Mahila College,
Patna University.

–Sunita Sinha

Acknowledgements

First and foremost, I would like to express my gratitude to Bryan Reynolds, Professor & Head of Doctoral Studies, Department of Drama, Claire Trevor School of the Arts, University of California, Irvine for his valuable collaboration. I met him at the IVth World Shakespeare Conference of the Shakespeare Society of Eastern India, Calcutta, India, and after that the concept of co-editing a book came to my mind and the prestigious Man Booker Prize Winner for 2006, Kiran Desai seemed the most appropriate subject. It was extremely gracious of a scholar of Bryan Reynold's stature to accept the proposal and find time to see this project through. A wonderful person and a great co-editor, Bryan made editing simple, easy and absolutely delightful. For his collaboration, I am deeply indebted to him. Secondly, I want to extend my thanks to my family, colleagues and the contributors for providing support, talking things over, offering comments, assisting in the editing, and seeing me through this book. I also wish to express my gratitude to Dr. K.R. Gupta, Honorary Advisor, Atlantic Publishers & Distributors (P) Ltd., for the confidence evinced in me and for seeing the book through the press.

Sunita Sinha

I am grateful to many people for supporting this project. I am especially indebted to my family, friends, colleagues at the University of California, Irvine, and fellow members of the University of California Multi-Campus Research Group on International Performance and Culture for continually encouraging me to produce art and scholarship that strive to contribute valuably to the world. This collection on the extraordinary work of Kiran Desai has such aspirations. In her novels, Desai productively engages with some of the most important issues facing the world today, and, in different ways, the essays collected here collaborate in this enterprise through the dynamic interfaces of literary-cultural criticism. For the inspiration to imagine this book, I want to thank Kiran Desai. For the collaborative energy necessary to produce the book, I am most grateful to my friend and co-editor, Sunita Sinha. It is Sunita's own remarkable dynamism that most fuelled this project from its inception. Finally, I am indebted to Dr. K.R. Gupta for sharing our enthusiasm for *Critical Responses to Kiran Desai*.

Bryan Reynolds

Preface

The opportunity to co-edit the first collection of essays on the work of Kiran Desai is both a privilege and an honor for which we are deeply grateful. The various subject matters of Desai's two novels, *Hullabaloo in the Guava Orchard* (1998) and *The Inheritance of Loss* (2006), extend far beyond topics characteristic of postcolonial literature. This is especially the case for *The Inheritance of Loss*, which treats with tremendous insight, sensitivity, and often piercing irony, topical issues related to politics and terrorism as well as immigration, identity-formation, and subjectivity, and the nationalist, gender, cultural, ethnic, and class differences that inform these processes. *Hullabaloo in the Guava Orchard* is no less ingenious in its treatment of identity and subjectivity and the myth-making or mythical systems on which they are normally based. Accordingly, the essays collected here span a wide range of critical approaches, from psychoanalytic to reader-response to eco-criticism. They also span several areas of concern and inquiry, such as subjectivation, colonialization, representation, diaspora, globalization, and socio-economics. Our purpose in this preface, however, is not to summarize or critically engage with the essays, but rather to comment briefly on the phenomenon that Kiran Desai continues to become.

Desai occupies what Bryan Reynolds refers to as an "articulatory space," a term which combines the concepts "articulation," meaning a coming-together of disparate elements, and "space," meaning a dimension or dimensions of any kind, which always includes the dimension of "time," that can be occupied by anything or something in particular.[1] Kiran Desai played an instrumental role in producing what we want to call "Kiran-Desaispace." Others who have significantly contributed to Kiran-Desaispace include her publishers, fans, and adversaries, the organizations that have given her awards, such as the Betty Trask Award, the Man Booker Prize, and the National Book Critics Circle Fiction Award, the influential articulatory spaces that intersect with hers, such as, broadly, postcolonial, cultural, and gender studies spaces, and, more specifically, ex-patriot-Indianspace, Indiannovelistspace, and Anita-Desaispace, the latter of which relates to her mother, a famous, award-winning writer. All of these forces and intersecting articulatory spaces and the discourses that fuel them work to sustain and expand Kiran-Desaispace. As Reynolds writes elsewhere, "Articulatory spaces are fluid multifaceted, primarily abstract, spatiotemporal realms in which ideational streams, discourses, and performances negotiate and aggregate meanings, redefine their trajectories, boundaries, and strategies, while orbiting and informing subjects of critical speculation. Articulatory spaces furnish connectivity to otherwise disparate elements, generating clusters of coherence out of multiple ideas, events, feelings, subjects, and objects. Anything that can be thought of can have an articulatory space."[2] Thus, consider the present collection, given the number of esteemed scholars who have contributed to this volume and have put much thought and energy into the work of Desai, and the exceptionally high-quality and controversial nature of many of the essays, the collection is not only itself a product of the fast-developing Kiran-Desaispace, but it may also play a key role in its dissemination and permeation throughout the academic institutions that engage the collection in its courses and dialogues as well as throughout the proliferating body of literary and cultural criticism devoted partially or entirely to the work of Kiran Desai.

Desai possesses what Reynolds refers to as "affective presence," the combined material, conceptual, emotional, ideological, and imaginary facets of an object, subject, event, or idea, with a level of intensity high enough to generate an articulatory space; in this case, associated specifically with her in conjunction with the subject matters of her work. In effect, that is, because of her extraordinary affective presence, as the voices of many scholars—from three continents—contributing to this collection testify, Desai has achieved significant "emulative authority." Someone has emulative authority when they are so remarkable in the eyes of other people that they want to become like him or her. Such authority inspires people to emulate him or her willfully, but it also inspires people to "come-to-be" like him or her unwittingly, as often occurs through sustained or intense association with a group of others: the group itself has affective presence or someone in the group possesses greater emulative authority than the others within the group, and this dynamic is typically under continuous negotiation, whether consciously or unconsciously. Hence, emulative authority develops out of profound engagements with specific identity-influencing forces.

An example of the force of emulative authority is that Kiran Desai chose, like her mother, to become a novelist. Other examples, immediately accessible to the reader, can be found in the affiliations with and disassociations from Kiran Desai articulated by the authors of the essays collected here. Together, as an activity emergent from the articulatory space of postcolonial studies, this collection hopes to achieve emulative authority as a conductor of critical discourses within the ebb and flow of Kiran-Desaispace—the now unavoidable interface—unavoidable because Desai is world-famous, of one of the most inspiring writers of the 21st century.

Sunita Sinha
Bryan Reynolds

NOTES

1. For more on "articulatory space" and the other terms quoted below (except "Kiran-Desaispace" which we are introducing here), see Bryan Reynolds, *Becoming Criminal: Transversal Performance and Cultural Dissidence in Early Modern England* (Baltimore: Johns Hopkins University Press, 2002); *Performing Transversally: Reimagining Shakespeare and the Critical Future* (New York: Palgrave Macmillan, 2003); *Transversal Enterprises in the Drama of Shakespeare and His Contemporaries: Fugitive Explorations* (London: Palgrave Macmillan, 2006); and *Transversal Subjects: From Montaigne to Deleuze after Derrida* (London: Palgrave Macmillan, 2008).
2. Reynolds, *Transversal Subjects: From Montaigne to Deleuze after Derrida*, 272-73.

Contents

Introduction

With Kiran Desai, a literary tradition is reborn. It is a literary inheritance Kiran Desai is proud to acknowledge: "To my mother I owe a debt so profound." As might be expected from the rich output of her cultural background, Kiran Desai has proved her literary legacy in formidable terms. With storytelling in her blood, Kiran Desai, daughter of the prominent Indian origin writer, Anita Desai, created literary history by being the youngest ever woman to win the prestigious Man Booker Prize for Fiction at the age of thirty-five. "Kiran Desai is the daughter of Anita: her arrival establishes the first dynasty of modern Indian fiction. But she is very much her own writer, the newest of all these voices, and welcome proof that India's encounter with the English language, far from proving abortive, continues to give birth to new children, endowed with lavish gifts"—Rushdie's prophetic lauding of Kiran Desai's writing prowess proved absolutely right.

Kiran Desai, first came to literary attention when in 1997, her excerpts found an honourable mention in Salman Rushdie edited anthology *Mirrorwork: Fifty Years of Indian Writing*. In 1998, came her celebrated debut, *Hullabaloo in the Guava Orchard*, which was published to unanimous acclaim in over twenty-two countries and went on to win the Betty Trask Award, a prize given by the Society of Authors for the best new novels by citizens of the Commonwealth of Nations under the age of thirty-five. In 2006, eight years later, with *The Inheritance of Loss*, Desai achieved a victory which had repeatedly eluded her mother Anita Desai, teaching Creative Writing at Massachusetts Institute of Technology, who had been thrice shortlisted for the Booker Prize: in 1980 for *Clear Light of Day*, in 1984 for *In Custody* and in 1999 for *Fasting, Feasting*.

The mantle of literary gravitas really does not weigh heavily on Kiran Desai. Published to extraordinary acclaim, *The Inheritance of Loss* heralds Kiran Desai as one of our most insightful novelists. With this mesmerizing gem of a novel, a prodigious effort of almost eight years, Kiran Desai has joined the ranks of literary stars like Jhumpa Lahiri, Arundhati Roy, Rohinton Mistry, Vikram Seth, to name a few.

From the mother to the daughter we see a literary tradition being built, starting from Anita Desai's psychological explorations in her fiction, to Kiran Desai's experiment in the making of a comic fable in *Hullabaloo in the Guava Orchard* and her insightful and often humorous commentary on multiculturism, globalization and postcolonial society in *The Inheritance of Loss*. After being declared a winner, Desai was inevitably asked about her mother's influence on her work, to which she said, that she owed a lot to her mother and that her prize winning novel, was as much "hers as it is mine." "It feels like a family endeavour." In an interview Kiran Desai talks of her famous mother as being a major influence on her own writing: "I'm sure she did have a big influence, because all my life I've grown up hearing her talk about writing and literature and books. It was wonderful to have her around when I was writing this book, to talk to her through this whole process." Often criticized for being her mother's daughter by those who prefer the mother's style and oeuvre, Desai has also been judged in isolation and acclaimed as a two novel old writer who has begun rather well. Kiran Desai may not have the same intensity that her mother weaves in her potent tales but she does not disappoint in producing a supremely funny and engaging novel in her joyous debut, *Hullabaloo in the Guava Orchard* (1998). The novel invariably reminds one of Shakespeare's *Hamlet*:

> Though this be madness, yet there is method in't.

Talking of *Hullabaloo*, Kiran Desai remarks, "I think my first book was filled with all that I loved most about India and knew I was in the inevitable process of losing. It was also very much a book that came from the happiness of realizing how much I loved to write." Although the publishers of *Hullabaloo* have been comparing the book to Arundhati Roy's *The God of Small Things*, Kiran Desai has less in common with Roy or Salman Rushdie than with the older generation of Indian writers including her mother Anita Desai and R.K. Narayan. As Narayan has done in his well-known Malgudi stories, Desai has conjured up a small Indian town poised midway between tradition and modernity and focused on the life of one of the anonymous inhabitants of that town—a dreamy, introspective fellow torn between his familial obligation and his own desire to be alone.

It is a whimsical tale that blends fable-esque magic with satiric comedy. Set in the fictitious village of Shahkot, the tale traces the chaotic progress of the monumentally unmotivated Sampath Chawla from a failed post office clerk to a guava tree inhabiting Guru. In Kiran Desai's Shahkot, it seems that the atmosphere of Narayan's Malgudi has been delicately captured and given a more boisterous build-up than Narayan's mildly Chekhovian humour is inclined to do. Kiran Desai, apparently, is fruitfully familiar with Evelyn Waugh's *Decline and Fall* and *A Handful of Dust* moving from a hilarious comedy to a macabre close. Avoiding the outspread tentacles of Arundhati Roy's characters in *The God of Small Things*, Kiran Desai concentrates within the limited boundaries of Shahkot as against Arundhati's trapezing from Kerala to Assam, with scattered relatives in Britain and America as well. The confines of Shahkot get a better and more concentrated build-up in the process and acquire a Narayanesque flavour of Malgudi.

In Anita Desai's *Voices in the City*, goddess Kali is presented as the presiding deity of the city of Calcutta. Kiran Desai's Shahkot is a miniature replica, where for once all characters are being assembled in the orchard to enact a crowded drama of action and atmosphere—the Brigadier with his marching orders to the subordinates; Sampath the godman, surrounded by devotees; Kulfi with her boiling cauldron; the drunken monkeys raiding the orchard; Pinky and her new love and the ice cream vendor and the spy, hoping to detect some flaw in the entire set-up. It is a mildly satirical portrait of the Indian cult of godman modelled on Narayan's Swami in

The Guide or Mauni Baba of Allahabad. Through a series of gossipy asides and subplots, this gentle comic satire offers a thoroughly funny, charming and occasionally touching insight into the absurdities of life in small town India. R.K. Narayan had stated that the incident of the reluctant holy man was based on a real event which he read about in a newspaper. Desai, too, says in an interview, talking of the process for writing this book: "I'd read a story in *The Times of India* and heard about a character from many people, a man who was a very famous hermit in India who really did climb up a tree, who lived in a tree for many years, until he died."

Hullabaloo is the story of Sampath, the ambitionless son of the middle-class family who wants to escape the looming responsibilities of his adult life. He decides to climb into a guava tree and live there in peaceful contemplation. The town's people start to revere him as a holy man and seek his counsel for their problems. His enigmatic responses only increase their awe for him. His father reacts by looking at the commercial possibilities of having many pilgrims coming to see Sampath. His mother spends her days searching the countryside for rare and unusual food to prepare for him. His sister struggles to maintain her independence but falls hopelessly in love with the Hungry Hop Ice boy. Inept bureaucrats, bungling army officials, a spy for the atheist society, and a herd of monkeys with a taste for liquor add to this hilariously irreverent story. From his perch, Sampath becomes comically misconstrued as a great visionary, a religious guru of sorts. He proceeds to find fame, fortune and eventually chaos—in the form of bumbling bureaucrats and a group of unruly, liquor-loving monkeys, who only Sampath can tame, by bestowing his wisdom upon the many people who make the pilgrimage to meet the Monkey Baba. The novel acquires the dimensions of the fable, when the drunken monkeys raise a hullabaloo in the guava orchard. There is in these scenes a manifestly Dickensian tilt towards the comic, particularly in Ammaji's repeated search for dentures in the company of young Pinky and the misbehaviour of the dentures falling now in the boiling curry and acquiring its special colour and flavour and then while tasting the ice cream her dentures get stuck in it. A book of rare humour and craft, *Hullabaloo in the Guava Orchard* traces the chaotic process of the monumentally unmotivated Sampath Chawla from failed post office clerk to guava tree inhabiting guru. Sampath as a godman inevitably draws comparisons with Raju in Narayan's *The Guide*, where Raju after serving time in prison advertantly becomes a spiritual saint for the people of Mangala when he takes refuge in an abandoned temple on the outskirts. The novel derives its strength from the steady fluidity in which the story unfolds itself by use of brilliantly lucid images and a distinct choice of unaffected words and phrases and an eccentric set of characters. In an interview, Kiran Desai classifies *Hullabaloo in the Guava Orchard*: "It is a comedy and it is satiric in many ways, I think, and it's fantastic. It reads very much like a folktale or a fairy tale." Kiran Desai had stated that she wrote the novel "very much for myself...but I think anyone with a sense of humour would enjoy it." True enough, through this radiant novel, Desai evokes a bright, buoyant world, which is wryly hilarious and enchanting.

From the sweet-natured playfulness of her joyous novel, *Hullabaloo in the Guava Orchard* to the exploration of such complex issues as colonialism, racism, immigration, young love, regret, hope, the role of family, and the myths of both India and America in *The Inheritance of Loss*, Desai makes clear her intentions to expand her reach from the narrow boundaries of her first novel to the global arena where luminaries like Salman Rushdie and Zadie Smith already perform. Unlike her first sprightly novel that ends in a raucous bang of comic eccentricity, the prevailing mood in *The Inheritance of Loss* is one of implacable bitterness and despair. Full of pathos and tenderness the novel presents its characters as ultimately frail human beings struggling in a search for love and happiness.

When talking of the characters in *The Inheritance of Loss*, and of her own life, she says, "The characters of my story are entirely fictional, but these journeys (of her grandparents) as well as my own provided insight into what it means to travel between East and West and it is this I wanted to capture. The fact that I live this particular life is no accident. It was my inheritance." It was this feeling of being caught between two continents that infuses *The Inheritance of Loss*—a story replete with sadness over globalization and with pleasure at the surviving intimacies of Indian village life.

Hermione Lee, the head judge for the Booker Prize, describes the book as "a magnificent novel of humane breadth and wisdom, comic tenderness and powerful political acuteness." John Sutherland, chairman of Man Booker judges, for 2008 said: "Desai's novel registers the multicultural reverberations of the new millennium with the sensitive instrumentality of fiction, as Jhabvala and Rushdie did previous eras.... It is a globalised novel for a globalised world." Both Rushdie and Rohinton Mistry believe that, with this her second novel, Desai has secured her place with the great contemporary Indian authors exploring life and society in India and elsewhere. Salman Rushdie had earlier described *Hullabaloo in the Guava Orchard* "as lush and intensely imagined." Her second novel, *The Inheritance of Loss*, too, has earned his complimentary blurb at the back of the new novel—"Kiran Desai is a terrific writer." Whereas, *Hullabaloo in the Guava Orchard* was a "charming, lyrical, fable about destiny," a "festival of comic eccentricity, exuding charisma, poetry and joy in language and life," *The Inheritance of Loss* is a majestic novel, "illuminating the pain of exile, the ambiguities of post-colonialism and the blinding drive for 'better life' when one person's wealth means another's poverty." It zips back and forth between Kalimpong, a tiny Himalayan burg, and the streets of New York City. Its primary setting is India, in this case the remote province of Kalimpong during the mid-1980's.

In this alternatively comical and contemplative novel, Desai effectively illuminates the pain of exile, like lingering effects of postcolonialism, the characters struggling as exiles to maintain their dignity and self-respect in the encroaching morass of Westernization. Dealing with all levels of society and different cultures, Desai reveals life's humour and brutality, its delicate emotions and passionate commitments so convincingly that, her mother's remarks seem to be no exaggeration: "I think Kiran's voice is extremely original, she brings something totally fresh and new to the writing scene."

Desai takes us to the northeastern Himalayas, where a rising insurgency challenges the old way of life. It's a good tale with a globalization undercurrent connecting India's Nepal border with New York City: "...there was a report of new dissatisfaction in the hills, gathering insurgency, men and guns. It was the Indian-Nepalese this time, fed up with being treated like the minority in a place where they were the majority. They wanted their own country, or at least their own state, in which to manage their own affair."

It spans continents, generations, cultures, religions and races. Desai has wonderfully presented the human face of globalization and showed how individuals living in different parts of the planet often intersect in surprising ways. A father's love for his son, that son's ambition to succeed, the bitterness of a lonely man living out his days on the edge of civilization, two sisters' yearning for the past, all of these lives are presented by Desai as fully realized and ultimately frail human beings in recognizable search for love and happiness. *The Inheritance of Loss* is not only a story, it is "a perspective, an inside look into post-independence India, with its roots dug in colonialism, its branches embracing Americanism, but its leaves brown and dusty with the age-old prejudices that govern people's minds; an India where a class of people still speak only English and squirm at the mention of their mother tongues; where a mother is proud because her daughter has chosen to marry an Englishman; where a foreigner is treated suspiciously in spite of his honest efforts to lay foundations of indigenous industries; where thousands of Indians enter America as illegal immigrants—in the eyes of their families, they are the heroes, but in reality, they sleep with mice on the kitchen floors of restaurants or in squalid suburbs of big cities."

The Inheritance of Loss opens with a teenage Indian girl, an orphan called Sai, living with her Cambridge-educated Anglophile grandfather, a retired judge in the town of Kalimpong on the Indian side of Himalayas. For the judge, all opportunity has passed him by. The hopes of his family rested on him, and he succeeded in leaving India for a difficult education in England. His color, his religion, his language all made him the embodiment of "other" in England, and he began to question his identity and his connection to India while there: "He retreated into a solitude that grew in weight day by day. The solitude became a habit, the habit became the man, and it crushed him into a shadow." The novel presents the judge, Jemubhai, cast away from the colonial times, carrying scathing memories of aborted attempts to acculturate into the metropolitan. He is one of those "ridiculous Indians," "who could not rid themselves of what they had broken their souls to learn" and those whose Anglophilia can only turn to self-hatred. As a student, isolated in racist England, the future judge feels "barely human at all" and leaps "when touched on the arm as if from an unbearable intimacy." Yet, on returning home he vented his anger and frustration on his innocent young wife because of her docility and her silent battle that she puts up by withdrawing into herself. Unloved, uncared and hated she lives a desultory life until the judge sends her back to her parents' home, their child, a daughter is born after the separation about whom the judge never knew. Alone and recluse the judge settles after his retirement in Cho Oyu, with a dog Mutt, whom he loves more than any human being and a cook for whom he has no feelings. To this cottage and to partake in the old man's arid life arrives Sai, his orphaned granddaughter, born to the judge's daughter.

After the death of her parents under the wheels of a bus in Moscow, when Sai arrives at Cho Oyu, the judge begins to confront his own sufferings as a victim of racism and colonialism as well as the violence he perpetrated against his wife. The judge, seems to have had his heart frozen long ago when he studied at Cambridge University and learned to despise his fellow Indians. The only creature he truly loves is Mutt, his dog. Living in a large, decaying house, her grandfather considers himself more British than Indian, far superior to hard-working but poverty-stricken people like his cook, Nandu, whose hopes for a better life for his son are the driving force in his life.

Fortunately for Sai, however, the cook at Cho Oyu cherishes her as if she were his own. His actual child Biju is living in New York, eking out a bare existence waiting tables and sleeping in a basement (even as his father imagines him to be amassing wealth and prestige). The story of Sai living in Kalimpong, near India's northeast border with Nepal, alternates with that of Biju, Nandu's son, an illegal immigrant trying to find work and a better life in New York.

Biju working in a series of decadent jobs epitomizes the plight of the illegal immigrant who has no future in his own country and endures deplorable conditions and semi-servitude working illegally in the US. With Biju we experience the world of illegal aliens, the "shadow class" condemned to movement, who spends much of his time dodging the authorities, moving from one ill-paid job to another. As Desai explores the aspirations of Sai and Biju, the hopes and expectations of their families, she also creates vivid pictures of the friends and relatives who surround them, evoking vibrant images of a broad cross-section of society and revealing the social and political history of India.

Inevitably, however, as Sai has grown older, the cook's love has no longer been enough, and now she turns her attentions to her young tutor, Gyan. Gyan, an ethnic Nepalese, loves Sai in return until he is swept away by a group of insurgents agitating for freedom from India and decides he needs to despise her and her bourgeois ways. Sai is young enough to live in the moment, which helps her overlook some of the issues with her boyfriend Gyan. Sai's identity and her relationship with India is very different from Gyan's. Sai belonged to a formerly powerful, educated and western thinking family and Gyan's Nepalese family lives in poverty, struggling to make ends meet while providing him with a good education. When Gyan's friends start to explore, first peacefully and then with violence, the inequalities present in India itself, he is caught up in the furore and clashes with Sai.

Both Sai and Gyan lose their innocence and love in the turmoil of unrest.

Meanwhile, on opposite sides of globe, Biju and his father lose themselves in the fantasy that is America; the cook hoping for better things for his son while the son, living the gruelling reality of life as a poor and illegal resident, is condemned to menial labour and abject living conditions. Biju longs for home. He is not immune from nostalgia. He can "feel the pulse of the forest, smell the humid air, the green black lushness; he could imagine all its different textures, the plumage of banana, the stark spear of the cactus, the delicate gesture of ferns."

Although the story has as its backdrop, Kalimpong and the Gorkhaland agitation, it is actually about loss—the loss of identity, nationality and loyalty, and the realization of this loss —the Gorkhaland agitation is merely a catalyst for the loss. The loss in her title is chiefly the loss of faith in India felt among the legions who overstay tourist visas and become illegal immigrants in the US. Longing is perhaps the thing that the characters in this novel do best. They long for home, they long for love, and they long for acceptance—yet rarely are they skilled at locating any of the above. As the insurgency grows in strength, however, all the characters of the novel come to share Sai's suspicion that life is more often defined by loss than by fulfillment. Desai wants us to explore the pain of the immigrant and the unfairness of a world in which, "one side travels to be a servant, and the other side travels to be treated like a king." Writing with wit and perception, Kiran Desai creates an elegant and thoughtful study of families, the losses each member must confront alone, and the lies each tells to make memories of the past more palatable. The Epigraph to the novel includes a line from Borges: "My humanity is in feeling we are all voices of the same poverty." But it isn't only physical poverty that Desai's characters seem to recognize. All of them seem to crave for a sense of belonging. What bind these seemingly disparate characters are a shared historical legacy and a common experience of impotence and humiliation.

A comparative study of Kiran Desai's *The Inheritance of Loss* and Anita Desai's *Fire on the Mountain* brings out some obvious similarities between the mother and the daughter in their respective storylines and choice of characters. Both the novels were written when the authors were between the age of thirty-five and forty. Both the novels establish the author's position in the realm of serious writing in Indian English literature. In Anita Desai's novel, the story centers around a reclusive old widow and her great granddaughter and Kiran Desai's book tells the story of a retired judge and his granddaughter. As Hermione Lee too perceives the similarity between the mother and the daughter: "It is clear to those of us who have read Anita Desai that Kiran Desai has learned from her mother's work," and she adds, "Both write not just about India but about Indian communities in the world."

A careful observer of behaviour, with a fine eye for revealing details, Desai brings her narratives and characters to life, illustrating her themes, without making moral judgments about her characters, creating neither saints nor villains, just ordinary people leading the best lives they can, using whatever resources are available. Her characters—both the major and the minor ones—are very real and compelling.

With these characters, Desai explores such complicated issues as colonialism, racism, immigration, young love, regret, hope and the myths of both India and America. Juggling between timeless wisdom and 21st century self-doubt, Kiran Desai combines in herself the naturalness of Tolstoy and the depth and resonance of Dickens laced with postmodern ambivalence. Thus, we can see that although Desai's second novel, "focusses on the fate of a few powerless individuals, it manages to explore, with intimacy and sight, just about every contemporary international issue; globalization, multiculturism, economic inequality and terrorist violence." A confident and talented writer, Desai's novels are full of wisdom and subtle parallels; it is both funny and bitterly sad, but generally optimistic. Never preachy, never predictable, Desai's scope is broad, looking at the consequences of large cultural and political forces for both people and individuals.

Critical Responses to Kiran Desai is a humble effort to acknowledge the writing prowess of Kiran Desai, the emerging distinctive voice in recent Indian English fiction. Writing with wit and perception, Kiran Desai renders serious insights into the contemporary events through a fascinating blend of magic, hilarity and wisdom and her buoyant language makes the reading joyous explorations. Hemione Lee rightly summed up the salience of Kiran Desai in these words: "A distinctive original voice, an audacious imagination that takes readers to undiscovered countries of the mind, a strong power of storytelling and a historical truthfulness." The twenty-three well-researched papers in the anthology offer an inclusive analysis of the dynamics of Kiran Desai's fictional oeuvre.

In the scholarly paper, "Globalization's Discontents: Reading 'Modernity' from the Shadows," Melissa Dennihy, discusses the issues of globalization and multiculturism taken up by Kiran Desai in her novel, *The Inheritance of Loss*. Desai, writing her novel from the "shadow class" sheds light on the ways in which the benefits of "modernity" for some are the cause of shame, self-loathing and solitude for others.

In her analytical paper, "Prizing Sameness? Kiran Desai and The Booker Prize," Ana Cristina Mendes critically discusses the star principle that has come to attach itself to Booker Prize winners, as well as to the cultural works themselves, and examines the current (hyper) visibility of postcolonial literature from the Indian diaspora resulting from niche marketing strategies developed predominantly by Anglo-American publishing houses.

In her perceptive analysis, "An Enchanting Enigma of Kiran Desai's Stylistic Nuances in *The Inheritance of Loss*," Devika makes an explorative analysis of Desai's, "stylistic sparks of aptness, her paucity of efforts in character development, their relationships and the surrounding scenario does not fall short of the beauty simultaneously ethereal and lingering." Her stylistic craftsmanship, her worth as an artist is firmly established and, "the story gets over but not the feel of it, simply because the language that unfolds it spellbinds."

Dr. Krishna Singh's innovative paper, "Representation of India in Kiran Desai's *The Inheritance of Loss*," presents the novel as a brilliant study of Indian culture—both in content and in form. Supported by Indian vocabulary, metaphors and imagery, the novel, "creates an atmosphere to transport the readers into that realm where India resides."

In "Aspects of Globalization in *The Inheritance of Loss*," Jackie Haque offers a competent analysis of the questions Desai poses on postcolonialism and globalization. With globalization as its epicentre, the book depicts the tug of war that is taking place between the Eastern and the Western culture.

In her scholarly paper, "Italo Calvino's *The Baron in the Trees* and Kiran Desai's *Hullabaloo in the Guava Orchard*: A Comparative Analysis," Elisa Armellino critically examines the parallelisms between the main themes in the two texts. Despite the historical and cultural differences, both works "offer an imaginative and witty portrayal of the world they describe."

In her well-researched paper, "Anatomising Immigrant Lives: Kiran Desai's *The Inheritance of Loss*," Reena Mitra discusses at length the immigrant experience as captured by Desai in her much-acclaimed novel.

In "*The Inheritance of Loss*: Individuals in Search of the Lost Identity," Sanghita Sen probes deftly into Desai's concern with hybridity, the issues of individual space and the lineage of colonial past and postcolonial present.

In "Of Love, Loss and Longing: A Lacanian Reading of Kiran Desai's *The Inheritance of Loss*" Anita Singh makes an insightful study of the movement from the imaginary to the symbolic order and back and forth and examines how this analysis identifies the nature of the movement, growth, and journey of the three characters—Biju, Gyan and Sai in the novel.

In an exhaustive analysis, "Kiran Desai's *The Inheritance of Loss*: A Study in Theme of Rootlessness, Alienation and Death," Gulrez Roshan Rehman offers a brilliant analysis of the sense of alienation arising out of double-selves, veneers, rootlessness and death characterized poignantly in Kiran Desai's *The Inheritance of Loss.*

In "Kiran Desai's *The Inheritance of Loss*: Politics of Being 'A Drab Immigrant'," Kripanath Mishra studies the novelist's remarkable insight into the contemporary issues such as the postcolonial discourse, the postmodern predicament, the pain of immigration, the impact of the forces of globalization on the current economy and culture as well as the dilemmas and passions, nostalgia and disillusionment, cross-border experience and sense of inequality, postcolonial chaos and despair which the immigrants experience.

"Conflicts of Globalization, Multiculturalism and Economic Inequality in Kiran Desai's *The Inheritance of Loss*," by Srutimala Duara explores Desai's keen eye for telling detail, profound wisdom and her concern with questions of identity and alienation.

In "*The Inheritance of Loss*: A Reading of the Ending," Purnendu Chatterjee critically examines the last chapter of the book in detail and rightly observes that, "a novel does not end in a final and finite vision but, in a slow cadence and creates a situation that is not delimited by the dimensions of time and space and may be variously interpreted."

In "Kiran Desai's *The Inheritance of Loss*: A Study in Insurgency," Sharada Iyer studies the arresting theme of Gorkhaland movement, woven by Kiran Desai into the texture of the novel rather sensitively and poignantly.

In "Memory and Nostalgia: The Diasporic Subject in *The Inheritance of Loss*," Nishi Pulugurtha describes the significance of memory and nostalgia in the act of rewriting history and revisiting the past, which happens to be the major concern of the "studies in homelessness."

In her analytical paper, "The Colonial Hangover and The Brown Sahib," Madhu Shalini focuses on the double awareness of the colonial inheritance as it works within a specific (Indian) culture and of a changing relationship among "communities, cultures and countries in the modern world."

In "Kiran Desai's *The Inheritance of Loss*: A Parable on the Predicament of Third World Immigrants," Beena Agrawal unveils the socio-political trauma of the "fragmented characters," seeking for "wholeness" in alien surroundings.

Vandana Singh, in her competent paper, "Deviating Ambit and Uprooted Sensibilities in *The Inheritance of Loss,*" focuses on the trauma and tribulations of hyphenated selves in exile in America and those interwoven in the postcolonial ideologies in India.

In her innovative paper, "An Eco-critical Reading of Kiran Desai's *The Inheritance of Loss,*" Neeta Kulshreshtha presents the eco-centred approach in Kiran Desai's novel which draws attention to the plight of man not only in the socio-political perspective but also in a manifestation of man's growing insensibility towards inherited environment.

In "Portrayal of Relations in Kiran Desai's *The Inheritance of Loss,*" Anju Bala Agrawal studies the novel as a saga of parallel stories of human relations in the changing Indian society.

In "Postmodern/Postcolonial Spatiality in Kiran Desai's *The Inheritance of Loss,*" Arpita Chattaraj explores the confluence of postmodernist (Soja's) "Third Space," which is a spatial manifestation of social structures in polyethnic, multicultural, globalised world, and postcolonial (Bhabha's) "Third Space," which is a spatial manifestation of cultural conflicts and crises in a specific historical and political context, in Kiran Desai's Booker awarded novel *The Inheritance of Loss*.

The paper "Reflective Moods in *The Inheritance of Loss*" by Shaleen Kumar Singh examines Desai's meditative mode, the weaving of the plot and the infusion of thought which make the novel, "exquisite."

Jati Sankar Mondal's scholarly paper, "'Imagi-nation': A Reading of Kiran Desai's *The Inheritance of Loss,*" analyses Desai's characters as representing a "nation" in miniature and the palimpestic design is shown as being created by various groups of people who are mainly differentiated by means of class, ethnicity, religion and language.

The book is multivocal, comprising scholarly critical approaches of eminent scholars and would prove to be very relevant and enlightening for the teachers and students of English literature.

Sunita Sinha
Bryan Reynolds

1

Globalization's Discontents: Reading "Modernity" from the Shadows

Melissa Dennihy

Reviews of *The Inheritance of Loss* featured in *The New York Times*, *BBC News*, and *The Guardian* all describe Kiran Desai's 2006 novel as a literary work grappling with the issues of "globalization" and "multiculturalism". Acknowledging the fact that the authors of these reviews have very limited spaces with which to summarize a 357-page book, their descriptions nevertheless fall extremely short of what Desai's novel actually achieves. In fact, *The Inheritance of Loss* is ultimately less concerned with globalization and multiculturalism than it is with the underlying processes that both contribute to and complicate these ideas. Perhaps, the most critical contribution Desai's novel makes to conversations about globalization and multiculturalism is its refusal to view either in the positive or "celebratory" light often attributed to them by mainstream Western thought. On the contrary, this novel offers a challenge not only to those who view globalization and multiculturalism as "positive" changes evidencing the progress achieved through "modernity," but also to those who are critical of globalization and multiculturalism, but fail to develop this criticism outside of a "Western" frame of analysis. By writing her novel from the perspective of the "shadow class" (which includes, for the sake of my argument, both Indians living in India and Indian immigrants living in England and America) Desai offers a way for her Western readers to re-think the effects of modernity, globalization, and "multiculturalism" from outside of the Western world; her novel works to shed light not only on the ways in which the very "benefits" of modernity for some are the cause of shame, self-loathing, and solitude for others, but also on the ways in which modernity and globalization both rely upon and, in many ways, replicate the same imperial and colonial processes that so many "positive-minded" modern Western thinkers would like to consider world systems of the past.

To begin, it is important not to underestimate the extent to which globalization has been heralded by many Western thinkers as the rise of a more positive, inclusive, and connected world order which allows for a previously unimaginable "leveling of the playing field" between Western and non-Western nations. Citing over fifteen theorists writing from 1989 to 1999, David Held and Anthony McGrew note that globalization has been described in various contexts as resulting in "instantaneous electronic communication (which) erodes the constraints of distance and time on social organization and interaction;" "accelerating interdependence (understood as the intensification of enmeshment among national economies and societies);" "a shrinking world (the erosion of borders and geographical barriers to socio-economic activity);" and, "global integration (and increased) consciousness of the global condition" (3). Similarly, The United Nations Development Programme (UNDP) in its 1999 report on global inequality, stated that "global markets, global technology, global ideas and global solidarity can enrich the lives of people everywhere, greatly expanding their choices" (433). Fredric Jameson notes the ways in which globalization and the "new communicational form(s)" which accompany it tends to create a sense of a "postmodern celebration of difference and differentiation: suddenly all the cultures around the world are placed in tolerant contact with each other in a kind of immense cultural pluralism which it would be very difficult not to welcome." Providing what we might consider a useful definition of "multiculturalism," Jameson goes on to add that—

> beyond the dawning celebration of cultural difference, and often very closely linked to it, is a celebration of the emergence of a whole immense range of groups, races, genders, ethnicities, into the speech of the public sphere; a falling away of those structures that condemned whole segments of the population to silence and to subalternity; a worldwide growth of popular democratization—why not?—which...is immediately expressed by a new richness and variety of cultures in the new world space. (56-57)

While aptly expressing the views of many of those who view globalization and multiculturalism as "positive" or "progressive," the irony with which Jameson writes in the above passage also encourages readers to pay attention to the important ways in which such "positive" views are, in fact, often riddled with contradiction and hypocrisy. As Desai's novel demonstrates, the "solidarity," "interconnectedness," and "democratization" mentioned in the above pieces often turn out to be merely surface-level assumptions of processes that are in fact far more problematic than initially meets the eye. For example, Held and McGrew also point to the ways in which globalization has been cited as causing "action at a distance"—"whereby the actions of social agents in one locale can come to have significant consequences for 'distant others'" (3). Yet, this statement prompts us to question to what extent those "distant others" (presumably members of non-Western nations who are subjected to the dominance of Western economics and culture) are able to have an equal impact upon the nations that so noticeably impact them. Desai's novel, for example, is full of instances where "Western elements" of the so-called "first world" have infiltrated into the "third world" space of Kalimpong: the novel opens with Sai reading National Geographic on the front porch of her "dark," "freez(ing)," "stone wall" home; later, we meet Sai's neighbors, sisters Lola and Noni, who are "sitting up in their beds, wrapped in Kulu shawls, sipping Sikkimese brandy, BBC news sputtering on the radio, falling over them in sparky explosions." On a trip to the library (during which time they contemplate having lunch at

"Let's B Veg") Sai, Lola and Noni, check out a variety of "British" books; Sai's choice is *Wuthering Heights* (1, 51, 239). Yet, while the impact that Western culture has upon these three ladies (amongst other characters in the novel) is more than apparent, the impact that Biju and other immigrants have upon America and its citizens is absolutely negligible—indeed, the depictions of the restaurants in which they work are of "first world" people on top (in the fashionable dining rooms) and "third world" people below (in the sweltering kitchens) Managers and owners are careful not to have this delicate balance upset (23, 25).

In this sense, Desai's novel demonstrates, virtually from start to finish, the ways in which the West insists upon forcing its (commercial) presence upon non-Western countries, while simultaneously refusing to acknowledge the presence of those same 'distant others'—even when they are no longer distant at all, but are, in fact, the very people cooking the meals that these Westerners eat. However, it is also important to pay attention to the ways in which Western elements infiltrate the non-Western world. One of the popular "positivist" views of globalization is that it offers non-Western nations new economic opportunities, new access to cheap commodities, and a chance to "experience" "modernity." Yet, the question rarely asked within such positive perspectives is at what cost are such things experienced? The cook and Gyan, for example, are two characters whose homes are marked by the struggle for modernity, a struggle which is nevertheless constantly mocked and destroyed by persistent poverty. Gyan's family's home is described as "modernity proffered in its meanest form, brand-new one day, in ruin the next;" the cook's tiny, almost unlivable quarters are nevertheless littered with various useless things, such as pieces of a watch that never worked, but is nevertheless too valuable to throw away (280, 327). On the other hand, for middle class characters such as Lola and Noni, who proudly invest in British jam and Marks and Spencer's underpants, the presence of poverty is less salient, and the notion of India as "home" becomes a distant idea; instead, "national histories, myths and ritual" are "diffus(ed)" in favor of a participation in a "new imagined community" (in this case, the sisters' abilities to imagine themselves as essentially part of England, rather than as citizens of India) (Held and McGrew, 14-15). The fact that this imagining of themselves as part of a Western community results in an extreme distancing from those around them is not something that the sisters lament; indeed, they often embrace the opportunity to poke fun at those who have not "succeeded" in embracing Western commodities and culture to the same extent that they have.

Yet, what ultimately results from an embracing of Western culture and commodities by such characters as Lola and Noni is not only the creating of rifts between citizens of different classes within India, but also the "uncoupling of the 'natural' link between," amongst other things, "languages and nations, languages and national memories, languages and national literature," creating the "condition for and enacting (of) the... fractures of cultures" (Mignolo, 42). Lola and Noni are not the only characters guilty of participation in this process; indeed, both Sai and her grandfather are virtually unable to speak the native language of Kalimpong, and conversely, read and study almost entirely in English. However, their detachments from the culture of the nation in which they live (detachments which are the result of having been educated within Western schools) not only help to create a "fracturing" of national culture within India, but also a "fracturing" of the minds and identities of these characters, who find themselves constantly torn between East and West, tradition and modernity, "Indianness" and "Britishness." Examples of the (psychological) colonization of Jemu, Sai, Lola and Noni (amongst others) abound throughout the novel: Lola, for example, speaks of Trinidadian-born British writer V.S. Naipaul as "strange, stuck in the past.... He has not progressed colonial neurosis;" her own daughter, who works for the BBC in the "completely cosmopolitan society" of England has, Lola wants it noted, no such "chip on her shoulder" (52). Sai's colonial mentality, although existing in a different form than Lola's, is quite present nevertheless: she learns at an early age that "cake was better than laddoos, fork spoon knife better than hands, sipping the blood of Christ... more civilized than garlanding a phallic symbol with marigolds. English was better than Hindi" (33). Upon her arrival at the judge's house, which ends Sai's education at the missionary school, the Judge decides to have Sai educated by Noni, explaining that he couldn't "send you [Sai] to a government school...you'd come out speaking with the wrong accent and picking your nose" (38). Troubling as his statement is, this is one of the more minor examples of Jemu's internalizing of a colonized mentality—not only does he consistently powder his own dark skin with white make-up, but Jemu also learns to mix "pity with shame" when thinking of his own parents' Indianness (42). Even the cook, perhaps the most subjected to inequality and unfair treatment, is not free of the internalization of a colonized mentality: he considers his working for Jemu to be "a severe comedown" since his father had "served white men only" (71).

It is crucial to note the ways in which the internalization of a colonized mentality is not lessened through the coming of "modernity" and "globalization," but, in many ways, exacerbated in new ways that it had not been in the imperial/colonial "past." Because of the continued infiltration of and easy (or at least easier) access to Western goods, concepts, and culture, people of previously colonized nations nevertheless continue to find themselves inundated with the very aspects of "Westernness" that are intended to most "appeal" to them and thus convince them to "prefer" Western culture over their own. As Stuart Hall notes, crucial to its maintaining of power is the West's ability to "make us [non-white people] see and experience ourselves as "Other." This becomes a "matter of imposed will and domination, by the power of inner compulsion and subjective conformation to the norm [in this case, commodities and concepts of Western culture/modernity]. That is the lesson—the somber majesty—of Fanon's insight into the colonized experience in *Black Skin, White Masks*" (236). Indeed, Jemu embodies a disturbingly apt description of what Fanon discusses within *Black Skin, White*

Masks—his willingness (indeed, eagerness) to literally don a "white mask" in denial of his own Indian identity is an act he engages in continuously from his return to India as a young man to his days of old age at the close of the novel. The result of this self-colonization is that Jemu comes to "env[y] the English" while "loath[ing] Indians," eventually causing him to be "despised by absolutely everyone, English and Indians, both" (131).

The solitude and isolation that Jemu experiences as a result of his psychological colonization is another indication of the ways in which globalization is usually far less "positive" than its proponents would make it seem. The notions of increased communication and interconnectedness which are often cited as major benefits of a globalized world hardly seem to exist within *The Inheritance of Loss*; indeed, it is not only the judge who is isolated from those around him, but the majority of the characters in the novel as a whole. The home in which the judge, Sai and the cook live together, for example, is considered by the boys who invade it to be a place of "intense solitude" (7). Although all three have shared the same space for many years, Sai and the judge barely speak, while Sai and the cook speak to one another in a "shallow mix" of English and Hindi where "the brokenness made it easier never to go deep, never to enter into anything that required an intricate vocabulary" (21). The cook and the judge fare even worse—despite having lived with one another "for more years than they had with anyone else, practically in the same room, closer to each other than to any other human being," there is "nothing, zero, no understanding" (344). This lack of communication between three people all sharing the same small space not only speaks to the ways in which the erosion of language and cultures as a result of modernity decreases connectedness rather than increasing it; it also speaks to the ways in which the forms of technology and communication which proponents of globalization conceive of as forming "connectedness" often have no impact upon many human beings whatsoever. Access to such connections is literally restricted to select groups of people in the Western world, resulting in the West's ability to develop further power over the "marginal and impoverished, cutting off their voices and concerns from the global conversation" (UNDP report, 428).

This cutting off of the voices of non-Western peoples within "global conversations" need not pertain exclusively to broader cultural, political, or economic conversations in the public sphere—indeed, one of the most painful ways in which Desai demonstrates the "downside" of globalization is through Biju's harrowing experiences while abroad. Biju's time in New York is one of intense solitude; he realizes almost immediately that he has been "abandoned amongst foreigners," not only those Americans who barely deign to acknowledge him, but also other immigrants and illegal aliens who are far too busy trying to survive for themselves and have no time to help Biju adapt to his new life (108). Far from experiencing the "extended 'family' made up of an immigrant community" that Gayatri Gopinath describes, Biju instead finds that immigrants "live intensely with others, only to have them disappear overnight" (Gopinath, 265; Desai, 112). The scene in which he delivers food to three Indian girls of the immigrant "middle-class" leaves Biju feeling as if he is "standing at [a] threshold" experiencing mixed emotions of "hunger, respect, loathing" (57). These experiences, amongst others, serve to suggest not only the disintegration of ties between people of shared cultures and backgrounds (a sharp contradiction to the argument that globalization creates interconnectedness between people of different cultures and backgrounds) but also that, far from creating "economic equality," globalization actually further pits people of poor nations against one another, creating a cruel sense of competition in which, for example, businessmen originally from Asia discuss with ease, while Biju serves them, the prospects of Asia itself as the "new frontier" in the global market of exploitation (151).

Aside from the ways in which Biju feels that he becomes "the only one displacing the air" in a space which should have "included family, friends," his lack of access to communication and information in New York is another excellent example of the ways in which the "benefits" of globalization are strictly limited to a select few (293). In a critique of the ways in which globalization, modernity and technology alter communication and information, Jameson writes that "rather than the return of startling reports from remote places," information in the global era begins to "slip insensibly in the direction of advertisements and publicity, of postmodern marketing, and finally of the export of TV programs" (56). Jameson's argument is an important one, one which we do see reflected in Desai's novel through Lola and Noni's obsession with their satellite television programs, which cause them to have virtually no idea of what is going on in the immediate world around them. However, Jameson seems to write his critique from an exclusively Western perspective here, failing to consider not only how those in the "remote places" he speaks of might get their information about the rest of the world, but also how those who come from the "remote places" to America or other "modern countries" are not able to access these forms of technology, communication, or information at all. Indeed, when Biju returns to Kalimpong at the end of the novel, the man at the bus station is "surprised at Biju's ignorance" about the political situation there—"How could he not know? Where had he come from? From America, No newspaper, no phone..." (340). This exchange also hints at the fact that information in the Western world is ultimately only concerned with information about the Western world—places such as Kalimpong are, it seems, rarely reported on. It is important to note that Biju's inability to communicate with his father or to get such news about India while in New York are both issues that plague him throughout the entirety of his stay. He and his father lament the fact that "they would never know how many of the[ir letters] went astray in all the rickety connections made along the way;" the cook often opens letters from Biju only to find the writing entirely washed away, confirming the fact that there is "literally an ocean between him and his son" (104, 132). Again, far from a sense of "connectedness" or "increased communication," the globalizing processes that lead Biju to his diaspora in New York further enforce the distance between father and son, reminding both that easy communication, quick plane flights home, and lengthy long-distance telephone calls are global "benefits" experienced only by those who can afford them.

Biju's fear of the telephone itself also speaks to the problematic ways in which the "shadow class" experiences life in America quite differently than do those who enjoy the benefits of the ever-desired "green card." Biju and fellow illegal aliens get up every morning "as soon as the clock str[ikes] 8:30" to call the immigration hotline and "t[ake] turns holding the receiver for what might be an all-day activity of line holding." If one person did finally get through, he would usually hang up out of fear that immigration had a superduper zing bing beep peeping high-alert electronic supersonic space speed machine that could

> transfer
>
> connect
>
> dial
>
> read
>
> trace the number through to their—
>
> *Illegality*. (90-91)

The ways in which Biju and his co-workers imagine the capabilities of technology indicate their extremely limited familiarity with the same forms of communication most Americans have taken completely for granted for the past several decades. However, even more problematic is the fact that their fear of the immigration hotline leaves many of them in the limbo of illegal status, usually resulting in deportment rather than eventual citizenship. As Leslie Sklair notes, citing Piven and Cloward, "people cannot defy institutions to which they have no access, and to which they make no contribution" (295). For Biju and other illegal immigrants in New York, the inability to effectively communicate with those in the immigration department only helps to further the continuation of a "shadow" existence, a fleeting and ephemeral life experienced in damp basements, dark alleyways, and crude kitchens. Far from experiencing America as a land of economic opportunity, the lives of Biju and those around him serve as grim challenges to any claims that globalization offers an increased chance for "equality" between the rich and the poor.

Yet, while Biju himself makes little to no impact upon "America" (even as "America" makes such a grave impact upon him, as well as upon the people he has left behind in India) the novel itself plays an important role in undercutting the idea of the "American dream," which is perhaps the most popular and idealized notion that is "exported" to other cultures through the processes of globalization—as Jameson notes, "American economic interest and American cultural influence coincide to produce the export of a way of life itself" (64, emphasis added). However, while characters such as Lola and Noni can imagine themselves as part of this way of life (or at least of a similar life lived by those in England) and while Biju's father can imagine his son as extraordinarily successful simply because he is in America, Biju himself learns quite quickly that America provides, in many ways, a far more painful and shameful way of life than he had ever experienced in India. His "early days" in America are spent "standing at a counter along with a row of men," immediately undercutting the notion of "individuality" so often expressed as an ideal of the American dream. Months later, Biju still considers himself as merely one amongst many others "making a start on miniature lives," suggesting that the idea that anybody can "make it" in America is also a myth. Indeed, a boy from Saeed's neighborhood that Biju sees with a "gold chain as fat as a bathtub attachment, his prosperity flashing out," is not a typically "successful" or "productive" member of American society, but is, rather, a street hustler (17, 84, 110).

However, while Biju's experiences do much to suggest to Western readers the ways in which America (and opportunity, prosperity, and individuality) are experienced entirely differently by non-Western people who migrate to the West, the fact that Biju writes completely exaggerated success stories within his letters home to his father in order not to disappoint him is another major problem to which Desai points. Because of the ways in which notions of the American Dream get "exported" to "distance places," belief in this dream becomes widespread amongst non-Western people, becoming for many, like Biju's father, one of (if not the only) major sources of hope for a brighter future. A refusal to let his father down leads Biju to perpetuate the idea that one truly can "make it" in America; this participation in the exportation of false American ideals is another negative process of globalization often overlooked or ignored by both Western and non-Western people alike. It is this very process which also allows for the continued belief in the need to send a son or daughter "overseas," despite the misery so many experiences while abroad. The fact that Biju's experiences so closely parallel the experiences Jemu had while abroad in England suggest that, despite the pain and suffering of these journeys, generations upon generations of people nevertheless still herald them as positive experiences which make those who undergo them part of a group of people who are amongst the "luckiest...in the whole world" (204).

Yet, it is perhaps the sorrow of the journeys and travels of immigrants which Desai most beautifully, and most painfully, depicts within her novel. Offering a sharp contradiction to the (Western) notion of movement as a form of liberation, freedom, or luxury, Desai describes people like Biju and Jemu as "condemned to movement" (112). The idea of movement as somehow damning or punishing plays a vital role in displaying the "underside" of globalization, particularly since many Western people consider movement—not just the freedom afforded them by cars and public transport, but also the luxury afforded them by quick, cheap travel overseas on planes or cruise ships—as something that is taken for granted, an "obvious" benefit of modernity and globalization. Desai uses this idea of movement not only to display the differences between those who move "freely" or "leisurely" and those who are forced to move, but also to give a sense of how movement, for immigrants, contributes to their erasure from everyday life. In an interview with *The Guardian*, Desai describes the immigrants in the novel as people "in a basement you just see briefly as you pass by." As R. Radhakrishnan notes, the existences of those in spaces of diaspora, such as those of the "shadow class" in America in Desai's novel, become ones in which both the "home country and the country of residence become mere 'ghostly' locations" (123). Just as Biju's father in India becomes convinced that his son does not exist, Biju, too, begins to feel that he is hardly a person at all, but rather just a shadow being asked to quietly disappear (18). He and the other illegal aliens he lives with are described as a "shifting population of men camping out near the fuse box, the boiler, in the cubby holes, and in odd-shaped corners that once were pantries, maids' rooms, laundry rooms"—a far cry from the supposed "prosperity" and "security" said to be enjoyed by those who experience the "American Dream" (58).

Biju's literal movement—how he actually makes his way around New York—is another striking example of the disparities that exist between "Westerners" and "non-Westerners," citizens and immigrants, those who "benefit" from globalization and those who do not. Biju's job delivering General Tso's chicken and Szechuan wings to city residents has him "on a bicycle with the delivery bag on his handlebars, a tremulous figure between heaving buses, regurgitating taxis" (55). In one of the most poignant moments in the novel, Biju on his bicycle "beg[ins] to weep from the cold, and the weeping unpick[s] a deeper vein of grief—such a terrible groan issued from between the whimpers that he was shocked his sadness was so profound" (57). Yet, Biju's grief is far from the only sense of sadness readers are asked to sympathize with when learning of the tribulations that immigrants and immigrant-hopefuls undergo. Those who arrive outside of the Queen of Tarts bakery in New York looking for Saeed Saeed appear "looking weary as if they'd been traveling several lifetimes;" similarly, those waiting outside the American embassy in India in the hopes of getting a visa are described as "a crowd of shabby people [that] had been camping, it appeared, for days on end. Whole families that had traveled from distant villages...some individuals with no shoes, some with cracked ones; all smelling already of the ancient sweat of a never-ending journey" (105, 199). The notion of an "ancient" and "never-ending" journey not only suggests the profound difference between those who "go abroad" for a week-long vacation and those who will spend their lives struggling to travel with even a fraction of that ease; it also serves as grim reminder of the ways in which those outside of the Western world are condemned to endlessly repeat the same journeys that their ancestors before them were subjected to—the parallels between Biju's journey to America and Jemu's journey to England are testament to that very idea. Ultimately, then, Desai's representations of these immigrants profoundly display her sense of the "underside" of globalization within her novel—they become a reminder of the fact that ours is "still a world...where one side travels to be a servant, and the other side travels to be treated like a king" (295). Those on the wrong side, of course, become the "condemned" who, "over several generations," learn the inevitability of "hav[ing] their hearts always in other places, their minds thinking about people elsewhere; they could never be in a single existence at one time" (342).

These inequalities in economics, culture, quality of life, and ability to maintain relationships with one's family and one's people are perhaps the best examples of the fact that globalization is not a "new" world system that embraces "positive" ideals such as multiculturalism, progress, and modernity, but is, rather, a newer version of the same form of world domination upon which imperialism and colonialism were founded. Often, theorists of globalization attempt to posit it as precisely the opposite of what Desai's novel presents—as a world system which is somehow different from the ways in which dominant nations of the "past" exploited weaker nations. Antonio Negri and Michael Hardt, for example, argue that the "postmodernization of global economy" leads to a fading of the "distinct national colors of the imperialist map of the world.... Imperialism is over" (117). While their argument is meant to be a demonstration of the ways in which globalization (or "empire," as they frequently refer to it) represents a more insidious form of power which transcends nation-states, thus potentially spiraling out of the control of those in positions of national power, their insistence that "imperialism is over" nevertheless represents an extremely problematic refusal to acknowledge the ways in which globalization still relies upon the same processes of exploitation and manipulation that were used during colonialism and imperialism. Now, however, this exploitation appears in a "trendier" or more "marketable" form—Saeed Saeed's job at Banana Republic, for example, is an extremely desirable position for an American immigrant from Africa, even though he will "sell to urban sophisticates the black turtleneck of the season, in a shop whose name was synonymous with colonial exploitation and the rapacious ruin of the third world" (112). As Pankaj Mishra notes in her review of the novel, the fact that Saeed has little choice but to eagerly accept this job, despite all of the horrible history behind the corporation's success, indicates a kind of humiliation that "people in the West are 'scarcely aware of,'" but which is a humiliation that is nevertheless "experienced by most of the world's population." Mishra adds that it is this "invisible emotional reality [which] Desai uncovers as she describes the lives of people fated to experience modern life as a continuous affront to their notions of order, dignity, and justice." In this sense, one of the most powerful moves Desai's novel makes is to insist that the shift from "colonization" to "postcolonialism" to "globalization" is hardly indicative of a sort of global progress; rather, it is merely the "recast[ing] in a new vocabulary" of "old ideas and prejudices [that have] not vanish[ed]" (Mignolo, 37). The ease and eagerness with which people of the Western world embrace ideas of globalization and multiculturalism represent what Anne McClintock might call a "premature" "celebrat[ion]" which is "obfuscatory in more ways than one"—most importantly, in its ability to obscure the relationship between past and present, and to refuse to acknowledge the fact that what is "the new age of globalization" for some is merely the "linger[ing] age of colonization" for others (McClintock, 13; Desai, 313).

Yet, even amidst its despair, sorrow, grief and pain, *The Inheritance of Loss* is still, in many ways, a novel of humor, irony, and joy, subtly but effectively ridiculing globalization and its consequences, not just as pernicious and horrible and oppressive, but also as laughable, absurd and incomprehensible. Images and descriptions which make a mockery of modernity abound throughout the novel: Lola imagining "tikka masal whizzing by [the English countryside] on buses, bicycles, Rolls-Royces" as the equivalent of a scene from To the Manor Born; her ability to "purr with pride" over the "sanitized elegance of her daughter's voice, triumphant over any horrors the world might thrust upon others;" Saeed describing the ridiculousness of the American habit of "everyone go[ing] shopping separately" ("separately they cook their dinner, together they eat their separate food. The fridge they divide up, and into their own place—their own place!—they put what is left in a separate box. One of the roommates, she put her name on the box so it say who it belong to!") as compared to the notion of a communal sharing of food such as Saeed learned from life in Zanzibar; Biju hearing of a man who owned a big "white house" with a white Lexus parked out front, even though to afford the house he had to leave it entirely unfurnished, and could only send pictures of the outside of it to relatives in India; cruise ships hiring a "basic drudge staff, all of whom would appear at the final gala dinner in suits and bow ties, skating on ice, standing on one another's shoulders, with pineapples on their heads, and flambéing crepes;" a tourist in India stopping to take a picture of a beaten and raped woman, yelling "Got it, babe...!" while his wife looks on in horror (52-53, 107, 166, 196, 289). Moments such as these, which so beautifully mingle the grotesque and the elegant, the ridiculous and the all-too-real, the absurd and the commonplace, achieve much more than merely rousing a few laughs from the critical reader—rather, they ask the critical reader to stop and think about why she/he is laughing. Ultimately, Desai's novel does not only demand that Western readers carefully consider how globalization effects others; it also prompts them to give some serious consideration as to why they so eagerly participate in this destructive system themselves.

For, if there is anything Desai's novel demonstrates by the time it concludes, it is that, although the influences of globalization often seem "inevitable" or "unavoidable" in our current moment, there are ways to challenge and counter-act globalization's principles, ideologies, and (most importantly) its consequences. As the novel comes to a close, moments of realization begin to occur which suggest, in small ways, alternatives to the "global lifestyle" and its many horrifying effects. The cook, for one, knows that "money isn't everything. There was that simple happiness of looking after someone and having someone look after you" (95). His realization is one that points toward a true sense of connectedness and communication between individuals, a connectedness which many have lost, but which Biju's return demonstrates is not irretrievable. Similarly, Jemu's realization that Sai is the "granddaughter whom he didn't hate" represents a small "miracle" that demonstrates the possibility of beginning to unlearn both self-loathing and the hatred of others; a possibility which, it seems, exists only through an interaction with and acknowledgement of the past, rather than a continual avoidance of it (similar to the avoidance that globalization's proponents encourage when they present it as "different from" colonization) (230). Perhaps most importantly, Sai comes to the critical conclusion at the novel's close that one must not live "safely" within one's "own tiny happiness" when there is an entire "globe twirling on its axis" (356). This perspective, arguably the novel's most important conclusion, seems to simultaneously act as the greatest indictment of globalization's ideologies. For all of its lauding of connectivity, communication, and multiculturalism, the global system ultimately allows for—indeed, encourages—an increasingly problematic and widespread sense of isolation (individual, cultural, national) which limits individuals' abilities to consider the large-scale consequences that their actions have. To think outside of one's "own tiny happiness" and to consider the rest of the world can be for many, as it is for Sai, "a glimmer of strength...[and] resolve" (356).

The Inheritance of Loss ultimately attempts to subtly suggest to readers that fulfillment, all too often sought through (selfish) material "happiness," can indeed still be found through emotional experiences and human interaction. Increasingly, the novel begins to focus on "simpler pleasures"—the image of "two figures leaping at each other" in the morning dawn, or Sai's realization that "music, alcohol, and friendship together could create a grand civilization" (244, 357). Moments such as these remind us of what we all too often forget through the rush and hustle of "modern" living, the disconnected communication provided by technology, and the privileging of commodities and meaningless concepts over human interaction, emotion, and engagement. None of these things, *The Inheritance of Loss* ultimately insists, have become permanently lost with the rise of the modernity—rather, they represent the "shimmering" of "honesty" and "humanity," much of which has been lost in the global world, but which might, nevertheless, be found again, if only with some effort and willingness to pay closer attention to the beauty of the world in which we live (Kirchner).

All too often, theorists of globalization conceive of it as "inscribed with a preordained logic which presumes a singular historical trajectory or end condition;" it becomes viewed as the "last of [several] stages of global transformation" (Held and McGrew, 7; Mignolo, 33). Yet, it is precisely this very notion of globalization as an "unchangeable" force or an "end" of the progress of civilization that makes it appear so unchallengeable to so many. What Desai reminds us continually throughout *The Inheritance of Loss*, however, is that none of us is larger than the natural world in which we live—as she notes, "the mist charging down like a dragon" is engaged in the process of "dissolving, undoing, making ridiculous the drawing of borders" (10). Desai's insistence on historical systems of domination such as colonization and globalization as constructed by human-kind, and as mere moments within an interrelated history, serves as a crucial reminder that none of these "global transformations" are "natural" or "inevitable;" as such, it follows that none of them are unchangeable. The question Desai's novel poses to Western readers is whether or not they are ready to participate in bringing about the necessary change. Regardless of whether the

Western world wishes to acknowledge it, novels like *The Inheritance of Loss* shed light on the fact that the "shadow class" cannot remain in the shadows forever—eventually, those reaping the benefits of globalization will have to face the destruction and violence that globalization, imperialism and colonization impose and have imposed upon other people and other nations. It seems advisable that the West comes face to face with these "shadows" sooner rather than later, for shadows are always, in some sense, reflections of the self. The destruction the West has caused and continues to cause others will, if unacknowledged, eventually come full circle; the potential, then, to save humanity as a whole, rather than to destroy it completely, seems a wonderful and hopeful idea that Desai's novel beautifully, subtly, and powerfully suggests.

WORKS CITED

Barton, Laura. "A Passage from India." *The Guardian*. 12 October 2006. http://books.guardian.co.uk/manbooker2006/story/0,1920237,00.html

Desai, Kiran. *The Inheritance of Loss*. New York: Grove Press, 2006.

Gopinath, Gayatri. "Nostalgia, Desire, Diaspora: South Asian Sexualities in Motion." *Theorizing Diaspora: A Reader*. Ed. Jana Evans Braziel and Anita Mannur. Malden (MA): Blackwell Publishing, 2003, 261-79.

Hall, Stuart. "Cultural Identity and Diaspora." *Theorizing Diaspora: A Reader*. Ed. Jana Evans Braziel and Anita Mannur. Malden (MA): Blackwell Publishing, 2003, 233-46.

Hardt, Michael and Antonio Negri. "Globalization as Empire." *The Global Transformations Reader: An Introduction to the Globalization Debate*. 2nd ed. Ed. David Held and Anthony McGrew. Cambridge: Polity Press, 2003, 116-20.

Held, David and Anthony McGrew. "The Great Globalization Debate: An Introduction." *The Global Transformations Reader: An Introduction to the Globalization Debate*. 2nd ed. Ed. David Held and Anthony McGrew. Cambridge: Polity Press, 2003, 1-50.

Jameson, Fredric. "Notes on Globalization as a Philosophical Issue." *The Cultures of Globalization*. Ed. Fredric Jameson and Masao Miyoshi. Durham: Duke University Press, 1998, 54-77.

Kirchner, Bharti. "*The Inheritance of Loss*: A Moving Tale of Honesty and Horror." *The Seattle Times*. 20 January 2006.

http://seattletimes.nwsource.com/html/books/2002750135_inheritance22.html

McClintock, Anne. *Imperial Leather: Race, Gender and Sexuality in the Colonial Contest*. New York: Routledge, 1995.

Mignolo, Walter D. "Globalization, Civilization Processes, and the Relocation of Languages and Cultures." *The Cultures of Globalization*. Ed. Fredric Jameson and Masao Miyoshi. Durham: Duke University Press, 1998, 32-53.

Mishra, Pankaj. "Wounded by the West." *The New York Times*. 12 February 2006.

http://www.iht.com/articles/2006/02/09/arts/idbriefs11a.php

Pryor, Fiona. "Review: *The Inheritance of Loss*." *BBC News*. 10 October 2006. http://news.bbc.co.uk/2/hi/entertainment/5413704.stm

Radhakrishnan, R. "Ethnicity in the Age of Diaspora." *Theorizing Diaspora: A Reader*. Ed. Jana Evans Braziel and Anita Mannur. Malden (MA): Blackwell Publishing, 2003, 119-31.

Sklair, Leslie. "Social Movements and Global Capitalism." *The Cultures of Globalization*. Ed. Fredric Jameson and Masao Miyoshi. Durham: Duke University Press, 1998, 291-311.

The Global Transformations Reader: An Introduction to the Globalization Debate. 2nd ed. Ed. David Held and Anthony McGrew. Cambridge: Polity Press, 2003, 423-29.

United Nations Development Programme. "Patterns of Global Inequality: UNDP Report 1999."

2

Prizing Sameness? Kiran Desai and The Booker Prize

Ana Cristina Mendes

In the course of an interview given to the Man Booker Prize for Fiction website by Kiran Desai, the recipient of the award in 2006, the interviewer recalls that, briefly after winning, the writer had confessed that she would have liked to have been in India because there "they care for the Booker so much" ("Kiran Desai") Desai clarifies her earlier assertion regarding the high public profile of the prize in the subcontinent: "Indians have always followed the Booker—an old link, I suppose, and the fact that the prize is often given to books particularly pertinent to us" (*ibid.*). It has without a doubt been quite distinctive of the Booker—the London-based literary award attributed annually to "the best novel written in English" by "citizens of the Commonwealth or the Republic of Ireland"—to promote fiction that concerns the British colonial history and what might be understood as its postcolonial present. Furthermore, the prize, with its eligibility prerequisites of Commonwealth or the Republic of Ireland nationality, "refers to the imperial history of Great Britain and the concomitant colonial structure of its publishing industry" (Squires, 45). Still, Desai might be referring also to the unprecedented visibility garnered by diasporic Indian authors writing in English in the last decades, and their favouring by the Booker and its shortlist.

Recent investigations of the politics of the book-prize industry have situated literary awards as a particular form of cultural capital within a contemporary "economy of cultural prestige." James F. English in his recent wide-ranging study "The Economy of Prestige: Prizes, Awards, and the Circulation of Cultural Value" (2005) notes the remarkable rise of prizes in literature and the arts, and identifies the cultural capital of prestige at the very heart of that industry. English argues that this economy of cultural prestige displays a more sweeping globalisation than what has taken place in the economy of material commodities. Moreover, according to John Street, "[t]he prize is a device for conveying market-relevant data," significant because "[c]onsumers need information in advance of their purchase of cultural goods" (820). In other words, those of Richard Todd, in what still remains today as the most comprehensive overview of the cultural politics of the Booker phenomenon: Consuming Fictions: The Booker Prize and Fiction in Britain Today (1996)—the Booker acts as "a consumer guide to serious literary fiction" (61). This, it might be added, is what makes the British literary prize such a huge promotional venture and hence responsible for the hypervisibility of Indian fiction written in English in the global market, a role that led Graham Huggan to understand it as "a popular retailer of the 'postcolonial exotic'" (117).

During an interview, Indra Sinha, an Indian writer whose novel *Animal's People* was shortlisted for the Booker in 2007, pondered over the recurrent charges of exoticism attached to the prize and criticised how the British reading audience has a tendency to suspect a tokenistic inclusion of "people from faraway exotic places" on its shortlist: "And then they say things like, "Three desis on the Booker List"? It shouldn't be like that, really, because it completely demeans and denigrates your book. And it's a bit sad if it's imputed that you are really there because of tokenism" (Naravane). The spectre of tokenism haunting the prize, or the accusation of winning because of "brownie points" (as Arundhati Roy put it after receiving the Booker[1]) and the interrelated perceived co-optation of postcolonial literature by the prize, were remarkably satirised in a sketch, broadcast in 1998, of the British comic television series *Goodness Gracious Me.*[2] This sketch depicts an interview conducted in the context of a literary chat show—"The Book Programme"—which sets out to "discuss the phenomenal success of Asian writers in Western literature." The show's host is joined by three authors on the Booker shortlist, including the fictional character Anita Devi, a probable pun on an eternal Booker bridesmaid Anita Desai: thrice Booker nominated, the first writer from the Indian subcontinent to have a novel shortlisted with *Clear Light of Day* in 1980, subsequently twice nominated with *In Custody* (1984) and *Fasting, Feasting* (1999) and mother to Booker prize winner Kiran Desai. The host questions Anita Devi if there is not "a certain amount of band wagging jumping going on, following the successes of such writers as Vikram Seth and Arundhati Roy," and if she does not feel "the glut of novels by Asian authors" to be "just a fad." Devi rebuts these allegations, while celebrating and essentialising Asian writers as "natural authors" on account of "the rich depth of [their] cultural experience."

The ensuing discussion lampoons the fashionable critical discourse surrounding literature in English by diasporic Indians, namely the celebration of the fertile creative ground made up of "the indelible scars" left by colonisation and by the fight for independence, and the disparagement of Eurocentric interpretations and imperialist preconceptions. The Booker nominated books featured on the show are, according to their authors, inspired by "the thousands of years of civilization," "the duality of the immigrant experience" and "the tradition of the pictorial in Indian literature." As it turns out, these shortlisted novels are a children's book and a colouring book, and were nominated merely because of their authors' Asian-sounding name, as is the case of the outlandish Indira Pakistani character who is, in fact, the white actor Jeffrey Archer, but whose book made the shortlist just the same. When Meera Syal, performing the role of Anita Devi, confidently declares (tongue-in-cheek) that her work—suitably titled *The Little Bear That Goes Shopping* because it deals in reality with a little bear that goes shopping—did not make the Booker shortlist because of her name, she seems to be echoing the (debatable) comment by Pico Iyer: "When a traditional English name takes the prize (...)—A.S. Byatt, say, or Kingsley Amis—it seems almost anomalous."[3]

Focusing on the Booker prize, the broad purpose of this essay is twofold: (1) to look at the star principle that has come to attach itself to Booker prize winners, as well as to the cultural works themselves, and (2) to examine the current (hyper) visibility of postcolonial literature from the Indian diaspora resulting from niche marketing strategies developed predominantly by Anglo-American publishing houses. This essay—"Prizing Sameness?"—has been titled in the interrogative mode so as to accommodate the ambivalence with which cultural commentators, such as the creative team behind *Goodness Gracious Me*, have regarded the canonisation of postcolonial authors and their works by the Booker. The broadcast date of that comic sketch is significant: in 1998, there was a boom in Indian writing in English following Roy's *The God of Small Things* winning of the prize the preceding year. Writers such as Roy have been perceived as having commodified their literary works, benefiting from their postcolonial associations to sell the "postcolonial exotic" in the context of the Booker prize industry (Huggan). In this respect, a scene in Mira Nair's film *Monsoon Wedding* (2001) depicts the aura of profitability and prosperity surrounding the act of writing in English by Indians, when a member of the Verma family makes known that she has applied for a creative writing course in the US, her entrepreneur uncle supports her immediately: "Lots of money in writing these days. Look at that girl who won the Booker: she became a millionaire overnight."

Not only does the sketch from *Goodness Gracious Me* introduce issues of commodification and marketability, connected with the commercial achievements of postcolonial literature, and to which the Booker is certainly no stranger, but it also helps clear the way for questioning whether or not a "postcolonial card" is being played—and if indeed it is, by whom—in the prize's acclaim of postcolonial writers, in this case, of Indian descent. In trying to address this interrogation, the focus will rest on the Man Booker Prize 2006 competition, specifically, by looking at how the winner Kiran Desai might be construed as a postcolonial commodity. With Desai as case study, this essay attempts to map out what Arjun Appadurai has designated as the "social life of things" (1986), i.e. the connotations that commodities—here, postcolonial authors circulating as commodities—come to acquire during their exchange. Accordingly, the writer is to be seen as a product in the global literary marketplace, held to standards of financial viability.

It is commonly agreed that Salman Rushdie's Booker in 1981 and Booker of Bookers in 1993 with *Midnight's Children* paved the way for the success of Indian fiction written in English in a large-scale literary marketplace. His influence was crucial in making the New Yorker (in a commemorative special fiction issue dedicated to Indian writing on the occasion of the 50th anniversary of the country's independence) dub "India's leading novelists" following in his wake as "Rushdie's Children." The label was without delay ridiculed by Amitava Kumar in a review of that issue: "We grew up in India under the stultifying shadow of the nationalist myth that we were all the children of Mahatma Gandhi. Now, if the New Yorker is to be believed, we are all the children of Salman Rushdie" (*The God*, 84).

Kiran Desai, one of Rushdie's "daughters," was hailed by the New Yorker as part of that emergent young crop of Indian novelists writing in English when she was just working on her debut novel, *Hullabaloo in the Guava Orchard* (1998). In fact, her only published work at that time was precisely the short piece included in that fiction issue. Still, the New Yorker was not the only stakeholder involved in turning this diasporic writer into a valuable cultural commodity: Rushdie gave her as "welcome proof that India's encounter with the English language, far from proving abortive, continues to give birth to new children, endowed with lavish gifts" ("Introduction", xxii). This "proof" consisted of an extract of her first novel, by then titled *Strange Happenings in the Guava Orchard*, which he included in his and Elizabeth West's collection *The Vintage Book of Indian Writing: 1947-1997* (1997) a selection of "the best Indian writing of the half-century since the country's independence" (ix).

Accounting for the growing status and rising notoriety of "'Indo-Anglian's literature" a decade ago in the (infamous) introduction to that co-edited anthology, Rushdie concluded that "On the map of world literature (...) India has been undersized for too long. This anthology celebrates the writers who are ensuring that, fifty years after India's independence, that age of obscurity is coming to an end" (xxii). When Desai's novel was published the next year, Rushdie's previous promotional push was boosted: his blurb "Lush and Intensely Imagined" features on the front cover and right under the title of the book, while the authorizing words originally written in the prologue to his and West's collection are included in a three-page opening section under the heading "Further Acclaim for Hullabaloo in the Guava Orchard."

Desai's second book, *The Inheritance of Loss*, winner of the Booker in 2006, has been decried (or praised, according to one's perspective) as a Rushdiesque novel. For instance, Will Self, noting that the Booker has tended to celebrate books that represent "the creative collision of English-language fiction with an explosive, post-colonial world," stated that "Desai's victory seemed like a mainstream choice" and that the novel "for all its individual sparkle and originality, is nothing if not a post-Rushdie novel." On another occasion, *The Inheritance of Loss* was regarded by a representative of the British booksellers Waterstone's as maintaining "the fine tradition of Booker winners set in India" such as its predecessors *The God of Small Things* and *Midnight's Children* (Jury). Earlier, one of the blurbs included in her debut novel read: "Desai spins a hilarious tale with a smattering of Rushdiesque flourish (*India Today*)." In fact, her work seemed to follow a step behind Rushdie, moving from a narrative with "lots of heat and dust, sweating men, lisping saris, and honking traffic, as well as plenty of yakking Indians" (Kumar "Louder", 83) in

Hullabaloo in the Guava Orchard, to a more transnational setting in *The Inheritance of Loss*, a novel which spans the Asian and the American continents to account from the travails of illegal immigrants in New York.

Rushdie, revered as the gatekeeper of Indian writing in English (to a certain extent because of his Bookers) frequently embraces the idea of acting as patron for upcoming writers[4] and granted a seal of approval to Desai with his words full of praise. Both this acclamation and the comparisons made between her and Rushdie's work add cultural capital to her novels and inform the judgement of prospective readers, but who gets the return from this investment when her work is made to circulate in the global literary marketplace? If, as James F. English contends, "the investment of foreign symbolic capital in emergent symbolic markets has been seen (...) as a means of sustaining less overtly and directly the old patterns of imperial control over symbolic economies and hence over cultural practice itself" (298). What are we to make of Rushdie's heavy endorsement of Kiran Desai? When an interviewer asked him last year how significant is marketing to literature, he answered that it was "[n]ot [important] to literature but it's very important for the bank balance of the writer" (Sawhney). Unless we regard Rushdie as fully co-opted by the metropolitan literary industry, hence inescapably part and parcel of the promotional circuit of postcolonial literature, there might be some difficulties in applying the reasoning that English describes. Praise extol.

What is Desai's standing as an Indian diasporic writer and winner of the Booker? If we adapt Huggan's general understanding of the award as an instance of "prizing (cultural) otherness" and recast it, with reference to this writer, as an example of prizing sameness, she is to be regarded as an author who is simultaneously marketed as the exotic other and as the recognizable exotic, made familiar through the comparisons with Rushdie, the "Booker heavyweight" (Muir) himself. Thus, in Huggan's phrasing, "diversity is translated and given a reassuringly familiar aesthetic cast" (27). In fact, only after the connections to Rushdie and parallels with his work had been drawn, were Desai and her work made ready for metropolitan consumption. The prior history of her commodification as postcolonial author, and the fact that her mother was shortlisted three times for the Booker but never won, serve the commercial logic of the Booker prize. As Street remarks, "[a]rtists' previous success (and the reputation attached to it) are essential to the prize becoming a media event. If the shortlist consisted of unknowns, then it would not attract media attention" (838).

If Desai is packaged, priced and thrown out on the market with the help of exoticising marketing strategies, is not Rushdie, the postcolonial lobbyist, the one playing the postcolonial card? Is he not displaying a self-awareness of the field of meaning already constructed around the label "Rushdie"? In all probabilities, he is one of the best examples to demonstrate how postcolonial cultural artefacts are commodified and made to circulate in a context of "postcoloniality," i.e. "a global condition of cross-cultural symbolic exchange" (Huggan, ix) displaying an overt "contradiction between anti-colonial ideologies and neo-colonial market schemes" (Huggan, 413).

Is he strategically playing with the perception, established in both the publishing industry and in academic circles, of "Rushdie" as buzzword? Or is he an unavoidable part of the global cultural economy and its marketing tactic of commodifying a postcolonial writer, as much as his blurb in Desai's *Hullabaloo in the Guava Orchard* is an integral component of the novel's promotional logic? Rushdie may well be redistributing cultural capital, but does this in any way contribute to the restructuring of the metropolitan publishing industry?

In the article "Is Salman Rushdie God?" Kumar denounces a partial view of Indian writers of English that should merit the attention of critics:

> I agree that "writers like Rushdie" or "not like Rushdie" continue to be categories under which most hacks prefer to slot Indian writers. But isn't this a short-coming and shouldn't we be critical of this habit? (...) And don't the

> writers who have emerged in India in the past two decades deserve more than what is given them when we treat them as clones? Yes, it is true that the writers who followed in the wake of Rushdie were inspired by his example, but it is important to take serious note of the different directions in which their work has gone. Their work, I believe, is a creative comment on Rushdie and his extraordinary output. Today, it is impossible to read any new work of Rushdie without also bringing into the discussion the new works by those who are patronizingly regarded as his literary offspring.

In fact, "writers like Rushdie" or "not like Rushdie" is the measure—albeit a very limited one—Indian writers of English are still categorised by. These labels are also used as a way to enhance the cultural capital of the Booker shortlist. Indeed, the impact of the prize on the consumption of literary texts comes mostly from labelling: it distinguishes a cultural commodity through ascription of, among others, exotic qualities, with decisions resulting, in this case, in (postcolonial) canonisation. More than selling books, the Booker contributes to the canonisation of writers, and nowhere is this more evident than in Rushdie's case, an effect that also extends to his "children." I set out to inquire whether a "postcolonial card" was being played in the Booker prize given its favouring of authors coming from nations of the erstwhile British Empire or belonging to minority communities in Britain (Huggan, xii). I conclude by admitting to having somewhat dodged the question when I ended up replacing the "postcolonial card" by the "Rushdie card." It is with the idea of interrogation that I wish to conclude: when the "Rushdie card" is played, who gets the upper hand?

NOTES

1. Jason Cowley. "Guest Column." *India Today International*, 27 Oct., 1997: 23, in Toor 17.
2. Second series, episode three (19'43" – 22'07").
3. "The Empire Writes Back." *Time*, 8 February 1993: 46, in Huggan 110.

4. Check, for example, Rushdie "The Best." Most recently, he has commended Ketaki Sheth for her book of photographs on Mumbai—*Bomay Mix Street Photographs* (Stockport and New York: Dewi Lewis Publishing and Sepia International, 2007)—extolling her work in the back cover with these words: "Ketaki Sheth's photographs, so formally interesting, so sharply seen, so deeply felt, give these street lives the greatest gift such work can offer: the dignity of art."

REFERENCES

Appadurai, Arjun. "Introduction: Commodities and the Politics of Value." *The Social Life of Things: Commodities in Cultural Perspective.* Ed. Arjun Appadurai. Cambridge: Cambridge University Press, 1986, 3-63.

Desai, Kiran. *Hullabaloo in the Guava Orchard.* London: Faber, 1998.

——. *The Inheritance of Loss.* London: Hamish Hamilton, 2006.

English, James F. *The Economy of Prestige: Prizes, Awards, and the Circulation of Cultural Value.* Cambridge and London: Harvard University Press, 2005.

Goodness Gracious Me. Dir. Nick Wood. BBC, 1998.

Huggan, Graham. *The Postcolonial Exotic: Marketing the Margins.* London and New York: Routledge, 2001.

"Kiran Desai: Exclusive Interview." n/d. 01 April 2008 http://www.themanbookerprize.com/perspective/qanda/40

Kumar, Amitava. "The God of Small Things: The West Reads India's 50 years." *Race & Class,* 39 (1998), 83-94.

——. "Louder than Bombs: What's So Hot About Indian Writing?", *Transition,* 79 (1999), 80-101.

——. "Is Salman Rushdie God?", *Tehelka,* 6 August 2005. 01 April 2008 http://www.amitavakumar.com/articles/rushdie2.html

Jury, Louise. "Outsider Desai Is Youngest Woman to Win Man Booker." *The Independent,* 11 October 2006. 01 April 2008

http://www.independent.co.uk/arts-entertainment/books/news/outsider-desai-is-youngest-woman-to-win-man-booker-419525.html

Monsoon Wedding. Dir. Mira Nair. Mirabai Films, 2001.

Muir, Kate. "Exclusive Interview with Salman Rushdie." *The Times,* 04 April 2008. 05 April 2008

http://entertainment.timesonline.co.uk/tol/arts_and_entertainment/books/article3681048.ece

Naravane, Vaiju. "Eyes Wide Open." *The Hindu,* 07 October 2007. 01 April 2008 http://www.thehindu.com/thehindu/lr/2007/10/07/stories/200710075 0110100.htm

Rushdie, Salman. "Introduction." *The Vintage Book of Indian Writing: 1947-1997*. Eds. Salman Rushdie and Elizabeth West. London: Vintage, 1997, ix-xxii.

——. "The Best of Young British Novelists." *Step Across This Line: Collected Non-Fiction 1992-2002*. London: Vintage, 2003, 34-39.

Sawhney, Anubha "An Indian is Not a Freak in London: Rushdie." *The Times of India,* 21 January 2007. 01 April 2008 http://timesofindia.indiatimes.com/articleshow/msid-1343391, prtpage-1.cms

Self, Will. "If the Veil Sucks, So Does the Extremism of Its Foes." *The Evening Standard,* 12 October 2006. 01 April 2008 http://www.encyclopedia.com/doc/1G1 - 152709631.html

Squires, Claire. "A Common Ground? Book Prize Culture in Europe." *The Public,* 11. 4 (2004), 37-48.

Street, John. "'Showbusiness of a Serious Kind': A Cultural Politics of the Arts Prize." *Media, Culture and Society,* 27.6 (2005), 819-40.

Todd, Richard. *Consuming Fictions: The Booker Prize and Fiction in Britain Today*. London: Bloomsbury, 1996.

Toor, Saadia. "Indo-chic: The Cultural Politics of Consumption in Post-liberalization India." *SOAS Literary Review*, 2 (2000), 1-33.

3

An Enchanting Enigma of Kiran Desai's Stylistic Nuances in *The Inheritance of Loss*

Devika

An inevitable comparison between the mother, an established literary personality and the daughter an upcoming but widely appreciated and acknowledged literary writer does not blur the sheen of the daughter's talent. The absence of experience in literary arena of stalwarts fails to intimidate her entry in the foray; no wonder, appreciation for her is immediate and instant:

> Desai might not be the first desi Booker prizewinner—she follows the esteemed footsteps of Arundhati Roy, V.S. Naipaul and Salman Rushdie—but at 35, she is the youngest winner ever. The inheritance of a literary life, however, is one that comes from her mother, novelist Anita Desai, who herself has been shortlisted for the Booker Prize several times.[1]

However, the adulation has spared her exalted humanity by allowing her to be down to earth in her approach. Instead of classifying this myriad work, she prefers to leave the liberty with the readers to read and interpret it the way they seem germane. Kiran Desai seems to be quite candid in her confession when she prefers not to classify her novel either as a comedy, a fable, a combination of styles:

> I wouldn't really—it is a comedy and it is satiric in many ways I think, and it's fantastic. It reads very much like a folktale or a fairy tale so I think it has different sides, different words can be used to describe it. It depends on how you read it, I suppose.[2]

Richly received, this work of hers is analyzed from different angles; the shifting angles sometimes change the focus of the work also but the effect seems to get hold of readers in one or another form; whatever the focus point of approval may be "(w)e do not need to agree with this vision in order to marvel at Desai's artistic power in expressing it."[3]

To provide the information, without any biased backup, yet curled in the delicacy of intricacy, Kiran Desai seems to bank on compactness, crispness and compression surprisingly exuding plethora of details. Her consciousness of its effects seems to assure her of the indelible impact, desired and effortlessly poured. Her practice of using many punctuation marks, earmarking chucks of information, gives immense delight to the readers. Her description of the place, activity and the role of the cook are clubbed together in one simple yet elegant line: "Here, at the back, inside the cavernous kitchen, was the cook, trying to light the damp wood." (1)[4] Though her fervour for long winding sentences never subsides yet she could be as crisp whenever the situation needs it, sometimes to suggest the shift and other times to accentuate the effect.

When suggestiveness is required or nothing else or more is to be conveyed, the use of a word or even a phrase instead of a properly developed sentence yields better and focused impression. Though sentences like "A kind man" (16), "Liars and cheats" (18), "Bruises. Blood" (275), etc. are not grammatically correct but the clarity of the meaning gets nowhere distorted. In fact, the bare but essential details retain their charisma. The mere mention of the words like "Ill. Dead. Maimed" (80), "Disease. War. Famine" (47), "Dead? Dying? Diseased?" (98), etc. is sufficient to conjure the image of destruction and deprivation. To retain the ineffable aura, compactness is used for expressions like "Inefficient beyond belief" (42), "Fun over. Back to work" (94), etc. When she refers to "(c)ompressed childhood, (and) lingering old age" (19) juxtaposition of adjectives to highlight the cruelty of life exudes all charm. Diversity of approach for the same thing has enriched the impact of approach. Repetition of phrases to show alarm and intensity is also not without the intended impact: "Beware. Beware. Keep away. Distrust" (22), "On and on" (30). The whole of the paragraph is of one phrase which is full of suggestiveness, a tool deftly employed by Coleridge in *The Rime of the Ancient Mariner*.

Indubitably, Kiran Desai basks in the abundance of one word sentences, one phrase sentences, one phrase paragraphs or one word paragraphs, but it nowhere indicates the inability to create long and winding sentences. The following sentences running into various lines might seem threatening but it is by no means a vague expression:

> The two of them had been fools feeling they were doing something exciting just by occupying this picturesque cottage, by seducing themselves with those old travel books in the library, searching fir a certain angled light with which to romance themselves, to locate what had been conjured only as a tale to tell before the Royal Geographic Society, when the author returned to give a talk accompanied by sherry and a scrolled certificate of honor spritzed with gold for an exploration of the far Himalayan kingdoms—but fare from what? (247)

Her preference to bank on one line paragraphs might seem to be not a much practiced habit but she utilizes it to show sometimes the disjointedness and the other times the much required shifting link: "But it was 4:30 already and she excused him with the thickening mist" (2). One line description seems to heighten the effect in the absence of supporting details when she writes: "They had come for the judge's hunting rifles" (4). The expression "(s)he felt intensely, fearfully female" (5) might have lost its intensity had the focus been there on minute fill-ins. That one line could be only a simple and short sentence or an elongating one, the need of the expression buttresses it: "They sipped and ate, all of existence passed over by nonexistence, the gate leading nowhere, and they watched the tea spill copious ribbony curls of vapour, watched their breath join the mist slowly twisting and turning, twisting and turning" (4).

Writers, who cherish the enviable position in the arena of creative writing, somehow follow the dictum of show not tell rather religiously. Primarily, though not always, her predilection has resulted in the creation of sentences like "She jigsawed the cups, saucers, teapot, milk, sugar, strainer, Marie and Delite biscuits all to fit upon the tray" (3).

However, the temptation to dwell on details takes the lead when the writer finds it hard to curtail the urge. The way of pleading of the servant is also accompanied by added details to explain how the suppression has blended well with their blood: "His lines had been honed over centuries, passed down through generations, for poor people needed certain lines; the script was always the same, and they had no option but to beg for mercy. The cook knew instinctively how to cry" (6).

Choice of simple but wonderful words, sometimes, is too pleasant to resist. The description of political boundaries is delicately defined with one simple sentence like "Here…it had always been a messy map" (9). Instead of highlighting it in an unpleasant and objectionable way, the point is put forward indirectly with multifold and pointed force. In the novel, crispness of the narration is maintained, which is quite a significant achievement, though the story line sometimes gets knarred. Quite compressed about the change in culture, she uses merely one line to hit the right chord; she tells it but restrains from making it an accusation. The shift in the cultural norms is clear when "the women took off their salwars and wore their kurtas like dresses" (22). Ultimately, though, Desai's success is due more to her finely-tuned observation of the complexities of our world, not just to luck. "Just as the dialogue is simplified and made more and more simple, I think people's emotional responses grow more and more complicated. We tend to place our identities in many different places—we have complicated identities."[5]

The temptation to use exactly the word they want to, makes writers sometimes coin their own ways of narration, the one being the use of nouns as verbs. "He wintered here" (52) when there was "great amount of warring" (9) and "pigeons (kept) shuttlecocking" (62) somehow, he never got to know "the fertile cauliflowering within his son's skull" (59). Nouns are used not merely as verbs but adjectives also. The judge always failed to his "wife...a martaryed and religious mother" (56) and got furious with her for something like "GNLF rally rallying" (215).

Onomatopoeia cherishes an enviable preference with poets but it has been not totally ignored by the fiction writers also. Doris Lessing in her *The Golden Notebook*, banks on these sounds when she writes, "Frrrrrr, frrr, frrr, say the banana trees" (430).[6] Onomatopoeia seems to have fascinated Kiran Desai considerably well as she entertains the readers with a rich dash of it in her novel. Her fondness for using sounds, even when something has already been explained vouchsafes for it. Her characters may be frightened but something keeps their spirits up: "He felt frightened but also a little proud. "Ai yai yai ai yai yai," he said to himself" (120). On the streets where vehicles "(b)acked up and went whroom whroom whrooming!.." (316), he also enjoys the sound of "a comical horn, PAWpumPOM paw or TWEE-deee-deee DEE-TWEE-deee-deee" (286). Immediate attention is caught by the sound of "silver grasses...shuu shuuuu, shu shuuu" (102), the telephone that "rang again and then again. Tring tring tring tring" (97), "the way someone would not blow her nose but went sur-sur-sur in the library" (68), "stones hit the rooftops, BANG BANG BANG BANG" (275) and "(b)ut the door shut itself along with all the doors in the house. Bang bang bang" (105).

If unusual or less used sounds are used then, proper explanation leaves nil scope for confusion. The sound used for cutting wood is properly accompanied by expression also, such as "Rrrr-rrrr, you would hear them, and the sound of wood being sawed" (224-25). Interjections like, "Oof ho" (56), "Oooo BABY! Look at them l e g s! Oooooooo weeee!" (100), etc. make the narrative more lively and more close to real way of conversation. The seasonal music "trrrr whonk, wee wee butt ock butt ock of frogs" (230) is properly synthesized by the sounds when "cows mooed oo aaw, oo aaw" (57). Her imagination becomes immensely fertile as per as sounds are concerned, because not only sounds are given place but to show the increase in volume, letter size is also taken care of, which narrates the increase in volume and duration:

> "PaaaaaaWWW!" (49) She, however, does not feel satisfied with merely unraveling the most common and acceptable sounds, she invents and implements her own sounds also, but the sounds are explained so as not to let the readers be bamboozled by her new coinages. "a thun thun in the legs and arms and sometimes a chun chun" (72). Sounds are even utilized as verbs. Sai's condition was pitied even by "(t)he nuns tsk-tsked because they knew Sai was a special problem" (28).

The need to intermix the two languages is felt and directly transliteration is used; Hindi words and sentences are liberally used. To get the real essence, where translation would have taken the regional touch away, she prefers to use the regional words. The servant merely gives way to his ever-persisting worry when he laments, "Hamara kya hoga, hai hai, humara kya hoga" (8). Conversation tone is kept intact when people feel and utter, "Bhai, dekho, aesa hai..." (95), "Arre, Biju...to sunao kahani," she always said, "batao...what's the story?" (146), "Hota hai hota hai" (179), etc. They eulogize "Angrezi khana" (14), prefer not to talk to a "hubshi" (16) and keep their "chappals" (203) and "durries" (203) very handy. To attain perfection, his son tries hard and the father is very proud about his son's hard work: "Bar bar karta rehta hai" (11). Though she writes in a foreign language, but instead of taking extreme stances, she prefers to remain level-headed as per the utility of the language is concerned, "Perhaps that's why they had been so happy to learn a new tongue in the first place: the self-consciousness of it, the effort of it, the grammar of it, pulled you up; a new language provided distance and kept the heart intact" (208). As a reality check, however, advanced Indian might seem to be but in the presence of the elders one they pay their obeisance in the most humble manner, "Namaste, Kusum Auntie, aayiye, baethiye, khayiye!" (50). The greetings to even the unknown fellows are full of respect, "Namaste, babaji" (75). The humbleness to appreciate the help or favour of others makes words flow from the mouth, "Dhanayawad. Shukria" (50). 'Worthless' appears less significant and out of proportion for her to replace it with the regional and seemingly appropriate words "Bilkul Bekaar..." (139). Of course, the aroma and taste of vegetables is kept intact in "loki, tinda, kathal, kaddu, patrel, and the local saag" (176). While he revels in his day dreaming thinking "(s)hopping ke liye jayeange, bhel puri khange...dollars me kamaenge, pum pum pum" (298). However, reality sneers at it as an "Ekdum bekaar!" (300) approach.

It fails to stand as a mere gimmick because the language used is more close to what people normally speak. Like Emily Bronte in her *Wuthering Heights*, who allows her servants to talk in the language the way they really do, Kiran Desai, has used the trusted technique of well-established writers to impart a touch of genuine happenings in her novel. Instead of dabbling with the artificiality and stiffness of perfection, words are written otherwise and the impact is immediate. It saves the explanation that non-natives are talking when they speak, "caan of saalmon, maaan" (22), "Baaad teee. Baaad teee" (61), "Oh myeee Gaaaawd!" (78), "You GO, gurllll!!!" (149), "but I don' taaalk to my relateev..." (138), "Goimta be a beeeg man, reech man, vhat you say? Ya vanna nice cheekan karry?" (147). Her spellings like "bee-oo-tee-ful country" (131), "POEtatto" (131), "TOEmatto" (131), etc. remind the readers of Arundhati Roy who in *The God of Small Things* has preferred to make many words out of the single word like pronunciation, "Their Prer NUN sea ayshun was perfect" (154).[7] Sometimes, she prefers not to leave the things for the readers to understand on their own and explains immediately, "Who aez thees?" "Very Indian-trying-to-be-American accent" (137). Her penchant to bank on word to word translation has resulted in expression like "such sweet sweet cheeks" (213). Quite interestingly, sometimes, she uses Indianised English, where the idiom is first written in Hindi and then literally translated: "No ghas phoos, no twigs and leaves!" (212).

Her enthusiasm to entertain her readers with the language really spoken by her characters sometimes loses its charm, especially when she allows them to use intense abuses, though she succeeds in retaining her charm as long as she restricts her vocabulary to the normal colloquial expressions. The coverage varies from simple stupid expressions like "Amreeka nehi, bephkuph" (182), "Hubshi hubshi bandar bandar" (185), etc. to the most intense ones like "sala!" (148), "Bitch, whore, cunt, sali" (181), etc. Plethora of abuses like "Pigs pigs, sons of pigs, sooar ka baccha," "Uloo ka patha, son of an owl, low-down son-of-a-bitch Indian" (23) might seem to entertain the readers with the originality of the people's standard but the essentiality of putting the abuses appears to be questionable sometimes. To impart genuine touch by making use of abuses does not appear to be necessary for stating their condition and treatment.

Her paragraph construction varies from one word paragraphs to one line paragraphs to sprawled ones. Through the ensuing line cum paragraph awareness about this electronic era which has changed the standard of living is reflected through equally visually rich way:

> They put down the phone hurriedly then, worried that imagination had a superduper zing bing beep peeping high-alert electronic supersonic space speed machine that
> could
> transfer
> connect
> dial
> read
> trace the number through to their—
> *Illegality*. (81)

Her sprawled description is not used all the times, sometimes she turns out to be too cruel for words to let them slip out of her grasp and she too becomes the spokesperson. The stretch of the fear is pictorially represented with no nonsense approach. However, her creativity in the area of paragraph construction is variedly rich; a rare combination of phrases with a sentence nowhere betrays the sense of perfection. The less explanation leads to more impact as is clear from the following combined lines or combined paragraphs:

> Black flag day on April 13.
>
> A seventy-two-hour strike in May.
>
> No national celebrations. No Republic Day, Independence Day, or Gandhi's birthday.
>
> Boycott of elections with the slogan "We will not stay in other people's state of West Bengal."
>
> Nonpayment of taxes and loans (very clever)
>
> Burning of the Indo-Nepal treaty of 1950. (192)

Liberally indulging in the practice of dashes within the chapter to highlight the disjointedness, she garners the desired impact. The practice frees her from the drudgery of explaining those details which could be made more apposite by just allowing them to speak for themselves through nonverbal signs:

> Biju at le Colonial for the authentic colonial experience
>
> On top, rich colonial, and down below, poor native. Colombian, Tunisian, Ecuadorian, Gambian.
>
> On to the Stars and Stripes Diner. All American flag on top, all Guatemalan flag below.
>
> Plus one Indian flag when Biju arrived. (21)

The information conveyed through the following piece of information religiously displays the impact of these signs, may be more richly as it allows readers the application of their individual imaginative interpretations:

Noni and Sai picked up the physics book again.

Then they put it down again. (69)

The scene related to the description of snakes and their roles is incorporated not with a tinge of overemphasis or underplaying but just with a balanced outlook. The policemen neither make fun of religious rites nor fall victim to it; they just depend on their reasoning and feel free to share, "Pray to them and they will always protect you, and they will never bite you" (13). This trend of showing faith in the cultural beliefs has caught the attention of literary writers, who flaunt its sacredness without making it preposterous. Preeti Singh in *Circles of Silence: An Indian Love Story* also treads on the same line when she allows a pious man to prophesize the future events in the life of a baby, "He continued in a voice low and ominous, 'His own will eat him up'" (6)[8] which eventually takes place in great precision. Like Preeti Singh, Kiran Desai also projects Indian beliefs without letting it become trivial or flippant. When she says, "(v)ery auspicious in Tibet, rain and sunshine at the same time" (196), she does not intend to make fun of the people as superstitious boors but simply states the beliefs of the people there, allowing them their dignity of independent and customary instincts.

Like omniscient approach of Henry Fielding, Kiran Desai also prefers to give personal remarks and judgment about the characters and situations but with great restraint. However, the urge sometimes becomes too overpowering and she makes no effort to curtail her opinionated thinking. In the sentences like, "Jemubhai's father owned a modest business procuring false witnesses to appear in court (Who would think his son, so many years later, would become a judge?)" (57), "He found he began to be mistaken for something he wasn't—a man of dignity" (119), "He isn't scared of anything at all. Even when he was very small he would pick up mice by the tail, lift frogs by the neck...", Biju in this picture did not look fearless but appeared frozen, life his parents" (14), etc. the added explanation serves the purpose. Indubitably, omniscient writer streak is also used judiciously but sometimes the desire overpowers the reason.

Projection of people, situations and things are meticulously drawn. Apropos to the decay settling in the society, things are shown as having delicacy whereas beings are shown as commodity, something so prominently taking place in this modern wasteland. Sai's prominence gets highlighted in her first meeting with the cook: "She had first met the cook when she had been delivered from St. Augustine's in Dehra Dun" (19). When she got to know of her parents' death "(s)he tried to cry, but she couldn't" (28). Psychologically deprived of protection and emotionally drained of bonding, what else she could do except try to cry for something which should come naturally to her? When she comes to stay with her grandfather she finds out "Oh, Grandfather more lizard than human. Dogs more human than dog" (32). The servant is also allowed to think according to his limited mentality when "(h)e would receive a daughter-in-law to serve him food, crick-crack his toes, grandchildren to swat like flies" (17). Interestingly, new raw expressions unconsciously bring a smile on the lips of the reader.

Her similes are not merely decorative but functional also; though her indulgence in similes is not very profuse, but it does not highlight her nonchalance for it, because whenever she makes use of them, it does give the impression of being an intrinsic part. The beauty of her similes is that whatever requires delicacy but no description fits in very easily in her comparisons. Juxtaposition of something intensely delicate yet fierce and powerful could not result in a better simile than a "soul (that) tremble(s) like a candle" (68). Relegation of values, heritage and culture need not be lectured about because the dilapidated condition of "monasteries (that) dangled like spiders" (128) speaks volumes about it. However, "people wish to cling to him like a plank during a shipwreck" (76), when void stares in their faces. Pompous backup of people like "the judge sitting poised like a heron over his chessboard" (88) nowhere compensates for the barren fertility. They are to remain contended dwelling amidst "walls swelled like sails" (73). Life is given to inanimate things and improper and inhuman treatment is left for the animate beings. Death is given its dignity where "spiders lay scattered like dead blossoms on the attic floor" (12). Concretely dead is made abstractly delicate where "the fancy wrought-iron gates to hang like lace between the banks" (12).

Tragedy of life gets unfolded through "(a) mad lady with tin cans hanging from her ears and dressed in tailor scraps, who had been roasting a dead bird on some coals by the side of the road, waved to the procession like a queen" (157), "Kanchenjunga smoking like a volcano or a cigar" (231) remained a silent observer of such people "who lived like a leaf in the apple tree" (199) because "broken umbrellas hanging oddly like injured birds" (158) could no longer protect them from sun and rain. "Mater and Pater finally became reconciled to India, went like mice into an ashram" (198). "The wealth that seemed to protect them like a blanket was the very thing that left them exposed" (242). Mixed feelings, like the ever shifting reality, rarely fall short of truth in its stark plainness. When it dawned on her, she could not help "trembling like a whisker from terror" (244) who "shut her mouth like a fish, and astonishment flooded over her gills" (215). She had a hard time to believe that she had stopped being a part of the ladies' group "making an overexcited noise like women in a sari shop" (172) while "he lay on his back and kicked his legs in the air like a cockroach" (233) and sometimes "silently moving an expressionless face like a sunflower" (143). As a result "(h)e looked like a bandit teddy bear" (242) and now, no longer "applause rang like a downpour" (223) for them. Like "(t)he anger, once released, like a genie from a bottle, could never again be curtailed" (305). Similarly, the charm of life once loosened, has bid them adieu.

Her stylistic sparks of aptness sometimes seem to be perfect, especially when the reference is to the dilemmas, reflection of realities or self analysis. Situation of Sai accurately blends well with her reflection in various household objects: "Round and fat she was in the spoons, long and thin in the knives, pocked by insects and tiddlers in the pond; golden in one light, ashen in another; back then to the mirror; but the mirror fickle as ever, showed one thing, then another and left her, as usual, without an answer" (74). Reflection of the true will-of-the-wisp condition of human beings, lost in the hubbub of mundane regularities, makes the beings aware of their failure to recognize their own reflections. Reflecting the human tendency of indulging in the chain of endless desires, she philosophizes, "The more pampered you are the more pampered you will be, the more presents you receive the more presents you will get, the more presents you receive the more you are admired, the more you will be admired the more you are admired the more presents you will get the more pampered you will be" (95). No wonder, she readily agrees with the statement, "A journey once begun, has no end" (111). Ungrammatical structures like "(w)hen it came time" (79) also seem to highlight the complexity of topsy-turvy occurrence of situations.

People exhibit "(s)hocked silence" (138) and nurture "the hate, pure, purer" (161) when they see common man "(h)and in hand with goondas" (218) or when they come across "(t)hieving, ignorant people" (168). They talk about "(c)heese" and get a reply in "(k)ya cheez?" (217). When human beings are expected to be loyal to their friends, they, somehow prefer to be taciturn and businesslike in their suggestive approach, "Return. No problem. Take rest. Have a holiday" (221). Urgency might skip the action but it never misses the tongue, when people brag about trivialities enshrouded in seriousness, "Flap! Wrap! Things to do! No time to waste! Nation calls!" (226). Sai, as a representative of modern dwellers, prefers to see things from her perspective; to her everything appears to be gloomy because when suddenly she finds herself an orphan: "Sai imagined a sullen bulky architecture, heavyset, solid-muscled, bulldog-jowled, in Soviet shades of grey, under grey Soviet skies, all around grey Soviet peoples eating grey Soviet foods" (27). Robert Browning's optimism does not seem to hold much water when people fail to listen and appreciate the voice and call of humanity about "all was right with the world" (65). The writer succeeds in maintaining the charm in chucks for the immediate effect; however, if not in relation to the whole, the sentences in isolation do feed the demanding urge for beautiful expression, especially when she introduces musical sounds to counterbalance the drabness in expressions like "homeworkless, one day, and delivered her bottom bright as a baboon's, so that she without shame quickly acquired some" (29). "Bulb began to buzz like the beetle on its back skittering over the table" (33), etc.

In her effort to show not tell, Kiran Desai gets mixed results as sometimes the impact pierces through whereas sometimes it simply goes unnoticed. The cook's doubts are very much clear when he thinks, "His son might, might, could! occupy the seat" (59). After dwelling on the elaborate details stating the deteriorating condition of Darjeeling, she makes her characters repeat the same, sometimes she takes it too far and repetition does not allow the charm to sustain the aura. "Darjeeling has really gone downhill," the ladies said with the satisfaction, and meant it not just literally. "Remember how lovely it used to be?" (197) However, expressions of anger, clearly shouting the thoughts of people indulged in, don't require additional explanation to state it otherwise. Use of capitals does the job for the writer: "BECAUSE I'M BORED TO DEATH BY YOU, THAT'S WHY" (163) or "THEY DON'T WANT YOU!!!!" (164). There is wonderful depiction of a cook's culinary skills or his mnemonic skills, when words keep gushing out of the mouth of the cook, with the force of bullets, without any break. Sometimes to highlight the connectivity among the words, Kiran Desai, avoiding the explanative drooling, purely banks on the stringed connectivity in phrases like "washing-bloody-kukris-in-the-mother-waters-of-the-Teesta speech" (238). "All kinds of Hindu-mantra-Tantra-Mother-Earth-native-peoples-single-energy-organic Shakti-ganja-crystal-shaman-intuition stuff" (296), etc. Connectivity of words to highlight the chain of series is somewhat in the same fashion as flaunted by Toni Morrison in her works.

The thinning line between the animals and humans is beautifully depicted by Kiran Desai with the help of the characters in the novel especially through the contrastive treatment meted out to the pet and the wife by the judge. "Mutt was waiting for him at the gate, and the judge's expression softened—he blew his horn to signal his arrival. In a second she went from being the unhappiest dog in the world to the happiest and Jemubhai's heart grew young with pleasure" (209). Animal imagery is prominently used to highlight the degraded status of human beings because in the prevalent changing scenario, objects seem to get better attention then the animals. Human beings are shown "greedy, eating like a fat pig" (259). And the tragedy of the situation reaches an apex when the magistrate finds his pet more beloved than his wife and gives a bitchy treatment to his beloved wife. Irony of the situation is made more intense by putting the dog in the situation of his wife who was completely neglected, ill-treated and forced to consider herself and her life worthless. Instead of thinking of his wife as his companion, he fondly remembers his time spent with the dog, "He pictured the two of them cozy in bed: good night, good morning" (292). When the pet gets stolen, the judge reaches on the verge of losing his mental balance and start shouting for it to come back:

> Please come home, my dear, my lovely girl,
> Princess, Duchess, Queen,
> Soo-soo, Poo-poo, Cuckoo, good good smelly smell,
> Naughty girl,
> Treat-treat time, dinnertime,
> Diamond Pearl,
> Teatime! Biscuit!
> Sweetheart! Chicki!
> Catch the bone! (293)

Kiran Desai fails to control herself from acting as an omniscient writer as far as the cruelty of the husband for the wife is concerned. Despite projecting it through the incidents, she buttresses it with explanation also, "Now Jemubhai wondered if he had killed his wife for the sake of false ideals. Stolen her dignity, shamed his family, shamed hers, turned her into the embodiment of their humiliation" (308). Not only the wife, the granddaughter also feels the lack of warmth and acceptance as is clear from the ensuing sentence: "Sai realized that her own delivery to the Kalimpong in such a manner was merely part of the monotony" (199). "The luckiest boy in the whole world" (187) remains lucky for none as he fails to fulfil his duties as a husband, son, father as well as grandfather. A man who showers all his affection on his pet whereas treats his wife worse than a slave; the hatred and negligence exercised towards her are ample proof of his being the luckiest man in the whole world.

To lay emphasis on details, to highlight the intensity or just to draw the attention of the readers, repetition is exhaustively used, sometimes with success and sometimes with futility. Following expressions bear the testimony to this authentication: "he did, he did, a mistake" (216). "He knew, he knew" (217). "Who had his pride. Knew he was something. Knew his mother knew he was something" (217). "He would laugh and laugh" (219). "I'm telling you, my friend, they will get you; if they won't the robbers will; if the robbers won't, some disease will; if not some disease, the heat will; if not the heat, those mad Sardarjis will bring down your plane before you even arrive" (269). "He was a martyr, a man; a man, in fact, of ambition, principle" (250). "The more she did, the more she did, the more she did" (252). "More moisture in the air than air" (235). "They knew. He knew. They knew he knew. They pretended they didn't know he knew." (135) "Holy cow unholy cow" (135). "Shameshameshameshame to the family" (169) "sorry, sorry, oh so so sorry" (200). "Yes yes yes yes" (204), "they would respond with an indiscriminate machine-gun-fire of NO!NO!NO!NO!NO!" (184). "The solitude became a habit, the habit became the man, and it crushed him into a shadow" (39), etc.

As a writer, sometimes her womanhood seems to take hold of her when she does not hesitate to announce, "Yes, our women are the best in the world," said another woman, "and our men are the absolute gadhas in the whole wide world" (297). Giving vent to the bitterness for taking away the treasure from India, Kiran speaks as the representative of Indians, brutally hurt by slavery. Acutely conscious of it but subconsciously reflecting it, she lets her pen go loose, "What bastards they were!"..."Goras—get away with everything don't they? Bloody white people. They're responsible for all the crimes of the century!" (206). The frustration and deep buried antagonism lead to:

> Jaw clenched unclenched hands clenched unclenched clenched.
>
> ...
>
> Jaw clenched unclenched hands clenched unclenched clenched unclenched.... (206)

Her queries seem to keep flowing through the questioning spirit of her characters: "And have we been rewarded? Have we been given compensation? Are we given respect?" (158). She does indulge in brilliantly expressing the concerns for humanity but somehow falls short of relating it as intensely to her main characters: "Millions risked death, were humiliated, hated, lost their families—YET there were so many here" (189).

Her decision of neither letting her characters evolve, nor providing suitable opportunities to prove themselves, nor to react to the situations in a judicious or prune way, dims the charm of her narration; however, a rare beauty of expression marks her work an enjoyable reading by providing the readers with some of the most exquisite framings. Her expression about the place where "the sound of the jhora that ran deep in the décolleté of the mountain" (34), is strong enough to bewitch the imagination. The cook also enjoys himself when "(r)emembrance, now authentic, shone from the cook's eyes" (88). Not only the cook, both the sisters also revel in the beauty of this ethnic place: "Deeper into Lola's intoxication, when the fire died low, she became serene, drew a pure memory from the depths" (153), "Lola and Noni could hear him and feel safe until the mountains once again shimmered in pure 2k" (45), etc. Grand background against hollow existence reflects the real condition of the judge:

> Outside, passionately colored birds swooped and whistled, and the Himalayas rose layer upon layer until those gleaming peaks proved a man to be so small that is made sense to give it all up, empty it all out. The judge could lice here, in this shell, this skull, with the solace of being a foreigner in his own country, for his time he would not learn the language. (29)

Beauty of expression, whenever it is reflected in its pristine form, does not require any reference to indulge in its lingering and soothing enjoyment. Her sentences like "And in fact, Buddha died of greed for pork" (196), while "(t)he meat charred on the grill, the blood beaded on the surface, and then the blood also began to bubble and boil" (136) highlight the intensity of the deprivation or may be final adieu. "Death whispered into Sai's ear, life leaped in her pulse, her heart plummeted, up they twirled" (31), but Sai is oblivious to "moth wings at the brink of eternity and dust" (198), and busy enjoying life with Gyan "when he tried to test the depths of her eyes with his, her glance proved too slippery to hold; he picked it up and dropped it, retrieved it, dropped it again until it slid away and hid" (125). Initially, "All day, the colors had been those of dusk, mist moving like a water creature across the great flanks of mountains possessed of ocean shadows and depths" (1), but finally all seem to be blessed by the power of serenity in nature when "The five peaks of Kanchenjunga turned golden with the kind of luminous light that made you feel, if briefly, that truth was apparent. All you needed to do was to reach out and pluck it" (324). Her efforts have duly resulted in effervescence praise: "Desai's prose has uncanny flexibility and poise. She can describe the onset of the monsoon in the Himalayas and a rat in the slums of Manhattan with equal skill. She is also adept at using physical descriptions to evoke complex states of mind."

Putting all the threads together, Kiran Desai's attempt to weave gossamer of reality with a distinct touch of an artist, does impress the readers to enjoy her stylistic nuances; her paucity of efforts in character development cannot be easily ignored but her attempt to provide them with a language to express themselves, their relationships and the surrounding scenario does not fall short of the beauty simultaneously ethereal and lingering. In an attempt to display it realistically, her overindulgence in certain tactics, like using abuses or explaining again the same information already revealed through the characters makes her a perfectly human writer, reserving places for peccadilloes. Despite weakened by some aspects, her stylistic craftsmanship does not need any accolade to prove its worth and leave a long lasting impression on the minds of readers. The way characters are introduced, the way abrupt turns are introduced, the way irony of the situation is projected, the way frustration is let loose, the way ambitions are trampled, crashed and kicked, her worth as an artist is firmly established; the story gets over but not the feel of it, simply because the language that unfolds it spellbinds.

REFERENCES

http://niralimagazine.com/2006/12/legacies-loss-literature/ 14.3.08

http://www.randomhouse.com/boldtype/0599/desai/interview.html 14.3.08

http://www.nytimes.com/2006/02/12/books/review/12mishra.html?_r=1& oref=slogin 14.3.08

http://www.nytimes.com/2006/02/12/books/review/12mishra.html?_r=1 oref=slogin 14.3.08

Ahmad, Nakasha. *Nirali Magazine*, LLC Published on December 20, 2006. http://niralimagazine.com/2006/12/legacies-loss-literature/ 14.3.08

Desai, Kiran. *The Inheritance of Loss*. New Delhi: Penguin Books, 2006. All the references quoted from this book are cited from the edition quoted above.

Lessing, Doris. *The Golden Notebook*. 1972. New ed. London: Granada Publishing House, 1977.

Roy, Arundhati. *The God of Small Things*. New Delhi: IndiaInk, 1997.

Singh, Preeti. *Circles of Silence: An Indian Love Story*. Great Britain: Hodder & Stoughton, 2002.

4

Representation of India in Kiran Desai's *The Inheritance of Loss*

Krishna Singh

Kiran Desai, the winner of the prestigious Man Booker Prize, 2006, for her second novel *The Inheritance of Loss* (2006) explores colonial neurosis, multiculturalism, modernity, immigrants' bitter experiences, insurgency and the game of possession, gender-bias, racial discrimination, changing human relations, impact of globalization, *Isthal Puran*-type delineation of the North-East of India, postcolonial chaos and despair, ethno-racial and historical relationships between people from different cultures and backgrounds. Love, longing and losses are dexterously handled in a humane manner articulating diasporic experiences of the novelist who is an Indian citizen but a Permanent Resident of America. Kiran Desai is deeply interested in India—the India of 1980s—honestly represents the mixed image of India. The present paper endeavours to bring forth the various aspects of India and its people. Desai observes everything through the "lens of being Indian," without that perspective, she acknowledged, "she can't write" (wiki/kirandesai). During Jaipur Literature Festival, in an interview she expressed her pleasant experience: "It's best time to be an Indian writer.... I do know that present day India isn't really my subject" (*The Times of India*, Jan. 22, 2007). It was only when she began to writing about the immigrant experience in New York that she realized she would have to return to India. But she finds India has changed, it belongs to the Indian author living in India. The subjects belong to them. She goes back to India of the 1980s. It is this feeling of being caught between two continents that infuses the novel. At times it appears to rejoice in the intermingling of cultures; at others it seems to inspire a wistful melancholy. But, "re-discovering her Indian-ness was vital to her, she tells Laura Barton" (*Guardian*, Thursday, October 12, 2006). Consequently, she makes the novel an Indian treating subjects concerning Indian life in India as well as in abroad. She superbly elaborates all these in a highly experimented English, i.e. uses Indian slangs, dialectic words, abuses of various regions, vulgar and obscene expressions, colloquial vocabulary—introduce an element of naturalism; highly congenial to portrait the image and sensibility of India.

Politically, India was hit by insurgency. It imposed a big threat to law and order. Entire novel is set in the backdrop of insurgency rising in the North-East, i.e. GNLF movement which disrupted the normal life, tourism, business and peace. Out of fifty-three chapters of the novel more than eighteen chapters are exclusively devoted to describe insurgency to highlight the dismal picture of the region. Poverty, unemployment, socio-economic backwardness, xenophobia, discriminatory policies and the government's apathy to seek remedies are deeply rooted in the separatist movements rampant in the whole country. No part is spared; it's alarming and anticipates disastrous consequences: "Separatist movement here, separatist movement there, terrorists, guerillas, insurgents, rebels, agitators, instigators, and all they learn from one another, of course—the Neps have been encouraged by the Sikhs and their Khalistan, by ULFA, NEFA, PLA; Jharkhand, Bodoland, Gorkhaland; Tripura, Mizoram, Manipur, Kashmir, Punjab, Assam...". (128-29). The close nexus among these makes the political problem more grim and intractable. Desai curtly blames the policy makers for these violent movements: "This state making, the biggest mistake that fool Nehru made. Under his rules any group of idiots can stand up demanding a new state and get it, too...it all started with Sikkim. The Neps played such a dirty trick and began to get grand ideas—now they think they can do the same thing again" (128). The genesis of GNLF Movement is narrated by a man clambered up on the bench:

> In 1947, brothers and sisters, the British left granting India her freedom, granting the Muslims Pakistan, granting special provisions for the scheduled castes and tribes, leaving everything taken care of, brothers and sisters—Except us. EXCEPT US, The Nepalis of India. At that time, in April of 1947, the Communist Party of India demanded a Gorkhaland, but the request was ignored...we are laborers on the tea plantations, coolies dragging heavy loads, soldiers. And are we allowed to become doctors and government workers, owners of tea plantations? No! We are kept at the level of servants. (158)

"Gorkhaland for Gorkhas" (7) is the motto of the movement; the activists work on universal guerilla fashion. Kukri sickles, axes, kitchen knives, spade or any kind of firearm they look for to make the movement more and more violent to force the government to grant statehood. Assam, Nagaland, Mizoram and Punjab were on fire with the assassination of Indira Gandhi; and Sikhs with their kanga, kachha, etc. still wishing "to add a sixth K, Khalistan, their own country in which to live with the other five Ks" (108). Socio-cultural and political identity and quest for autonomy furthers and kindles the fire of agitation. Indian Nepalese are "fed up being treated like the minority in a place where they were the majority. They wanted their own country or at least their own state, in which to manage their own affairs" (9). Gyan's involvement in the separatist movement is the reflection of young Indians' deep-rooted frustration, for which Gyan even sacrifices the love of Sai. A feeling of "martyrdom crept over him" (175) and he was overwhelmed and swayed by this vortex. Arson, looting, strike, bundh and the violent reactions were the commonplaces of the time. The novel opens and ends with insurgency. In the opening chapter, Jemu's house is besieged and a hunting rifle is plundered; chapter fifty-two ends with Bijou robbed by Gurkha mercenaries and chased by dogs in the jungle. The partition of India and the emergence of Pakistan is indeed, Desai poignantly reacts: "First heart attack to our country...that has never been healed" (129).

The novel portraits the Indian society as poverty-stricken; moreover illiteracy, unemployment, xenophobia, cultural conflicts, traditional values, customs, practices; and multiplicity of languages, religions, faiths constitute the very structure of the society in which the novelist is deeply interested. Though she draws a dismal picture of the Indian society, she has a humanistic approach—even characters, i.e. Jemu, Sai, Gyan, Biju, Cook, Lola, Noni, Booty, Potty and Bela all are helpless and feel inferior by their subject position—Desai, very candidly and humane manner treats them. Poverty is the root cause of GNLF movement and migration. Gyan's involvement in GNLF movement and frustration caused by the extreme polarities he witnesses between the poor and the rich brings drastic changes in his attitude and love. He is upset to undertake long walk in the cold for the small amount of money the Judge paid him. It maddened him that: "People lived here (Cho Oyu) in this enormous house and property, taking hot baths, sleeping alone in spacious rooms...cutlets and peas dinner..." (162). He is born of poverty and proudly Indian—his family's house still made of mud with a thatch roof. Cook and Biju epitomize the distress of common men. Biju migrates to America because he is badly hit by poverty; he bears every kind of exploitation for the sake of money. Cook renders yeoman services to Jemu. On the contrary, Jemu humiliates and kicks the Cook. It pained Sai's heart to see how poverty has worked on Cook: "A poverty-stricken man growing into an ancient at fast-forward. Compressed childhood, lingering old age.... There was age in his temperament, his kettle, his clothes, his kitchen, his voice, his face, in the undisturbed dirt, the undisturbed settled smell of a lifetime of cooking, smoke, and kerosene" (19). Cook advises Biju: "Just make sure you are saving money" (18) so that they might overcome poverty. Sai's journey from Dehradoon to Darjeeling notices the panorama of village life and India looks as old as ever; realistic description arrests our attention: "Women walked by with firewood on their heads, too poor for blouses under their saris.... It was early in the morning and the railways tracks were lined with rows of bare bottoms...defecating onto the tracks, rinsing their bottoms with water from a can" (30). Chapatis, jalebis, samosa, fish, chips, pakora, tea, chhang, laddoos, chooran, srikhand, fresh milk, etc. figure in regular meals of the society gradually experiencing transition and replacing them with Angrezi Khana. But all over Kalimpong modernity began to ıail.

The novel is a brilliant study of Indian culture—the culture in its transitional phase. Changes are brought out by "colonial neurosis," craze for the Western values, manners, language and glamorous life style; impact of modernization, consumerism, globalization and deep-rooted reaction to indigenous values which failed to sustain life. Characters feel inferior, bounded and defeated by their Indian heritage confronted with colonialism; consequently, they develop grotesque complexes which mar their mutuality and reciprocal relationship. Jemu, Lola, Pixie, Noni, Biju, Cook, Sai, Gyan all are generic, reflect the pain of transition. Despite political freedom, cultural slavery is directly manifested through these characters. They are in a "to be or not to be" position; fail to assimilate new culture and give up original culture in totality. There remains identity crisis which most of the Indians face despite postcolonial reactions in which endeavour is to revitalize indigenous culture and its values. Jemu originally belongs to Piphit, goes to Cambridge for higher studies, selected in I.C.S.; becomes a judge. In this entire process of making, he goes on adopting the West as a model of excellence; he sacrifices his native values. He even changes the name of his desi wife Bela to Nimi; condemns her for her socio-cultural practices; whereas Sai, the granddaughter is commended because she is Westernized Indian brought up by English nuns. Jemu is the finest example of an Anglophile—"being a foreigner in his own country..." (29). Jemu and Sai are type of "estranged Indian living in India" (210). Gyan also satirizes: "You (Jemu and Sai) are like slaves, that's what you are, running after the West, embarrassing yourself" (163). Biju stands for young crazy men of the Third World who dream a plan to go to the West for money making; unflinchingly, they sacrifice original culture and social conventions. When Biju gets full timer waiter position in New York, he sends reactions to his father: "Uniform and food will be given by them. *Angrezi Khana* only, no Indian food, and the owner is not from India. He is from America itself" (14). "He works for the Americans," the Cook reports the contents of Biju's letter to everyone as a thing of pride and high honour in the society. Gyan is also intimidated by Jemu's affluence, very English accent and superior ways. Lola, Noni, Pixie and Mrs. Sen are also camouflaged by British ways. Lola advises her daughter Pixie to leave India because "India is a sinking ship...*the doors won't stay open for ever...*" (47).

Multiculturalism is another characteristic feature of Indian society. Jemu, Sai, Biju, Cook, Lola, Noni, Booty, Potty, Gyan, Mr. and Mrs. Mistry belong to different cultural backgrounds. Desai herself inherited multiculturalism from her parents and grandparents. Her maternal grandmother was a German; grandfather was a refugee from Bangladesh. Her paternal grandparents came from Gujarat, and her grandfather was educated in England. Although she has not lived in India since she was 14, she returns to the family home in Delhi every year. She maintains convivial attitude to all cultures and mildly exposes the vanity and hypocrisy imbibed in them.

Immigration problem is one of the most striking problems. Most of the Indians and Third World citizens face such problem in Europe and America. Desai herself has spent more than twenty years in America, she still holds on Indian passport; struggling to get American citizenship; increasingly, she, too, is unsure that she would really want to surrender her citizenship. It was her own experience and intimate talks with immigrants in America she could highlight the problem so emphatically. Biju, Saeed, Harish Harry, Saran, Jeev, Rishi, Mr. Lalkaka and thousands of Africans, Latin Americans and Asians working in American and Europe exemplify the bitter experiences of the immigrants. Father Booty is another example of illegal immigrant who lives in India for forty-five years, while he has the visa for two weeks only. Later he is forced to leave the country. Biju spends his early days working as waiter in New York soon there was "green card check" (16) on employees. He was relieved by the manager, who advised him: "just disappear quietly..." (16). Saeed applied for the immigration lottery each year, but Indians were not allowed to apply hence Biju continued to dodge authorities, moving from one ill-paid job to another for thirty years. He is frightened to see the lot of illegal immigrants: "...there were those who lived and died illegal in America and never saw their families, not for ten years, twenty, thirty, never again" (99). He is overwhelmed by fugitive role, nostalgic reminiscences and racial discrimination; soon he is disillusioned by the West. Immigrants' painful experience is embittered by racial discrimination. Biju, whose hopes are very lofty; feels ecstatic when selected to work in New York; soon he encounters with the working conditions, racial discrimination and immigration laws; he is enlisted as "shadow class" (102), discovers authentic colonial experience how Third World natives are exploited and humiliated in the West: "They drew the lines at crucial junctures" (23) and "on the top, rich colonial, and down below, poor native; Colombian, Tunisian, Ecuadorian.... Above all, the restaurant was French, but below in the kitchen it was Mexican and Indian" (21). Even the glamorous image of the West changes into hatred: "There was a whole world in the basement kitchens in New York" (22). "...the habit of hate had accompanied Biju, and he found that he possessed an awe of White people, who arguably had done India great harm" (77). Jemu also experiences racial discrimination against Indians while he was studying in England and thereafter too. Gyan and GNLF activists find Delhi has adopted discriminatory policies against Gorkhaland.

Nature and landscape description occupies large canvas of the novel; though it extends from Manhattan to Himalayas, it is central to Piphit, Kalimpong, Cho Oyu, and Darjeeling. Topography, scenic beauty, variety of vegetation, changing colours of the sky, patches of clouds, rain, mist, mountain tops, Teesta river, thick forests, cluster of houses, vapour, ice, zig-zag roads and seasonal changes, etc. define nature in the novel. It is sensuous beauty which delights the novelist very much, simultaneously, it is contrasted with rising insurgency and it's violent outbreak disrupting normal life. Her treatment of nature is highly poetic and Wordsworthian finding deeper import in it. The novel opens with nature description: "All day, the colors had been those of dusk, mist moving like a water creature across the great flanks of mountains possessed of ocean shadows and depths. Briefly visible above the vapor, Kanchenjunga was a far peak whittled out of ice, gathering the last of the light, a plume of snow blown high by the storms at its summit" (1). Desai's observation is very keen, acute and specific; even the different parts of a tree embody sensuous beauty as well as represent the psychic conditions of the inhabitants: "Kanchenjunga glowed macabre, trees stretched away on either side, trunks pale, leaves black, and beyond, between the pillars of the trees, a path led to the house" (19). Sometimes, she juxtaposes and blends together various objects and presents an elaborate portrayal, free from "pathetic fallacy" (phrase coined by John Ruskin to signify fidelity between object and its delineation). The vicinity of Cho Oyu is marked by it:

> ...a wetter climate, a rusty green landscape, creaking and bobbing in the wind. They drove past tea stalls on stilts, chicken being sold in round cane baskets, and Durga Puja goddesses being constructed in shacks...paddy fields and warehouses...to the right, the Teesta river came leaping at them between white banks of sand. Space and sun crashed through the window.... By the riverbank, wild water racing by, the late evening sun in polka dots through the trees, they parted company. To the east was Kalimpong barely managing to stay on the saddle between the Deolo and the Ringkingpong hills. To the west was Darjeeling, skidding down the Singalila mountains...not a street light anywhere in Kalimpong, and the lamps in the houses were so dim you saw them only as you passed...forest making ssss tseu tsts seuuu sounds. (30-31)

Her involvement in nature and landscapes of India confirms her unending interest and diasporic articulation. Unlike Wordsworth, Desai hardly tries to divinize nature or feels the presence of God anywhere. She investigates parallel development in changing seasons and incidents of violence: "*The incidents of horror grew*, through the changing of the seasons, through winter and a flowery spring, summer, then rain and winter again. Roads were closed, there was curfew every night, and Kalimpong was trapped in its own madness. You couldn't leave the hillsides; nobody even left their houses if they could help it but stayed locked in and barricaded" (279). Nature is, here, subservient to human emotions and actions; gives force and meaning and aesthetic beauty as well. *The Sunday Express* has eulogized Desai's portrayal of nature and landscapes and masterly use of language: "Descriptions of the mountains and the people of Kalimpong, the changing seasons and the inner mindscapes of her characters are mesmerizing; her use of language is virtuoso, and her ideas sparkle" (Courtesy: Internet).

The novel is essentially a study of losses—loss of culture, loss of identity, loss of human relations, loss of emotional binding, loss of human values, loss of rationality, loss of peace and harmony, loss of human beings' faith in each, etc. Sense of loss is an integral part of every character's life; they are insecure, and unmoored, struggling to survive in the modern world, unsure of whether they will ever see the benefits of globalization; characters unnecessarily feel inferior due to their Indian heritage. Historical events have deep personal import that last people's lifetime and even beyond. Jemu who originally hails from Piphit; goes to Cambridge for higher studies, selected in I.C.S. and becomes a judge. He is so much impressed and immersed in Western values, he loses his original Indian identity and feels "foreigner in his own country" (29). He is one of those ridiculous Indians who can't rid themselves of what they had broken their souls to learn and whose Anglophilia can only turn into self-hatred. These Indians are also unwanted anachronism in post-colonial India, where long-suppressed peoples have begun to awaken to their dereliction, to express their anger and despair; GNLF movement is an outburst of that reaction and Gyan's xenophobia is rooted in it. Jemu can't free himself from "colonial neurosis" (46). He envied the English. He loathed Indians. "He worked at being English with the passion of hatred and for what he would become, he would be despised by absolutely everyone, English and Indians both" (119). Jemu loses peace by the arrival of Sai and Biju and GNLF activities; strongly misses the glorious past and Mutt for whom he laments loudly. Due to insurgency North-East loses three Ts: "Tea! Timber! Tourism" (225). Sai also loses indigenous cultural values. In the process of academic learning in a convent school Western Christian values enter into her blood. Though she remains "full of contradictions" (30) she also suffers from identity crisis. The biggest loss she feels profoundly is the love of Gyan. Biju who goes to New York with bright hopes, soon discovers authentic colonial experience how Third World poor natives are exploited and humiliated in the West: "They drew the lines at crucial junctures" (23) and "on the top, rich colonial, and down below, poor native; Columbian, Tunisian, Ecuadorian.... Above all, the restaurant was French, but below in the kitchen it was Mexican and Indian" (21). White men also shout: "Uloo ka Patta son of an owl, low down son-of-a-bitch Indian" (23). Even the glamorous picture of the West changes into hatred: "There was a whole world in the basement kitchens of New York" (22). He also faces tough and discriminatory immigration laws in America, fails to procure green card; listed "shadow class" (102) of illegal immigrants in New York and spends thirty years time dodging the authorities, moving from one ill-paid job to another. His bitter experience in America and home sickness compels him for homecoming. Even in his own country he finds total loss of peace, law and order. He is robbed by GNLF activists and chased by dogs. Biju emerges as a generic figure, represents young crazy men of the Third World who dream a plan to go to the West and face tough ordeals there. Lola, Noni, Pixie and Mrs. Sen are also trapped by British ways. Lola advises her daughter Pixie, a BBC reporter: "Better leave (India) sooner than later.... India is a sinking ship. Don't want to be pushy, darling, sweetie, thinking of your happiness only, but the doors won't stay open for ever..." (47). Lola and Noni are publicly humiliated by Pradhan of GNLF, violate the dignity of genteel women while both the sisters go to complain against encroachment in Mon Ami. Loss of dignity and dreamland (Mon Ami) make them helpless. Father Booty, who runs a dairy in Kalimpong, spends forty-five years as an illegal immigrant, while he has the visa for two weeks only. Later he is forced to leave the country. Consequently, he lost "every thing but his memories" (257). Gyan sacrifices the love of Sai for his Gorkhaland. Cook loses his honour when he is cruelly beaten by Jemu on the missing of Mutt. Almost all of Desai's characters have been stunted by their encounters with the West.

Kiran Desai makes the novel Indian—both by contents and form. Whether its topography, idyllic beauty or the elaborate description of insurgency, description of mountains, mist, changing seasons, Kalimpong, Cho Oyu, Darjeeling, Piphit, immigration problem, culture conflicts, the inhabitants or the inner mindscapes of characters, Desai frees herself from the stereo-typed Euro-centric models and honestly and independently depicts India. Her use of language is another powerful technique to create the manifest sense of Indian-ness. She prefers American English and tries to make it Indianized. She has encountered with American and British writers of English and studied creative writing at Columbia University. Subsequently, she has experimented a lot with the language. Use of popular slangs, dialectic words, abuses of various regions, vulgar and obscene expressions introduce an element of naturalism; Indian vocabulary, Indian metaphors and imagery, etc. are highly supportive to fillip the portrayal of picture and sensibility of India. Indian vocabulary creates a congenial atmosphere to transport the reader into that realm where India resides.

Every chapter in the novel begins with topical line, italicized; thereafter, the novelist elaborates and illustrates the topic. Chapter one *All Day* introduces major characters, secluded life in Kalimpong, Kanchenjunga, Judge, Sai, Gyan,

Biju Cook, Mutt, insurgency in North-East and romance of Gyan and Sai. Chapter three *All the Way in America* elaborates immigrants' bitter experiences, disillusionment and racial discrimination. Chapter seven *Oh, Grandfather more Lizard than Human* focuses on Jemu's character—dehumanized and Anglophile. Chapter nine *Oh my God* introduces Lola, Noni and their craze for the West and changing identity. Chapter fifteen *In Kalimpong* topography and scenic beauty of the region is highlighted. Chapter twenty *Gyan and Sai* deals with love and insurgency. Chapter twenty seven *Moody and restless* expresses the unrest of Gyan. Chapter forty *The Incidents of horror Grew* portraits the increasing insurgency in Kalimpong.

Use of popular slangs, dialectic words, abuses of various regions, vulgar and obscene expressions are frequently used: *nakhara, pakora, huzoor, chhang, mia-bibi, mithai, pitaji, Angrezi Khana, salwars, kamaal hai, Baap re!, laddoos, dhotis, jhora, pallu, Budhoo, choksee, Neps, Namaste, aiyiye, baethiye, khaiye, dhanayawad, shukuria, chapattis, jalebi, haveli, tika, chokra, murga-murgi, bania, dhobi, hubshi, haat, atta, srikhand, kundan, peepal, choolah, rasta roko, phata phat, Bilkul Bekar, Jai Gorkha, Saag, bhai, Goras, ghas phoos, goondas, sukhtara, susu fucking oil, ber, chooran, jamun, tatti, roti-namak, gadhas, murdabad, parathas, tamasha, chappals, desi,* etc.

Even full length expressions figure significantly: "*Humara kya hoga, hai hai, humara kya hoga*" (8), "*Bar bar karta rahata hai*" (11), "*O! Yeh ladki zara si deewani lagti hai...*" (51), "*Angrez ki tarah. Angrez Jaise,*" (105), "*rasta rook*" (107), "*Gas maar raha hai*" (217), "*Jai Gorkha*" (7), etc.

Abuses and vulgar expressions: "*Sooar ka bachha*," "*uloo ka patha*" (23), "*sala*" (148), "*bephkuph*" (182), "*bhenchoot*" (287), "*sala machoot*" (289), and "*gadhas*" (297), etc. Indian imagery and metaphors are also used: "cheeks like two Simla apples" (262); the technical terms also get place, i.e. "24 k" (45). Obscene descriptions read like a blue film; for Desai they are not obscene or pornographic. She narrates them very candidly. Jemu's sex with his wife Bela reads like this: "...he clamped down on her, tussled her to the floor, and as more of that perfect rose complexion, blasted into million mates, came filtering down, in a dense frustration of lust and fury—penis uncoiling, mottled purple-black as if with rage, blundering, uncovering the chute he had heard rumour of—he stuffed his way ungracefully into her" (169).

Whenever she tries to emphasize an expression, she adopts four different methods:

(1) Size of the letter/letters goes on increasing: "ooooo!" (49).

(2) Use of capital letters: "But I don't NEED to go. / Oh, but you MUST" (154). "Except us. EXCEPT US. The Nepalis of India" (158). "BECAUSE I'M BORED TO DEATH BY YOU, THAT'S WHY" (163).

(3) Number and size of the letters go on increasing: "paaaaawww," (49), "*twe tweeeeee twhoo*" (50).

(4) Use of italics: "*Because of people like you!*" "*...three Ts: Tea! Timber! Tourism!*" (225). "*You are the one who is stupid*" (304).

Use of Periphrasis: "Indian foreigner" (220)—Father Booty who spends forty-five years in India. And "first heart attack to our country" (129)—partition of India.

Use of Hyperbaton:

"Muttoncurrymuttonpulaovegetablecurryvegetablepulao...". (207)—busy restaurant waiter speaks.

Rhetorical Questions: "And are we allowed to become doctors and government workers, owners of the tea plantations?" (158)—a GNLF activist addresses the crowd and answer is implied.

No Punctuation: for fast action, Desai does not use any punctuation: "Cups plates beds chairs wiring light fixtures..." (43).

Desai uses crispy, terse, pithy, broken and cryptic sentences; and interestingly, she too has frequently used elaborate, detailed, run on lines, poetically gifted to describe nature and landscapes. Sonali Das finds the instances of "transliterations and situation modified language" (*The Critical Endeavour*, p. 42).

The Inheritance of Loss was the result of eight years' work, writing of broken people, difficult lives; writing not just about India but Indian communities in the world. It was quite difficult, emotional experience for Desai, because she was devastated and sad by the end of the book where "loss" predominates. Binnie Kirshenbaum has rightly commented about the novel: "A nation's tragedies, great and small, are revealed through the hopes and the dreams, the innocence and the arrogance, the love betrayed and the all, too, human failings of a superbly realized cast of characters. Kiran Desai writes of Post-colonial India, of its poor as well as its privileged, with a cold eye and a warm heart" (Courtesy: Internet). Political, social, cultural, economical, immigration, nature and landscape, Indianized English all aspects are dealt in and described in a comprehensive manner which is not only entertaining but also highly informative.

REFERENCES

Desai, Kiran. *Hullabaloo in the Guava Orchard*. London: Faber and Faber, 1998.

——. *The Inheritance of Loss*. New Delhi: Penguin Books India, 2006.

Das, Sonali. "Kiran Desai's *The Inheritance of Loss:* A Study in Humanism", *The Critical Endeavour*. Volume XII, December, 2006.

Mishra, Pankaj. NYTimes.com/2006/books/review.

Raveendran, P.P. "The Indian Diaspora", *Littcrit*. Vol. 27, No. 1&2 Jun.-Dec., 2001.

The Times of India. New Delhi: Monday, January 22, 2007.

http//www.orkut.com/community.aspx

http://www.Sawnet.org/books/authors.pp? Desai+ Koran

http://en.Wikipedia.org/wiki/Kiran

http://Search.barnes and noble.com/

http://www.powell.com

www.browse.com/biographies

5

Aspects of Globalization in *The Inheritance of Loss*

Jackie Haque

Kiran Desai won the Man Booker Prize of 2006 for her work *The Inheritance of Loss*. It was her second novel which she took seven years to complete. Desai accepted the Booker Prize by saying, "To my mother, I owe a debt so profound and so great that this book feels as much hers as it does mine." Her mother, Anita Desai, is also a renowned writer by her own right. Days of working side by side with her mother in the sleepy New York village of Cold Spring as they toiled over their respective manuscripts, capping some evenings with dinner and rum, Desai described when she was interviewed by Dinitia Smith for *The New York Times*.

The Inheritance of Loss is set in quite different background than that of her first book *Hullabaloo in Guava Orchard*, which is a story about a middle-class post-office clerk who wants to avoid his failure and jumps on the guava tree in order to become a hermit. All the characters revolve around the guava tree.

The second novel is of a different note, the story unfolds as a young teenager comes from a convent to live in Kalimpong, a Himalayan town in the Indian state of West Bengal. To its west there was Darjeeling. Her parents lived in Russia in the days when India was falling out of love with it; both of whom were killed there. Her grandfather Jemubhai is a retired judge who lives in Cho Oyu a house built by a Scotsman while living in

India as an employee of the colonial empire. Even though the house is dwindled, the judge retains his sahib-like etiquettes picked up from the English while studying there. It is said that the book in a way is Desai's autobiography as her own grandfather went to Cambridge just the way Jemubhai Patel did. Desai does acknowledge that the novel was a family story.

The parallel story is of Biju's diaspora to the melting pot of the United States of America. Biju is the son of the cook who brings up Sai as his own with the limited resources in Cho Oyu. The novel deals with globalization, immigration, terrorism and racism from an Indian perspective. Desai squeezes in all of which with utmost sincerity; but like her predecessors she was not spared from the criticism that she portrayed the Indo-Nepali community with negativity. They said she depicted them as "crooks, thieves and beggars." She even got the threat that her book would be burnt on the streets of Kalimpong. *The Inheritance of Loss* deals with Nepali insurgency and she mentions in an interview that she feels sympathy for the cause. In this paper I want to explore the themes of globalization in *The Inheritance of Loss*.

On a cool, foggy winter's day Sai's home is attacked by some hooligans who forced themselves in Cho Oyu and demanded tea and refreshments, they also took away guns owned by the judge Jemubhai. The only three and half inhabitants who resided in the lush green hillside bungalow were left terrified by the episode. When the judge sent the cook to the police station for filing a complaint the police actually suspect that the cook himself might be involved in the robbery.

As Sai was falling in love with her math tutor at her tender age of sixteen, the Indo-Nepali rebels in the mountain town were stepping up movement for their demand for a separate homeland.

The slogan was "Gorkahland for Gorkhas." Just like in 1971 when the Bengalis wanted their independence from Pakistan, "it was the Nepalese this time fed up with being treated like the minority in a place where they were the majority." It was a declaration of the need for a homeland for the ethnic minority community in India. Kiran Desai is very much conscious about the politics of the Himalayan town of Kalimpong and has portrayed this with uncanny precision.

It's worthwhile to mention the time of history in which Desai was setting the plot of her novel. The '60s, '70s and '80s, the cold war between two global blocs was at its height. The USA and the then Soviet Union were in a ruthless competition in globalizing their respective ideas. One was trying to globalize socialism and the other capitalism. In the process of this tug-of-war, that particular time in history saw huge numbers of countries gaining independence. Independence itself emanates from the people's sense of freedom. However, at that time in history, these two global powers were instilling the sense of freedom in many countries across the world for suiting their own needs.

As we make our journey through the novel *The Inheritance of Loss*, we feel that Desai poses questions on post-colonialism and globalisation. The judge who is devoid of any feelings for his family members especially his granddaughter is an embodiment of a "sahib" who had lived in India as government official of the colonial rule. Like the real sahib he had a pet dog named Mutt. The judge bestowed all his affection to Mutt. He calls the dog "little pearl" whereas he addresses Sai as a "Stupid fool." Sai was growing up in a house where the dog was more human than dog. We come to know from the narrative that Jemubhai used to force himself upon his young wife as she didn't like to commune with him. Neither does he have any friends apart from Mr. Bose whom he is reluctant to meet. Mr Bose mounted a court case that Indian ICS men should be paid equal to the white ICS men. They lost the case. Years later his son also fought a case against his employer Shell oil and he too had lost. But their battle for justice went on so fought again and again.

> The man with the white curly wig and a dark face covered in powder, bringing down his hammer, always against the native, in a world that was still colonial.

Biju on the other hand was changing his job from one Indian restaurant to another either because he was not liked by the owner or vice versa. Even though the American dream has sought him to a foreign land who thought himself to be the "Luckiest boy on the whole wide world" when he got the American visa; Biju couldn't set his heart to fulfill his American dream. Through the eyes of Biju, Ms Desai shows how the melting pot where Mexicans, Indians, Pakistanis, Colombian, Tunisians, Gambians, Trinidadians, Guyanese, Ecuadorian, Kenyan all get muddled up, yet remains so unique.

The Inheritance of Loss has globalisation as its epicenter. Sometimes it's the west which is trying to globalize its ideals as in the case of the judge and Sai and his westernized neighbourhood on the other hand India is the power which is being spread across the west. So the book is actually depicting the tug-of-war that is taking place between the western culture and the eastern one.

The colonial encounter can be seen as an adversarial confrontation between two competing nationalisms. It is known that colonialism comes from the violent and expansionist energies of European nationalism. So the history of decolonization has been articulated through the resistant counter energies of anti-colonial nationalism. This anti-colonial nationalism is needed in aspiring the oppressed and colonized people of the world. Post-colonialism is just another name for globalization of culture and histories.

Cho Oyu, the judge's house is abundant with foreign materials or ideals there is *National Geographic*, a western magazine which inspires people to care about the planet. Sai reading it as the dog Mutt snores gently in her sleep. The judge has a cook who prepares "Angregi khana" for him. Ham roll ejected from the can and fried in thick ruddy slices, of Tuna fish Soufile, Khari biscuit pie (17). The judge always had bed tea in the mornings.

Upon arriving at the port in England he was marveled at "a white person to pick up a brown person's bag." He started comparing the English (Boxy) with the Indian (loopy) cows.

After coming from Cambridge with a UK degree Jemubhai couldn't accept others at the same rank as himself. He ill-treated everyone including his young bride whom he left just as soon as he got married. As Sai arrived at Kalimpong the judge was very disturbed. Later, he found that his granddaughter was like him; convent going Indian girl brought up by English nuns. But the cook was quite disappointed when he found that Sai was only coming from Dehra Dun and not as far away as America!

Even as a school boy, the judge admired Queen Victoria's portrait in his school. He was so deeply impressed by a woman so plain had such great influence! On his way to earn his degree in the UK his mother packed some food and bananas with him "just in case;" he thought of his mother's love as "undignified love, Indian love, stinking unaesthetic love" and threw the food away in the ocean. The same judge years later felt unimaginable pain at the thought of his pet dog Mutt being lost; he went frantic with the fear that Mutt might have been killed.

In the judge's neighborhood all the houses had names like Mon Ami; a French name. When Lalita was transformed into the Anglican version Lola went to see the GNLF chief as his men were building huts in Mon Ami's vegetable garden he refused to accept the name as Indian or Nepalese. Pixie alias Piyali Bannerji was a BBC reporter and Lola never gave up the opportunity to take pride in it. When Mrs Sen's daughter Munmun got a job in CNN she considered her daughter as an asset to her country and good enough to compete with her neighbour Lola.

The vegetable garden in Mon Ami had broccoli which were procured from England. They even preserved a Jam Jar which inscribed "By appointment to Her Majesty the Queen Jam and Marmalade manufacturers."

As Biju's plight in the hot center of Galaxy one can't help think of Jhumpa Lahiri or Zadie Smith's depiction of the second generation Indian born desis in the west. *The Namesake* and *White Teeth* both present the conflict of the first generation to hold on the tradition of the country of origin and that of assimilation by the second generation. Biju's employer Harish Hari runs an all Indian food shop named Gandhi Café where he tries to uphold the Indianness whereas his daughter was totally Americanized.

> Nose ring found compatible with combat boots and clothes in camouflage print from the army-navy surplus. (149)

When her parents confronted her by slapping her or telling her "You Go girl!" she answers:

> I didn't ask to be born.... You had me for your own selfish reasons, wanted a servant, didn't you? But in this country, Dad, nobody's going to wipe your ass for free.

Harish Harry and his wife are beyond belief by their daughter's actions. And the romances, "the Indian-white combinations" were a problem for them, it was difficult for them to handle culturally. Even the white customers who were his bread and butter infuriated him:

> Every time one enters my shop I smile—Hi How ya doing? But all I want to do is break their necks. I can't but maybe my son will and that is my great hope.

Like all immigrants it's the money that brought them to this country; some of them get the money that come to get others don't but in the process they lose their most valuable possessions. Their next generation, their children who don't feel as their parents do about India. To them it's just another country from where their earlier generation came from.

While in Kalimpong there was a strong sense of presence of western culture what we see in the US it is quite the contrary. The Indian community is becoming increasingly popular in trade, and other fields of work. Earlier in the book we saw India swallowed the jewel coloured kingdom Sikkim, Darjeeling was annexed from Sikkim and Kalimpong belonged to Nepal. Kiran Desai shows that all Indians living in the US have adopted some mechanism of assimilating their culture, food, music in the host country. We hear some business man talking, "we need to get aggressive about Asia."

It's opening up, new frontier, millions of potential consumer, big buying power in the middle classes, China, India potential for cigarettes, diapers, Kentucky Fried, life insurance, water management, cell phones, big family people, always on the phone, all those men calling their mothers, all those mothers calling their many many children this country is done, Europe done, Latin America done, Africa is a basket case except for Oil. Asia is the next frontier. Is there oil anywhere there? They don't have oil? Do they?

Indian businessmen are portrayed as money making factories where the employers use the employees as their machine. They all hire illegal immigrants who can be made to work for long hours with minimum wages with no medical treatment. While Biju hurt his knee his employer gave him two days off but he refused to go the doctor. He had to be sponsored in order to go the doctor which meant going to the INS and saying that no US citizen can do the job so an Indian has to be hired.

> Millions risked death, were humiliated, hated, lost their families—YET there were so many here. (189)

In Kalimpong, Gyan had a strong sense of nationalism and had strong hatred for Sai's servile nature towards the west, Sai celebrated Christmas which infuriated Gyan and asked if she would celebrate Guru Nanak's birthday or Durga puja, Dussehra or the Tibbetan new year. When Sai tried to reason by saying that Christmas is as much a holiday as any other Indian holidays, Gyan retorted:

> You are just like slaves that's what you are running after the west embarrassing yourself. It's because of people like you we never get anywhere. (163)

And there the bitter-sweet relationship is sacrificed in the name of revolution for statehood.

But we come to know that Lola, Noni and father Booty all agreed that they didn't like English writers writing about India; "it turned stomach; delirium and fever somehow end with temples and snakes and preserve romance, spilled blood and miscarriage. It didn't correspond to truth English writers writing about England was good."

Biju's father's unfaltering dream of being rich or rather his son will earn enough money to change his luck as he lives in the best country in the world. He thought, "It was strange that India went first with day, a funny back to front fact that didn't see mirrored by any other circumstances involving the two countries."

Desai poses the question of pretension by the Asian community living in the west we see Biju's employer who refuses to acknowledge himself as a Gujarati. In case other people from Gujarat ask for undue favour. His friend Saeed from Zanzibar who is afraid that the whole of his hometown will come to stay with him. And so he unplugs the phone. The cook also sends messages to help this person and that to his son. When someone goes abroad it becomes customary to think that they have made it big there.

The dream to have the green card is the only dream that makes the immigrants suffer with out which was they were not going back home. There were illegal immigrants who had the desire to move into the mainstream.

> He was illegal, his taxi was illegal, the yellow paint was illegal, the whole family, and all the men in his village were here, perfectly infiltrated and working within the cab system of the city.

So they endure whatever come their way so strong is their passion for assimilation.

In Kalimpong as Sai, Father Booty, Uncle Potty Noni and Lola go to change their library books on their way they were near the bridge, the only bridge that connects the northern India, Uncle Father Booty decided to take a picture of a butterfly. His camera and the books from Gymkhana library were confiscated.

Before coming here Sai saw Gyan at a procession that was giving slogan "Gorkhaland for the Gorkhas," as soon as Sai saw him he ignored her completely. This reminds us of the Marxist procession in Arundhati Roy's *The God of Small Things* where Velutha was seen. Again, he ignored Rahel and Estha.

As the police came to inform Father Booty that his camera had focused the bridge that was spanning across the Teesta and as they searched everything in his house Father Booty was found to be illegally living in India. He had two weeks to leave.

Kiran Desai reveals in an interview that she depicts the darker side of immigration in *The Inheritance of Loss.* According to her, there are enormous gains but the losses are also significant. As people move from the native land they wonder where the center is and as Asians were taught to look at the west as the center of happiness. As one grows older one realizes that no matter which part of the world you are in there is someone else in some other part of the world and you don't know anything about that part of the world. Hence, half the story of their life takes place elsewhere therefore for all the characters in the book happiness is a complicated thing.

> And not pure. And not single in nature. Sai finds that there are many competing claims on what she thought was her little territory. Gyan believes his location of happiness is smaller than many of the other characters. And Biju is the one I find most hopeful. Because he makes an emotional decision in the end and not an economic one.

Even though Kiran Desai wanted to tell the story of a westernized community in the small town of Kalimpong overlooking the snowy edge of Kanchenjenga, she narrated her story from a very personal viewpoint, serious issues of globalisation, racism and immigration came up as she tells the story. She may not have put the issues of Nepali insurgency for the want of homeland for the Gorkhas from a heroic point of view, but she does present a story of some very alive, lonely people and their pain, happiness and loss, a loss they never wanted. They have inherited this sense of loss.

WORKS CITED

Desai, Kiran. *The Inheritance of Loss.* India: Penguin Books, 2006.

Gandhi Leela. *Post-colonial Theory: A Critical Introduction.* India: Oxford University Press, 1998.

http://edition.cnn.com/2007/WORLD/asiapcf/04/23/talkasia.desai/index.html

http://www.ohdave.net/2007/03/sunday-reading-kiran-desai.html

6

Italo Calvino's *The Baron in the Trees* and Kiran Desai's *Hullabaloo in the Guava Orchard*: A Comparative Analysis

Elisa Armellino

In an interview of some years ago, the young Indian novelist Kiran Desai revealed that the story in *Hullabaloo in the Guava Orchard* was inspired by a real event. As she explained:

> I started with a very small idea, really. I'd read a story in *The Times of India* and heard about a character from many people, a man who was a very famous hermit in India who really did climb up a tree, who lived in a tree for many, many years, until he died. He died last year, I believe. So I began to wonder what it was about someone like this who would do something as extreme as to spend his life in a tree. So it started really with that character, and then the story built up around it. (McWeeney—see web-site in Bibliography)

However, almost all readers who love the works by the great Italian writer Italo Calvino can easily identify many parallelisms between *The Baron in the Trees* (original title: *Il barone rampante*) and Desai's novel. The first and very obvious analogy is the fact that the main characters in the texts decide to spend their lives in trees. Nevertheless, what I will argue is that the tales have in common much more than this.

Some of the main themes with which they are concerned are the same and they are both examples of magic realism, though with slightly different meanings and implications.

Before dealing with the key-points more fully, a brief presentation of *The Baron in the Trees* is needed. This charming story was written in 1957 and forms, alongside *The Cloven Viscount* and *The Nonexistent Knight*, *The Ancestors* trilogy. I will define it as a 'novel' in this essay, though keeping in mind Italo Calvino's own words in his Preface to the work:

> There are two different words in English, novel and romance, for what in Italian is always called a *romanzo*. But although we have only a single word for them in Italian, the difference between the two kinds is felt. The three tales collected in this volume are what I think should be called romances in English. In the fifties, however, what was expected from Italian literature in general, and from me in particular, was novels. This is why they raised eyebrows when they appeared in Italy. (Calvino, 5)

The Italian author mentions here the fact that everybody was expecting a realistic work from him, whereas he offered to his readers a deeply imaginative and unrealistic one. The story begins in the small (invented) town of Ombrosa in Liguria. As the author, who spent all his childhood and adolesecence in this coastal region of Italy, points out: "It is natural when I tell imaginary stories that this country should be like the Riviera where I grew up. So the Ligurian landscape, where trees have almost disappeared today, in the Baron is transformed into a kind of apotheosis of vegetation" (Calvino, 9). This is, very briefly, the plot: Cosimo Piovaschi di Rondò is the twelve year old son of the Baron Arminio Piocasco di Rondò and spends his time living comfortably in his family castle. One day (it is the year 1767) he refuses to eat the snails he has been served at table and—after being scolded vehemently by his father—he climbs up a tree and decides never to come down again. Despite all attempts by his relatives at making him change his mind, Cosimo manages to stay among branches and leaves for the rest of his life. However, he is not content with remaining in the same place. Thus, he travels around from tree to tree and does more things than a man who spends his life keeping his feet on the ground is supposed to do. He falls in love with the young Viola, he meets several secondary characters (including thieves and a group of Spaniards who live in trees) he has his heart broken, and he becomes a Baron and finally goes back to Ombrosa, to his first arboreal home. From there—true to his principles until the very end—he departs by hanging on to the basket of a hot-air balloon.

From the account given, many elements in common between Calvino's and Desai's stories can already be identified. In *Hullabaloo in the Guava Orchard*, Sampath Chawla climbs up a tree after having a serious quarrel with his family because of his bad behaviour. Unlike Cosimo, he has not refused to eat something (when he takes the important decision he is already twenty years old). He has performed a striptease at his boss's daughter's wedding and thus lost his job at the local post office. The two types of rebellion are very different and yet they both reveal a sense of repulsion towards social impositions. Italo Calvino makes his main character choose a non-conformist way of life because of what seems—at a first glance—a very trivial reason. However, behind Cosimo's refusal of snails, deeper meanings are hidden. Cosimo is a young boy in love with nature, whereas his family cares only about social duties and social prestige. The snails on the table are the dead remnants of creatures which have been cruelly killed. They embody the dis-respect of his family (and, particularly, of his sister Battista) towards his most important values as a child and as a human being. The way in which Battista prepares and serves her dishes is almost grotesque and reveals how much hidden cruelty and resentment lies inside her towards the world she lives in:

> Battista was a really excellent cook, for she had the primary gifts in the culinary art, diligence and imagination, and when she took a hand no one ever knew what surprise might appear at table; once she made some pate toast, really exquisite, of rats' livers; this she never told us until we had eaten them and

> pronounced them good; and some grasshoppers' claws, crisp and sectioned, laid on an open tart in a mosaic; and pigs' tails roasted as if they were little cakes; and once she cooked a complete porcupine with all its quills, who knows why, probably just to give us all a shock at the raising of the dish cover, for even she, who usually ate everything however odd that she had prepared herself, refused to taste it, though it was a baby porcupine, rosy and certainly tender. (Calvino, 25)

Therefore, what makes Cosimo totally horrified are not snails per se but the meanings he attaches to his sister's behaviour. As the narrator (Bruno, Cosimo's younger brother) reveals: "Most of these peculiar dishes of hers were thought out just for effect, rather than for any pleasure in making us eat disgusting food with her.... Even more revolting than the sight of this dish was the thought of Battista zealously preparing them, of those thin hands of hers tearing the little creatures to pieces" (Calvino, 25). To run away and climb up a tree are actions which mark for ever (both mentally and physically) the distancing from his parents and from the ideas they maintain. It would be total nonsense for him to remain with them and adapt to their parameters. Therefore, from his point of view, the absurd idea of living in the trees is the only solution to escape from a too limited world. Almost the same can be said of Sampath's shocking behaviour at the wedding. Indeed, everyone in the story believes that he is a calm, quiet boy who could never dare break the most obvious rules of politeness and good social conduct. And yet, for many years, Sampath has hidden in the deepest recesses of his soul a total sense of disgust towards the life his father has carefully prepared for him. Unhappy with his job and with his existence in general, Sampath is an imaginative introverted boy who spends his time contemplating mysterious things in his mind or observing nature in admiration. His inner world is so rich that he is able to turn what is meaningless to others into something magnificent, as this passage demonstrates:

> The room was quite dark, since he had closed both the window and the door so he might conduct his

> exploration undisturbed. In order to survey himself in all his finery, he lit a candle by the mirror and watched as he metamorphosed into a glorious bird, a magnificent insect. The mirror was mottled, slightly clouded, speckled with age. He felt far away, lifted to another plane.... (Desai, 38)

His lack of interest in what society defines as successful achievements (to make a good career and to marry a beautiful wife, for example) deeply offends his father. As he confesses to his wife, talking about their son: "Ever since he was born, this boy has been progressing steadily in the wrong direction. Instead of trying to work his way upwards, he started on a downward climb and now he is almost as close to the bottom as he could ever be" (Desai, 26). The 'arboreal' route Sampath takes stands for a total rejection of his father's requests and hopes. Thus, both Desai's and Calvino's stories deal with difficult relationships between children and parents. In *The Baron in the Trees*, Cosimo's mother is described as a woman of almost 'military' manners:

> Our mother, the Generalessa, did not worry us, as even when serving herself at table she used brusque military manners, 'So! Noch ein wenig! Gut!' and no one found fault with her: she held us not to etiquette, but to discipline, supporting the Baron with parade-ground orders, 'Sitz ruhig! And clean your nose!' (Calvino, 24)

As Bruno—Cosimo's younger brother and also the narrator of the story—says, after explaining how uncomfortable it was to sit at table together: "So it can be seen why our family board brought all the antagonisms, the incompatibilities, between us, and all our follies and hypocrisies too; and why it was there that Cosimo's rebellion came to a head" (Calvino, 79).

However, there is something more in the two texts than a mere conflict between generations. At a deeper level, the stories revolve around the theme of alienation. Both Sampath and Cosimo suffer from a painful sense of displacement. They are different from other people; they have different needs, desires and feelings. Of course, this does not mean that they are akin to each other. On the contrary, they have quite different personalities. Cosimo lives in the 18th century, in the Age of Enlightenment. He embodies perfectly the faith in rational thinking, empiricism and sensism of his time. Though his decision to spend his life in trees may seem absurd, from above he is able to look at the world below with objectivity. He does not spend his time alone in the same place for all his life. He travels and sees the world, he keeps on studying and reading. Like the essayists of his time, he also writes a treatise, entitled *A Projected Constitution for an Ideal State Founded on the Tree-Tops*. Even the most important historical figures of the Enlightenment—like Jean Jacques Rousseau and Denis Diderot—are somehow in contact with him (whether because they meet him or because they know him by repute).

Thus, Cosimo is much more 'in' the real world than what might be supposed at first by a reader who begins to read his story. Indeed, he experiences many situations in life which range from love and battles to thievery. This is also a strong belief of the Enlightenment: only through experience (and through the help of reason) are human beings able to write on the *tabula rasa* which is initially their soul. Thus, Cosimo's rebellion against his parents is also a form of rebellion against given assumptions about the world which, according to him, need to be questioned and reshaped through a closer observation of things. Therefore, the principles of the Enlightenment are offered against the old fashioned principles of the Ancien Régime (the political and social system that used to exist in France before the Revolution of 1789). When Bruno describes the daily routine at home, he actually makes a parody of courtesan manners and privileges:

> Life at our home was a constant dress rehearsal for an appearance at court, either the Emperor of Austria's, King Louis's, or even the mountain court of Turin. When, for instance, a turkey was served, our father would watch carefully to see if we carved and boned it according to royal rules, and the Abbé scarcely dared touch a morsel lest he made some error of etiquette.... (Calvino, 79)

In Kiran Desai's novel, the young Sampath Chawla is—like Cosimo Piovaschi—a rebel and, yet, he is so in a different way. His whole existence is endowed with a sense of the supernatural. Like the main characters in Salman Rushdie's *Midnight Children*, his birth is an event of an almost mysterious and incredible kind. First of all, he was born when monsoons finally came to the village of Shahkot after months and months of terrible drought. In addition, immediately after rain began to pour down on roofs and streets, a Swiss relief plane dropped down Red Cross supplies greeted with happiness and joy by everyone. When Kulfi (Sampath's mother) finally holds her baby in her arms, she can see what the book describes as "a creature that looked as if he had come from another planet altogether, or had been discovered in the woods, like something alien and strange" (Desai, 12). All this makes people predict a marvellous future for Sampath:

> Attempting to include Kulfi in their high spirits, the neighbours assured her that her son was destined for greatness, that the world, large and mysterious beyond Shahkot, had taken notice of him. 'Look! Even people from Sweden have remembered to send a birthday present.' And: 'Let's name him Sampath,' they said. 'Good fortune.' (*ibid*)

However, Sampath's mother is the character who most influences the development of the child. She is the real 'sufferer,' the one who cannot stand the rules of society her husband strongly respects and adheres to. Indeed, she is an unhappy wife. She is married only because of her parents' imposition, since her family thought marriage was the only way to keep her craziness under control. As the narrator explains: "Clearly she was going mad. Yes, there it was—the eccentricity that had plagued her mother's side of the family for generations bubbling up yet again, just when they hoped the culprit genes had finally run into some dead end and been laid to rest" (Desai, 63).

From this point of view, we are now able to achieve a better understanding of the theme of alienation in the story. Sampath's decision to climb up the guava tree in his orchard and never go back is the rebellion his mother could not attempt. From another point of view, it is also the character's achievement of a full coming into being. Only in the tree can he resort to his inner strength and become what he is without being silenced by others. Indeed, both Italo Calvino's *The Baron in the Trees* and Kiran Desai's *Hullabaloo in the Guava Orchard* describe, like 'bildungsromans,' the growth of the main characters. In this sense, the climbing of trees in both tales is a metaphor for the re-discovery of the true self. Trees are primitive symbols of life and the cosmos. Both Cosimo and Sampath are in contact with the forces of nature thanks to their new 'privileged' position. However, the ways in which they develop their identities and exploit these forces are of a different kind. Cosimo Piovaschi resorts to books and culture, whereas Sampath Chawla is in an almost sacred state of spiritual awakening in which only nature finds a place. In addition, unlike Cosimo, he never moves from his tree. In Calvino's novel, the arboreal varieties mentioned are many. There is no one single tree, as there is no one single truth but many truths to discover through multifarious experiences. Thus, Cosimo senses Italian olive trees as friendly ones, which help him in his travellings by twitching easily under his hands and feet. He finds it more difficult to explore ficuses and pines, because of thorns and needles, and sees chestnuts as totally unhospitable homes, whereas he is in love with beeches and oaks. In Desai's work, Sampath remains on the same guava tree. Interestingly, in his mind the world he can observe from branches seems perfect and still:

> This orchard matched something he had imagined all his life: myriad green-skinned globes growing sweet-sour and marvellous upon a hillside with enough trees to fill the eye and enough fruit to scent the air.... Oh if he could exchange his life for this luxury of stillness, to be able to stay with his face held towards the afternoon like a sunflower and to learn all that was to know in this orchard; each small insects crawling by.... (Desai, 51)

Thus, his attitude is of a meditative kind. The world he sees from branches is a microcosm in which to find peace and rest. Like a detached philosopher, Sampath achieves a deeper awareness of things but does not take part in action. Indeed, Kiran Desai describes him as a spiritual guide—her satirical attack being against the 'creation' of gurus by the credulous. All the inhabitants of the village go to him, standing by the tree, and ask him for advice, receiving a few obscure sentences in reply. The only creatures who manage to break his almost sacred silence are the monkeys, which climb up the guava tree and sit near him or run in the garden and steal food from Kulfi. However, what really makes Sampath sad are not animals but humans. He is far less free than Cosimo: he cannot escape through forests; he can only remain on the same tree, wakened and bothered by devotees:

> About Samapth's tree there was a feeling of the air being stretched tight and wrapped around and around him. When he peered down, all he could see was an ugly sea of humanity. Nobody respected his visiting hours any more. Several men marched about the periphery of the orchard, banging the ground with sticks and blowing upon whistles.... (Desai, 184)

Thus, like Cosimo, he becomes very popular. Yet, unlike Calvino's hero, he wants to hide from society, whereas in *The Baron in the Trees* the narrator says: "What he [Cosimo] had in mind was an idea of a universal society. And every time he busied himself collecting people, either for a definite purpose such as guarding against fire or defending from wolves, or in confraternities of Trades such as the Perfect Wheelwrights..." (Calvino, 258).

From what has been said so far, it is clear that Cosimo is the prototype of the involved intellectual of his time (with—it must be added—a warrior-like spirit, since he is able to fight enemies in real battles) whereas Sampath is akin to the prototype of the spiritual, thoughtful man. Interestingly, the differences between the two characters mirror the stereotypes of Western and Oriental culture. However, what is important is that both authors, Calvino and Desai, portray their characters with much sense of humour and define their choices of living in trees as forms of rebellion against the dominant ways of thinking of their time. As a consequence, they dismantle all easy assumptions about life as a whole. This is what is really in common between their stories: the rejection of what is taken for granted without being questioned, the passive acceptance of reality without critical thinking.

In addition, as can be inferred from the ending of the novels, Cosimo and Sampath are also examples of loyalty towards themselves and their ideals. Interestingly, almost the same chain of events—though in a different context and with a different solution—is presented by Italo Calvino and Kiran Desai in the last chapter of their novels. In both of them, a crowd meets at the foot of the tree and stands there, looking at what is happening among the branches, until—in a final apotheosis—the 'heroes' are released from the burden of their existence by flying away after clutching the rope of a hot-air balloon (in *The Baron in the Trees*) and by turning into a guava fruit (in *Hullabaloo in the Guava Orchard*). After creating a sense of suspense for what comes next, the authors make their characters perform their last 'show' and then disappear. In different ways, this offers a final escape to them.

Cosimo has grown more and more tired of his life and falls ill. He is almost dying when a doctor climbs up his tree. Before thc doctor reaches him, the Baron vanishes in the sky:

> Some English aeronauts were experimenting with balloon flights along the coast.... Cosimo had raised his head too and was looking fixedly at the balloon. And then suddenly the balloon was caught in a gust of westerly wind.... The dying Cosio, at the second when the anchor rope passed near him, gave one of those leaps he used so often to do in his youth, gripped the rope, with his feet on the anchor and his body in a hunch, and so we say him fly away, taken by the wind, scarce braking the course of the balloon, and vanish out to the sea.... (Calvino, 285)

Thus, Calvino offers his character an almost spectacular 'sortie.' The same does not occur in Kiran Desai's novel. When military forces are called to oblige Sampath to get out of the tree and to send the monkeys away, the character disappears and, in his place, an enormous guava fruit is found. Readers may suppose the fruit is Sampath himself. Indeed, the guava fruit once made him think of the perfect shape of the universe:

> Here and there in the branches near him, the season's last guavas loomed from amidst the moonlit leaves. One, two, three of them...so ripe, so heavy, the slightest touch could make them fall from the tree. He picked one. Perfect Buddah shape. Mulling in its insides, unconcerned with the world.... Beautiful, distant fruit filled with an undiscovered constellation of young stars. He held it in its hands. It was cool, uneven to his touch. (Desai, 204)

This final transformation is, in a sense, the sublimation of Sampath's life. He remains in the tree all his life, despite the attempts of people to make him change his mind. In other words, he succeeds in being what he wanted to be: a person who is different from other people, and who is one and the same with nature. Yet, the only solution offered to him is metamorphosis. If he is to continue his life, he must necessarily change and leave his old self for ever behind.

What Kiran Desai does here, is to use magic realism to create a sense of the supernatural (Sampath must certainly possess some god-like qualities if he is able to turn himself into a guava fruit!) and to achieve comical effects. The enormous guava fruit is stolen by a monkey, which runs away while everybody tries to catch it.

Thus, in conclusion, Kiran Desai's *Hullabaloo in the Guava Orchard* seems in many ways in parallel to some of the main themes in Italo Calvino's *The Baron in the Trees*. Despite historical and cultural differences, both works offer an imaginative and witty portrayal of the world they describe and state the importance of finding new perspectives from which to look at life in a subtler, non-conformist way.

REFERENCES

Angulo, Elena. *Magic Realism: Social Context and Discourse*. New York: Garland, 1995.

Bock, Hedwig and Albert Wertheim. *Essays on Contemporary Post-Colonial Fiction*. Munchen: Hueber, 1986.

Calvino, Italo. *Our Ancestors: Three Novels: The Cloven Viscount; Baron in the Trees; The Non-Existent Knight*. London: Minerva, 1992.

Desai, Kiran. *Hullabaloo in the Guava Orchard*. London: Faber & Faber. 1998.

Di Carlo, Franco. *Come leggere in nostri antenati (Il visconte dimezzato, Il barone rampante, Il cavaliere inesistente)*, Milano: Mursia, 1978.

Durix, Jean-Pierre. *Mimesis, Genres and Post-Colonial Discourse: Deconstructing Magic Realism*. London: Macmillan Press, 1998.

Gorlier, Claudio and Isabella Maria Zoppi eds. *Cross-cultural Voices: Investigations into the Post-Colonial*. Roma: Bulzoni, 1997.

Perrella, Silvio. *Calvino*. Roma: Laterza, 1999.

Pescio Bottino, Germana. *Calvino*. Firenze: La Nuova Italia, 1967.

Rushdie, Salman. *Midnight's Children*. London: Cape, 1981.

Williams, Patrick and Laura Chrisman. *Colonial Discourse and Post-Colonial Theory: A Reader*. New York: Columbia University Press, 1994.

7

Anatomising Immigrant Lives: Kiran Desai's *The Inheritance of Loss*

Reena Mitra

A sizeable segment of contemporary writing in English today comprises fiction by women writers who lend their work insights and perceptions characteristic of their kind alone and who take sharp cognizance of a wide and varied range of experience indispensable for an understanding of the world around. A literary handiwork is conditioned by imaginative experience as well as by the past or prevailing social predicament. Kiran Desai, essentially a diasporic writer of Indian origin, is now, with a Booker Prize-winning novel, *The Inheritance of Loss* (2006) to her credit, vehemently and persistently claimed as an Indian English writer of fiction. This postulate, however, is largely justified in the light of the fact that both her novels deal primarily with life in India.

Kiran Desai, with the advantage of a globalised language as her medium—a language she uses to perfection—and the exposure to significant modern Western literary movements like post-modernism, has given a fresh orientation to fiction in English at the interpretative and construal level as also on the linguistic and stylistic plane. Most expatriate writers of the second generation of Indians abroad have a vague and diffident grasp of life as lived in contemporary India and tend to portray what are, in effect, "imaginary homelands" (to use Salman Rushdie's expression). What they depict most confidently is what they have seen from close quarters, i.e. the lives of Indian immigrants primarily in Great Britain and the United States of America. Kiran Desai, unlike this majority of writers living abroad, portrays both life in India in the recent past and the life of Indian Americans settled in the United States with a verisimilitude and a sureness of touch that is rare.

Kiran Desai's first novel, *Hullabaloo in the Guava Orchard* (1998) ran into a lot of flak on the ground that the treatment it gave to its central thematic motif of the Indian holy man and his credulous following in the nation was not a convincing one. This very theme had been more profoundly and persuasively explored about forty years ago in Bhabani Bhattacharya's novel, *He who Rides a Tiger* (1954) and R.K. Narayan's *The Guide* (1958). The author's chef d'œuvre, *The Inheritance of Loss*, however, is a work far more plausible than her maiden venture and analyzes confidently with equal ease the lacerating immigrant experience of the non-Nepalese in Darjeeling, Kalimpong and other neighbouring hilly areas holding forth with fortitude and resilience against the Gorkha National Liberation Front's demand for Gorkhaland and the ordeals faced by the Indians and nationals of other Third World countries in the capacity of expatriates making a sincere bid at self-actualization and assimilation in the country of adoption.

Robin Cohen in *Global Diasporas*[1] defines a diaspora as a community of people who have settled outside their natal country but acknowledge their loyalties towards and ties with the country of their origin by voicing or implying a sense of co-ethnicity with the people of their country back home or as fellow members of their diaspora. Victor Ramraj in his essay *Diasporas and Multiculturalism*[2] discriminates between immigrant/exile and expatriate writing and diasporic writing by asserting that immigrant writing would be more inclined towards the contemporary experience in the host society whereas diasporic works are likely to be more preoccupied with the idea of the deserted or imagined homeland. Kiran Desai has adeptly blended in her later novel immigrant and diasporic writing for on the one hand she depicts the problems confronted by immigrants like Biju in the United States and on the other, she delineates the heart-rending pangs of remaining away from one's homeland and being discriminated against for having permanently settled in a geographical area one does not belong to. Alienation and estrangement are inherent aspects of the migrant situation in which the individual's identity is torn between the old and new worlds of experience. Immigration itself being a facet of post-colonialism, relevant here is the statement drawn from *The Empire Writes Back*: "a major feature of post-colonial literature is the concern with placement and displacement."[3] The ramifications of these two terms, "placement" and "displacement" are multiple and the psycho-cultural issues involved are many.

Today, American writing in English including the works of the Indian diaspora has evolved into an amazingly diverse canvas catering to the experiences of people from different ethnic, racial and immigrant groups that are today incorporated into the social edifice of the United States of America. Kiran Desai, an established member of the Indian diaspora in the United States, makes the best of this prevalent multiculturalism in her country of adoption by re-living in *The Inheritance of Loss* a significant chunk of the history of India when inordinate insurgency born of the Nepalese Movement during the 1980s perpetrated heinous crimes on the pretext that the community was being persecuted and tormented in Bengal. They were not prepared to settle for anything less than statehood, a homeland in and around Darjeeling and Kalimpong. The GNLF men assaulted affluent Bengalis and people from other states who they believed had encroached upon their land. One such target was Jemubhai Patel, the Gujarati judge who had chosen to settle in Kalimpong after his retirement. Born in pre-Independence colonial India, Jemubhai had gone to England for advanced studies and had come back to India to serve under the British Government. He was totally detached from his family and there was no emotional bond that drew him to his wife and his only daughter. He lived alone in his old bungalow, Cho Oyu, which he had acquired in Kalimpong. His only companion here was his cook, who still, like his master, laboured largely under the influence of colonialism, and who, after having lost five mango trees to his brother in a court case, had left his village in Uttar Pradesh to work for the judge with whom he still remained. The only person who joined Jemubhai later in Cho Oyu was his grand-daughter, Sai, who arrived in Kalimpong after the unfortunate demise of her parents.

Another aspect of the immigrant experience is that of Biju, the only son of the cook who had migrated to the United States in the hope of a "better life." The cook had been lured by the prospect of a "legal employment in the U.S.A." and had manipulated some counterfeit recommendations for his son, which had finally helped Biju in being selected at the interview. At this achievement the cook was elated and started comparing himself with Mrs Sen whose daughter was also in America. To everyone he met he proudly announced:

> My son works in New York. He is the manager of a restaurant business...New York. Very big city. The cars and buildings are nothing like here. In that country there is enough food for everybody.... One day soon, my son will take me.[4]

The cook, however, was not aware of the exact nature of Biju's work in America. Being ignorant of his son's travails and anxieties abroad, he generously recommended to him the names of some of the local boys aspiring to go to America and asked the former to help them in getting jobs. Ironically, he was blissfully oblivious of the dire circumstances under which his own son worked to keep body and soul together.

Mrs Sen thought herself privileged in having a daughter who worked in America and did not forget to take a dig at her neighbour, Lola, whose daughter worked in England in the capacity of a BBC newsreader: "All these people who went to England are now feeling sorry."[5] For the cook, however, the difference between America and England remained vague. He was contented with whatever his son had achieved, little realizing that though his son and many others like him had acquired a tourist visa to go to America they were treated as illegal migrants after the expiry of the visa and were under stress from all sides. They could neither live honourably as immigrants nor relinquish their aspirations and come back to their native country. Biju, too, embroiled in this typical predicament had no standing and identity of his own. Like a fugitive on the run he had to switch from one job to another lest he be discovered and penalized as an illegal immigrant who had stayed on longer than permitted by law. Subjected to trenchant remarks that pierced his heart Biju had to labour under indignities that reminded him of the plight of the colonized way back in the past. He worked in numerous hotels and restaurants—French, Mexican, Italian, Indian—and invariably had to share a room downstairs with the other workers, some of whom, especially a Pakistani, he never got along with:

> The sound of their fight had travelled up the flight of steps and struck a clunky note, and they might upset the balance, perfectly first world on top, perfectly third world twenty-two steps below.[6]

The contempt for the inhabitants of the Third World countries is clearly evident. To add to the humiliation the wife of the proprietor of the Italian restaurant, Pinocchio, disdainfully observed that Biju "smelled" and the latter had finally to search for a new job for the lady was unappeaseable:

> She had hoped for poorer parts of Europe—Bulgarians perhaps, or Czechoslovakians. At least they might have something in common with them like religion or skin colour, grandfathers who ate cured sausages and looked like them.[7]

Biju very soon realized that people from the Third World countries were engaged in a losing battle for existence. Braving the severe cold in America was another front for which Biju had to brace himself:

> Biju smelled the first of the snow and found that it had the same pricking, difficult smell that existed inside the freezer; he felt the Thermocol scrunch of it underfoot. On the Hudson, the ice cracked loudly into pieces, and within the contours of this gray, broken river it seemed as if the city's inhabitants were being provided with a

> glimpse of something far and forlorn that they might use to consider their own loneliness.[8]

Alienation, estrangement, humiliation and bone-chilling frost, all contributed to the sense of utter loneliness experienced by Biju in America. His father's friend, Nandu, whom he had been banking upon for all kinds of help, callously gave him the cold shoulder and dismissed him with the advice that he should go back to India. Biju soon realized the prevalence of a deep divide between the legal and the illegal immigrants and knew that unless and until his immigration was formalized and given a legal sanction, he would not even be able to go back to his native land and would continue being exploited by some restaurant owners like Harish-Harry, who were busy making money at the cost of poor Indians and nationals of other Third World countries who did not have the authorized stamp on their papers. All his dreams melted away in the light of this realization of utter helplessness:

> The green card the green card. Without it he could not leave. To leave he wanted a green card. This was the absurdity. How he desired the triumphant. After the Green Card Return Home, thirsted for it....[9]

However, as we are made conscious of other characters in the novel, we see that Biju was not alone in his misery:

> ...it WAS so hard and YET there were so many here. It was terribly, terribly hard. Millions risked death, were humiliated, hated, lost their families—YET there were so many here.[10]

The novel thus underlines the collapse of the 'American dream' of the poor of the Third World countries like India. These underprivileged people are lured by the hope of better prospects abroad but the 'exile'[11] that they inflict upon themselves to live better, ironically compels them to live in disgrace and wretchedness. The following statement of Santana Haldar corroborates this view,

> Kiran Desai highlights that the process of globalization has its loopholes that the cartographical binaries have collapsed only for a blessed few. The poor people of the

> third world countries who dream of a better future and are lured by the affluence of the American society have no place in the world of their dream. They are compelled to suffer in their homeland and the exile they opt for only increases their suffering.[12]

The present study focuses on the mode in which Desai shows how the immigrants of the Third World countries are maltreated in America and are made to experience a sense of deprivation and an unnerving consciousness of being rootless. The fact that the cook's son, Biju, and all other illegal immigrants like him were generally made to stay in the basement quarters of a building, "at the bottom of Harlem"[13] is indicative of the subservient, menial status assigned to them. Like a spurned, rebuffed, jettisoned derelict, Biju makes his way to the Queen of Tarts bakery in the wee hours of the morning:

> ...watching for the cops who sometimes came leaping out: where are you going and what are you doing with whom at what time and why?

But immigration operated independently of Police, the better, perhaps, to bake the morning bread, and Biju fell, again and again, through the cracks in the system.[14]

The indignities suffered by Biju in the United States belied his father's hopes of experiencing "a sense of pride and achievement"[15] on the former's return home.

In *The Inheritance of Loss*, Kiran Desai perceptively depicts the lives of the gamut of Indian immigrants in the U.S.A.—the affluent and the successful as well as the poor and the hunted—and has tried to bring alive the drama of the erosion of identity in the case of those who have no claims over being minions of Lady Luck. The tension that prevails in the sensitive mind of an immigrant between the two socio-cultural environments and between the feelings of rootlessness and nostalgia and the desire to assimilate the new way of life leaves him with a lacerated self trying to piece itself together. Bharati Mukherjee in *Wife* and Anita Desai in *Cry, the Peacock*, both explore the inner space of near-neurotic immigrants abroad but Kiran Desai in the novel understudy is different in that her purpose is to expose the inhuman and discriminatory attitude of the Americans towards the poorer section of immigrants. Generally, however, all immigrants to Western countries, be it Canada, U.S.A. or England, to quote Bharati Mukherjee, are "lost souls, put upon and pathetic"[16] and they can be seen "...surrendering little bits of self every year, clutching the souvenirs of an ever-retreating past you'll never belong, anywhere."[17]

Whether cultures are inherited or consciously adopted as in the case of the migrant status, basic problems of the definition of identity are inescapable. As Paula M.L. Moya puts it in the Introduction to the work, *Reclaiming Identity*:

> .... The significance of identity depends partly on the fact that goods and resources are still distributed according to identity categories. Who we are—that is, who we perceive ourselves or are perceived by others to be—will significantly affect our life chances: where we can live, whom we will marry (or whether we can marry) and what kinds of educational and employment opportunities will be available to us.[18]

This is very true in the light of the identity crisis faced by the underprivileged section of the immigrants in America that Kiran Desai portrays in *The Inheritance of Loss*.

Another aspect of Kiran Desai's novel, *The Inheritance of Loss*, is her preoccupation with Indian history, like Rushdie's in his fiction. The strains of complexity in her treatment of history are evident from the fact that the human drama in the novel is played out against the backdrop of the insurgency born of the rise of the Nepalese Movement during the 1980s, a chunk of India's recent past. The theme of immigration pertaining to Saeed-Saeed's and Biju's visit to the U.S.A. is equally relevant to the migrant situation that prevails in Kalimpong and Darjeeling with regard to Jemubhai Patel, Sai, the cook, Noni and Lola. Gyan, the young Nepalese Mathematics tutor, however, finds himself in a dilemma when he has to choose between his beloved, Sai, and his native place, Kalimpong. He is "...caught between two worlds: one promising him Sai and adolescent love 'Free from history. Free from family demands and the built up debt of centuries'"[19] and the other, making him learn through a sense of virility and belonging, "as everyone does in this country, at one time or another, that old hatreds are endlessly retrievable."[20]

The ironical tale of a young nation turning against its own people rather than rejoicing at the termination of the colonial rule is deplorable. Unfortunately, despite widespread talk of globalization, to adapt the lines referring to Bapsi Sidhwa's *The Pakistani Bride*, "the differences between the cultural mores of the plains as opposed to those of the peoples who live in the mountains"[21] have re-emerged to draw accentuated borderlines between one region and another and for this, the natives and the immigrants are both responsible for neither group tries to accommodate to the other. The native Nepalese of the Kalimpong and Darjeeling region from the very beginning believed that they had been given a raw deal and justice had not been meted out to them. The immigrants from West Bengal who had settled there were equally unhappy with the conditions that had come to prevail and were now very suspicious of the local Nepalese residents. Lola (Lalita) for instance, voices her suspicion when she exclaims, "I tell you, these Neps can't be trusted. And they don't just rob. They think absolutely nothing of murdering, as well."[22] Robe Pope's words in this context are very illuminating:

> In every domain of language, literature and culture there is an acute tension and sometimes a flat contradiction between globalizing processes of standardization and localizing processes of differentiation.[23]

Kiran Desai with her priorities rooted firmly in Indian ethics would like to wish away such animosity between any two communities of men and would have peace and amity prevail. For a close realization of this blissful state the following clues to a future standpoint given by Sanjay Solanki in his essay, 'Past, Present and the Future in *The Inheritance of Loss*,' may help:

> The post colonial and multicultural perspectives entail a subtle reconfiguring of attitudes: no extreme and facile stance can overnight purge us of our colonial hangover

> and undo the material intellectual and cultural destruction that came in its wake. Nor formulaic posturing—like Jemu's masochistic Anglophilism or Biju's Anglophobia—can do in a world changing fast. Nor does the situation offer a luxury of glib solutions like the ones Lola, Noni and Mrs. Sen would seem to approve of. To be well placed in this feverish pace of the globalized world, what is required is the poise, neither seclusion, nor 'Macdonaldization' of society is the answer, especially for the Asian countries in which poverty is much more concentrated than in the European countries.[24]

Dr Tejinder Kaur of Punjabi University, Patiala, in the paper entitled "Problematizing Issues about Home, Homeland, Diaspora and Belongingness in Transnational and National Lands: A Study of Kiran Desai's *The Inheritance of Loss*," analyzes the issues raised by the author in her novel putting forth the contention that the latter, by setting her narrative in two parallel venues—New York City of contemporary America and Kalimpong, a small Indian town at the foothills of Mount Kanchenjunga in the Himalayan ranges—has brought into relief the commonality of problems of the two hubs of human insurgency, one tacit and the other vocal and strident. "Desai has portrayed," says Dr Kaur,

> the state of homelessness, displacement, exile, marginalization and lack of belongingness being experienced by the illegal and legal diaspora communities and individuals in America as well as by the people from other states, regions and communities from India residing in Kalimpong (national land).[25]

Desai has demonstrated in her novel the havoc wrought in human societies by initiations of migrations, settlements, journeys and movements, voluntarily or involuntarily made, of individuals and mass communities "from their homelands into new regions."[26]

The aptness of the poem by Jorge Luis Borges, "Boast of Quietness," chosen by Kiran Desai as an epigraph to the novel, adds immeasurably to the impact of the depiction of immigrants in the narrative, immigrants who, ironically enough, on the one hand, have lost touch with their homeland and on the other, they have lost their identity and cannot hope "to arrive" anywhere:

> ......
> They speak of homeland.
> My homeland is the rhythm of a guitar,
> a few portraits, an old sword,
> The willow grove's visible prayer as evening falls.
> Time is living me.
> ....
> My name is someone and anyone.
> I walk slowly, like one who comes from
> so far away he doesn't expect to arrive.[27]

The comment on *The Inheritance of Loss* published in the *Publishers Weekly* and cited on the front page of the novel reinforces our assessment of the novel here:

> Stunning...alternately comical and contemplative... (Desai) deftly shuttles between first and third worlds, illuminating the pain of exile, the ambiguities of post-colonialism, and the blinding desire for a "better life," when one person's wealth means another's poverty.[28]

To conclude, Kiran Desai in *The Inheritance of Loss* is, perhaps, prophetic in her depiction of the discriminatory attitude of the Americans towards the people of the Third World countries for one cannot ignore today the growing sensitivity towards national specificity as a mark of the future. Despite the general thrust on multiculturalism and multi-ethnicity in the world one cannot fail to observe the cultural distinction of each individual nation that defines the viewpoint of its people. The resolution to this issue of multiculturalism versus cultural distinction remains open-ended and one has only to mark the direction literary creativity takes in the future in terms of theme and intention.

Thus, suffice it here to say that though Kiran Desai has been hailed as a novelist whose characters are alive and kicking and as a narrator whose twin strands in the tale straddle continents portraying historical and racial relationships between peoples from different cultures and geographical backgrounds, her strength as a novelist lies in her brilliant negotiation of the English language which has conveyed a world of meaning and which has been put to varied use including that of humour—"a humour born out of darkness, the laughter of the dispossessed"[29] as Suketu Mehta, the author of *Maximum City* puts it.

NOTES

1. Robin Cohen, *Global Diasporas: An Introduction* (UCL Press, 1997).
2. Victor Ramraj, "Diasporas and Multiculturalism," *An Introduction to Post-colonial Theory*, eds. Childs Peter and Patrick Williams (Europe: Prentice Hall, 1997).
3. Bill Ashcroft, Gareth Griffith and Helen Tiffin, *The Empire Writes Back: Theory and Practice in Post-Colonial Literature* (London: Routledge, 1989), p. 8.
4. Kiran Desai, *The Inheritance of Loss* (London: Penguin Books, 2006), p. 84.
5. *Ibid.*, p. 85.
6. *Ibid.*, p. 23.
7. *Ibid.*, p. 48.
8. *Ibid.*, p. 51.
9. *Ibid.*, p. 99.
10. *Ibid.*, p. 189.
11. Edward Said in *Reflections on Exile and Other Literary and Cultural Essays* (Penguin Books, 2001) remarks that exile is "the unhealable rift forced between a human being and a native place, between the self and its true home: its essential sadness can never be surmounted" (p. 173). "...our age," says Said, "is indeed the age of the refugee, the displaced person, mass immigration" (p. 174). Thus, 'exile' in the present times is not always banishment. It is often a choice exercised in the hope of better prospects in life.
12. Santana Haldar, "Exile in Kiran Desai's *The Inheritance of Loss*," *The Atlantic Literary Review*, April-June, 2007, Vol. 8, No. 2, p. 87.
13. Kiran Desai, *op. cit.*, p. 51.
14. *Ibid.*, p. 75.
15. *Ibid.*, p. 20.

16. Bharati Mukherjee, "Introduction," *Darkness* (New Delhi: Penguin Books, 1985, rpt 1990), p. 2.
17. *Ibid.*
18. Paula M.L. Moya and Michael R. Hames—Garcia, eds., "Introduction," *Reclaiming Identity* (Hyderabad: Orient Longman, 2001, rpt. 2003), p. 8.
19. Kiran Desai, *op. cit.*, p. 157.
20. *Ibid.*, p. 161.
21. Huma Ibrahim, "Transnational Migrations," *Post-independence Voices in South Asian Writings*, eds., Alamgir Hashmi, Malashri Lal and Victor Ramraj (Islamabad, Pakistan): Alhamra Publishers, 2001), p. 39.
22. Kiran Desai, *op. cit.*, p. 45.
23. Robe Pope, *The English Studies* (Great Britain: Routledge, 2002), p. 139.
24. Sanjay Solanki, "Past, Present, and the Future in *The Inheritance of Loss*," *The Atlantic Literary Review*, April-June 2007, Vol. 8, No. 2, p. 81.
25. Tejinder Kaur, "Problematizing Issues About Home, Homeland, Diaspora and Belongingness in Transnational and National Lands: A Study of Kiran Desai's *The Inheritance of Loss*." http://in.mc946.mail.yahoo.com
26. Bill Ashcroft, Gareth Griffith and Helen Tiffin, eds., *Key Concepts in Post Colonial Studies* (London: Routledge, 1998).
27. Jorge Luis Borges, "Boast of Quietness" (poem cited in the epigraph of *The Inheritance of Loss*).
28. *Publishers' Weekly*, Review of Kiran Desai's *The Inheritance of Loss* cited on the front page of the novel.
29. Suketu Mehta, Review of *The Inheritance of Loss* cited on front page of the Penguin edition of the novel.

8

The Inheritance of Loss: Individuals in Search of the Lost Identity

Sanghita Sen

Miranda: "...I pitied thee, took pains to make thee speak, taught thee each hour one thing or the other. When thou didst not, savage, know thine own meaning, but wouldst gabble like a thing most brutish, I endow'd thy purposes with words that made them known...."

Caliban: "You taught me language, and my profit on't is, I know how to curse. The red plague rid you for learning me your language."

The Tempest, Act I, scene ii

INTRODUCTION

The aim of this paper is to critically examine Kiran Desai's Booker winning novel *The Inheritance of Loss* (2006) in terms of representation of individual and cultural identity, indexicalities of culture and people constructed, power-relations assumed in respect to these terms. Membership of a particular culture expressed through adaptation of several components such as language, ethnicity, religion, rituals, geographical location and education, are emblematic things in society (Blommaert, 2006). It becomes crucially political in terms of creating a *cultural regime*, particularly when the variety of *culture projects* itself as a supreme qualifier for entry into the world of opportunity, success and power while functioning as a tool to exercise control over the "dominated."

In this regime, behaviours conditioned by the "dominant" culture is considered to be a marker of "normalcy" and therefore "desirable." Thus, there is a series of efforts to create a colonial discourse "devoted" to manipulate the cultural orientation of chosen individuals originally belonging to the cultural boundary of the "other." This is to make sure that these chosen individuals "behave" not like the "other" but rather as a member of the community with the desired cultural accent and mindset representing the colonial stereotype.

The venture is directed upon creation of the construct "colonial stereotype" as "desirable" through a colonial discourse. The English people upheld their superior position over the natives in the colonies. Arthur C. Danto (1991) aptly points out:

> The superiority of Western civilization was never doubted, and one of the premises of Victorian anthropology was in effect that there is a moral direction in history as there is in evolution, that societies and species evolve toward optimality, and that Western Europe was history's masterpiece just as *Homo sapiens* was [sic] Nature's. (p. 338)

As far as India was concerned, the infamous Macaulay Minute of February 2, 1835, declared the superiority of colonial education over native education. The target recipient of colonial education was the males. It aimed to create a sort of inaccurate doubling of the colonized as a reflection of the colonizers. A particular variety of British culture is projected as a tool for linguistic and cultural homogenisation and normalisation in the present case. Adoption and adaptation of cultural accents itself appear to function as an *apparatus* (Althussar, 1977) vis a vis index of inclusion (and therefore exclusion) into a specific "culture" (Blommaert, 2007). While the stated agenda of such attempts of homogenisation is "inclusion," in practice it implies "exclusion" of those outside this cultural periphery by the same index. This proclamation of normalcy is crucial because it is potent to "elevate" a person from an arbitrarily assumed "lower" social stratum to the higher one along the social ladder. The culturally conditioned mindset here ensures the membership/participation in a particular culture to share its power relations. It is through acquiring a specific cultural affiliation that the "peripheral members" are promoted to the level of "core members" and are included at the cost of loss of a linguistic/cultural identity indexed in one's socio-economic space such as ethnicity, class and language. The colonial discourse projects the latter to be essentially either "deficient" or "inferior" representing the subject thus as a mimic individual (Bhabha, 1994) in its failure to be the perfect image of the underlying ideological agenda (Butler, 1997). This essay is an attempt to look into the creation of a subject position realising the above agenda through the colonial discourse the legacy of which is continued far beyond the colonial regime influencing the lives of individuals even in a post-colonial period.

Kiran Desai in her novel, *The Inheritance of Loss* (2006) attempts to locate the blurring lines of the history of Indian mental architecture from the colonial rule to the contemporary time. Desai skilfully demonstrates this through the convergence of the tormented past and an indeterminately positioned multicultural/multiethnic present. All through the narrative woven with assorted and generically complex composition, Desai offers a panoramic representation of a constructed reality where individuals are engaged in an incessant search for personal identity. Macrocosm and microcosm in the narrative coalesce to interweave each small event into the plot in terms of construction of an image of the "self" and the "other" that is essentially partial. Through a partial and mimic representation (Bhabha, 1994) of the individual Desai's narrative effectively confronts and challenges the murkiness of the individual identity constructed by the colonial discourse vis a vis agency to induce separation among and to exercise control over members of a culture well-known for peaceful co-existence for centuries in spite of differences. Her subtle examination of boundaries concurs with a concern for hybridity, the issue of individual space, the lineage of colonial past and post-colonial present.

Partial and Mimic Representation: Subverting the Colonial Discourse

As pointed out by Ashcroft (2005) "the mimicry of the post-colonial subject" can effectively destabilize or subvert the colonial discourse by establishing "an area of considerable political and cultural uncertainty in the structure of imperial dominance" (p. 142). A complete policy of normalisation regulates the native population to subliminally construct their own identities as colonial subjects realizing the agenda of the hegemonic power (Foucault, 1991; Ashcroft, 2005). What emerges in the process is the colonial stereotype instead of autonomous individuals governed by principles of an asymmetrical power relationship. Bhabha's (1994) inveterate argument demonstrates that a refractive encounter between the civilizing agenda and the post colonial materiality enables subversive and emerging forms of resistance tend to be ratified via the very tools for repression as well as manipulation employed by the colonial discourse. A reverse process is initiated by this, challenging the colonial agenda of creating a stereotype. He points out that the very mechanism that endorses the control and supremacy of the colonial discourse, in fact exposes its inherent vulnerability leading to its ultimate peaceful demise from within. An illustration of colonial imitation exemplifies the destabilization of the restructuring and civilizing mission by the shifting gaze of its punitive double in the gray area between "mimicry" and "mockery" (Bhabha, 1994).

Though the process is inverted by means of the reversal of gaze by its "disciplinary double" the mechanism relegates the individual into a constructed subject position that remains the same. By sharing the discursive practice the subversive and emerging positions through "the excess or slippage produced by the ambivalence of mimicry" not only ventures forth to discontinue the discourse, but also inculcates in the colonial subject an inderminacy leading to an "incomplete," "partial" and "virtual" presence (Bhabha, 1994). Mimicry becomes both "resemblance and menace" in that the "proliferation of inappropriate objects" ascertaining the strategic failure results in success of the colonial appropriation.

The Inheritance of Loss: A Journey to Lost Inheritance

An inescapable sense of inferiority is inculcated in the colonial subject by prolonged subjugation under colonial rule due to uncertain space(s) of individual in the cultural regime. This subsequently shapes and influences the architecture of the mind of several characters in the novel both as postcolonial subjects and the "disciplinary double." The very first chapter of the novel introduces the reader to five important characters in the novel. Whereas Sai, Gyan and Mutt, the dog, are introduced by their names; the judge and the cook are introduced by their respective designations. The judge's claustrophobic preoccupation with his own self is aptly but ironically portrayed by an image of an individual with a chessboard "playing against himself" (p. 1). The anonymous representation of the judge, a major character in the novel who is obsessively preoccupied with his own exiled world, immediately invokes into one's mind the image of the Boss created by Katherine Mansfield in *The Fly*. Sai, throughout the text, exposes a dynamicity of character though her grandfather's stagnant character is projected to cling onto his colonial subjecthood of which his designation is the primary token. Gyan, a representative of the insurgent group that invades the household of the judge can be seen as the "disciplinary double" in the narrative that tends to destabilize the discursive practice of the colonial cultural regime.

The leading question in the very beginning of the novel—"[c]ould fulfillment ever be felt as deeply as loss?" (p. 2)—sets the introspective and somber tone of the novel. The feeling of inferiority, indeterminacy and uncertainty leads individuals to a quest of identity through achieving professional success vis a vis social position either through participation in the colonial administration or the insurgent movement. The legacy that begins in this narrative with Jemubhai Patel appears to be inherited by members of later generations.

Jemubhai begins his quest for identity from a position of the "other" to become a member of the mainstream by way of putting on a persona with an endeavour to mark the "sameness" with the powerful in him. His futile efforts isolate him from the group he originally belongs to without granting him the much desired membership of the "desired" "civilized" class of the British in India. While Jemubhai's quest for identity is negotiated through adoption of normative parameters of the class of the powerful, Gyan's is negotiated through an apparent (though tentative) expression of "resistance" and directionless vengeance; while Biju takes resort to subjugation, and his father seeks it in an imagined socio-economic space achieved through his son's economic prosperity in a country much beyond his own reach. Whereas participation in colonial administration is viewed as a tool of empowerment for Jemubhai, the resistance to established government is seen as empowering for people that Gyan represents. In fact, incidents in Jemubhai's universe are re-enacted in lives of almost all major characters in the novel. On several occasions and instincts Gyan is represented as a dichotomy of Jemubhai. Instinctive responses such as misogyny, violence against their respective female counterparts, and identity crisis bind these two characters very closely. The narrative becomes a site for contest of identity issues mediated by individual perceptions of personal identity as well as the identity of the group. Whereas Jemubhai's search for identity creates a prototype subsequently to be represented in Biju's metaphorical as well as physical journey, which is partially Lazarian, Gyan's journey to seek his identity provides the antithesis, i.e. he undertakes the venture not through submission and subjugation but violent resistance through insurgency, a revisited form of subjugation to a new order by inversion of gaze.

Finally Jemubhai's relation and treatment to his wife appears to be a combination of both class and gender issue. Jemubhai looks down upon his wife not only because she is a woman and therefore is a subject to subjugation, but also because she represents the non-transformed Indian self Jemubhai himself is and which he despises so much. Her non-conformist defying presence in his household with her silent resistance to Jemubhai's oppressive behaviour appears as a constant reminder of Jemubhai's powerlessness/impotency, conformity and subjugation that he makes himself subject to for inclusion in the mainstream. Jemubhai's inherent vulnerability is exposed through his act of violence as a result of his inability to face the truth about his own callous submission to the system geared by her comment—"you are the one who is stupid" (p. 304). His violence to his wife exemplifies what Bhabha (1994) identifies as "the narcissistic demand of colonial authority." His wife's comment about his own "stupidity" immediately presents to him "a gaze of otherness" exposing the discernment of "the genealogical gaze" (Bhabha, 1994) shattering the unity of his constructed existence through which he upholds his "sovereignty" (Foucault, 1991).

Isolation is a prevalent motif throughout the narrative. In spite of desperate attempts conjugation of individuals to form a unified collective remains unachieved. By the end of the novel each appears to lose something valuable in their own personal lives. Jemubhai loses his dog, the only object of his attachment to this material world; Sai loses her love and probably an unperturbed trust in life; Gyan loses the cause for his resistance, Father Booty loses his long cherished dream and his "home;" the two sisters lose their peaceful musings and leisure; Biju loses all that he saved in his life in "exile" and his father, his imagined space. Though Biju apparently loses all that might have changed his individual identity in the society, the positive note in the novel is maintained through the possibility of redemption of identity marked by Biju's return to his own root without any condition; he represents an individual who exhibits faith in norms of both the external and internal worlds. The journey of each individual in the novel reduplicates Jemubhai's quest the primary concern of which appears to be a search of individual identity as part of the collective. If Jemubhai is the macrocosm in the narrative, each character in the novel plays microcosm to complete a cycle that has been initiated by Jemubhai Popatlal Patel.

This mundane macrocosm in *The Inheritance of Loss* is marked by "partial representation" of individual identity, split personalities, modified motivation, authorized "otherness," personal confusion and indeterminacy devoid of enthusiasm, a sense of individual identity in terms of completeness, security and specified agenda of life, where mockery and mimicry prevails as the order of life and existence (Bhabha, 1994). It appears to be the reason why Jemubhai—the representative anglicized Indian bureaucrat—betrays his long cherished 'western', 'rational' and 'civilized' persona (of the authorized other) at the loss of his pedigreed dog Mutt, his only connection to the material world, towards the end of the novel. The unexpected incident of a personal loss compels him to seek refuge in a self-imposed exile in the house that provides a microcosm of an idealized anglicized world in likeness with the colonial system. His characteristic vulnerability as part of his real person is exposed in a circumstance which is sudden, sure and on which, for the second time in his life, he didn't have any control.

The sudden disappearance of Mutt bound Jemubhai, Sai and the cook for their respective 'claustrophobic' sadness due to loss of something valuable in their lives, e.g. Mutt, the only object of attachment to the materialistic world for Jemubhai, an amorous alliance that promised a wide (non-existent) vista to Sai, a certain separation with uncertain fate between the cook and his son, Biju. The joint search party comprised of Jemubhai, Sai and the cook, looking for the dog becomes a symbolic individual inward quest for each member into their respective personal losses. With full awareness that wistful forgetfulness capacitates one to continue in their routine existence, he succumbs to memory—"One thing Jemubhai learned: a human can be transformed into anything. It was possible to forget and sometimes essential to do so" (p. 308). Jemubhai's delirious rambling, resembling the whine of an insane mind, marks the disintegration of the mimic persona of the "authorised other" and the futility of such an existence. The loss of the dog invokes in his mind his own violent act towards his wife and her subsequent forced acquittal from home as well as his own life. This "fusion of elements" (Eliot, 1920) constitutes what Eliot (1920) calls "the substantial unity" of the narrative in the novel—in a miniature and in parts in the reverse.

It is in this gloomy uncertainties of the disintegrating macrocosm of Jemubhai, Biju's arrival in India without any knowledge of the ongoing turmoil in his home reminds one about an individual's return from a space which is cut off from the space she/he belongs to and where such information about the insurgency and consequent changes do not have any information value. His whole existence is alienated from the representational space of the narrative to his lack of knowledge of the state of affairs in the home front, his worldly belongings, even the currency he offers are all very "different" yet he is unaware of it as is Jemubhai. It is because of a lack of awareness of the "difference" he appears to be happy after boarding the jeep driven by people who share the same culture and in spite of the "sameness" are going to rob him soon to reduce him to the position of literally an outsider—"he felt so lighthearted to be back, even this journey with these men didn't unsettle him" (p. 311).

In a context devoid of "real" and "complete" identity and individual space, existential insecurity as well as indeterminacy and delusion makes individual to live. This also simultaneously makes the individual (1) seek refuge in denouncement of one's own root and chase impossible as well as distant dreams of an imagined space as in case of Jemubhai and the cook; (2) take resort to violent self-assertion and insurgency as in case of Gyan; (3) uphold silent but strong resistance as in case of Mrs Jemubhai and (4) discover the futility of vainly ambitious pursuit of a target arbitrarily assigned to an individual externally as in case of Biju. The macrocosm in this novel is a mimic space in which the "self" deprived of autonomy and true representation awaits for a meaningful individual as well as collective identity to make sense of his/her fragmented subjugated self. A strange sense of absurdity characterizes this waiting, symbolizing a barren and callous universe where paranoia prevails without healing and hope. Though individuals appear to be in search of their lost inheritance and identity, they are forbidden by an apprehension about their own constructed self for "...the problems of the road [are] tedious" (p. 315).

The Inheritance of Loss is a narrative of fragmented representative mimic individuals where the issue of identity renders the family as well as individual relationship as a site for contest of assertion of identity and power, thereby ensuring the recognition of partial and mimic representation. So when individuals are confronted with the reality about their being relegated into the domain of helplessness, not only by an external, indifferent and politically motivated system that constructs their identity to exercise control over a group of people stripping off their individual autonomy but also as a passive participant in the process of construction of mimic individuals. Consequently, crawling back like parasites, she/he attempts to live afresh, renew life creating for their own self a crippled order. Jemubhai—a stranger to his own people, culture—more distant that anybody else—a non-White carrying out the 'white man's burden' in his own country where he himself is contextualised as a cultural alien—"[h]e had been recruited to bring his countrymen into the modern age, but he could only make it himself by cutting them off entirely, or they would show up reproachful, pointing out to him the lie he had become" (p. 306).

Conclusion

The novel illustrates the acute complexity emerging as a result of a subject's recognition of convictions and practices that had been proliferated since ages suddenly turn out to be volatile, replete with mutual isolation and consequent anxiety. The disconsolate, unfrequented prematurely old women, Noni and Lola, rocking to and fro in tune with their own are at-times-gloomy, at-times-happy musings of the olden days. Representing the two halves of a single solitary soul in a setting so disturbingly sinister seeking another millennium desperately —without the vitality of Dickens' Madam Defarge—they immediately remind one of a bare and barren world of carelessness and mutilated identity. In this anesthetized world of constructed representation individual's constant consideration of his/her powerlessness, ineffectuality of existence, infantile living prompts him/her to an extent of violating the normative boundaries in an imbecile attempt to create a personal space. A timidity of effort riddled with prufrockian indecisiveness and an existence marked by conformist compromises paves the way for a partial yet virtual representation of the individual. Such subjects do exist, yet their true "self" is nullified unless represented through discursive practices. As a result, a slight dwindled move in the status quo makes the individual behave in an insanely imbalanced way, e.g. Jemubhai's otherwise perfect behaviour that seems undisturbed in the time of crisis in his life is completely jeopardised on the loss of his high-bred dog, Mutt. Gyan who appears to be meek and introvert turns violent to Sai. Jemubhai's act of violence to his wife sets loose geared by his inherent fear about resistance symbolizing the agony of the colonial stereotype regarding resistance in general. All these exemplify how easily the veneer of civilization and imposed personality is swept aside in favour of "self-assertion" and "self-importance."

REFERENCES

Althusser, L. (1977) *Lenin and Philosophy and Other Essays*. London: New Left Books.

Ashcroft, Bill et al. (2005) *Post Colonial Studies: The Key Concepts*. London: Routledge.

Bhabha, Homi K. "Of Mimicry and Man: The Ambivalence of Colonial Discourse", *The Location of Culture*. London and New York: Routledge, 1994.

http://prelectur.stanford.edu/lecturers/bhabha/mimicry.html

Blommaert, J. (2007) Classroom Lecture on *Describing and Analysing Language* Module in MA in TESOL Programme of Institute of Education, University of London.

——. (2006) *Encyclopedia of Language and Linguistics*. 2nd Edition. London: Elseier Ltd.

Butler, J. (1997) *The Psychic Life of Power; Theories in Subjection*. Stanford, California: Stanford University Press.

Danto, A.C. (1991) "The Shape of Artistic Pasts, East and West", *Culture and Modernity: East-West Philosophic Perspectives*. ed. E. Deutsch. New Delhi: Motilal Banarasidass.

Desai, K. (2006) *The Inheritance of Loss*. New Delhi: Penguin Books.

Eliot, T.S. (1920) *The Sacred Wood*. London: Methune, Bartleby.com, 1996. www.bartleby.com/200/. [03.06.08].

Foucault, M. (1994) *Ethics; Subjectivity and Truth*. ed. P. Rabinow; trans. Robert Hurley et al. New York: The New Press.

Foucault, M. (1991) *Discipline and Punish*. Harmondsworth: Penguin Books.

9

Of Love, Loss and Longing: A Lacanian Reading of Kiran Desai's *The Inheritance of Loss*

Anita Singh

The epigraph of Desai's second novel *The Inheritance of Loss* contains Jorge Luis Borge's poem "The Boast of Quietness":

> ...I walk slowly, like one who comes from so far away he doesn't expect to arrive.

In the light of this poem we can understand the process of evolution from the imaginary order to the symbolic order in the Lacanian sense and the love, loss, longing and desire in the lives of three characters in the novel—Sai, Gyan and Biju and also explore the novel from Lacanian psychoanalytic perspective.

Set in 1980's the book tells the story of Jemubhai Popatlal Patel, a judge living out a discontented retirement in Kalimgpong, a hill station in the Himalayan foothills. The novel orbits around his granddaughter Sai who is brought under his care, after being orphaned. Her romantic involvement with Gyan her math's tutor leads to disillusionment and the realization that love could never find fulfillment. After his disenchantment with his love for Sai, Gyan a descendant of Nepali Gurkha falls in with a group of ethnic Nepalese insurgents. In a parallel narrative we are shown the life of Biju, the son of Sai's grandfather's cook who goes to New York as an illegal immigrant to fulfill a materialistic longing for prosperity. He too does not fare any better than Sai and Gyan in his journey of life. Embittered with the American dream of success he returns bruised and broken. Desai employs a kaleidoscopic technique to illuminate their parched lives. What binds these seemingly disparate characters is a common experience of a desire for completeness/wholeness and the consequent lack, loss, impotence and humiliation.

II

Lacan's notion of desire is at its heart, a desire for otherness—'a hole in the self' that the subject attempts to close through an endless metonymic chain of supplements: the perfect house, the perfect car, the perfect job, the perfect love, etc. but as soon as one supplement is acquired, desire moves onto something else. Lacan sees desire directed towards recognition and self-consciousness achieving its satisfaction only in another self. Since one recognizes oneself through an intersubjective relationship with the other, the other is the negative space of misrecognition.

Central to the conception of the human in Lacan is the notion that the unconscious, which governs all factors of human existence, is structured like a language. Lacan talks about three trajectories from infant to adult. He talks of three concepts—Need, Demand, Desire that roughly corresponds to three phases of development or three fields in which humans develops—the Real, the Imaginary and the Symbolic.

The Real, the phase of need, lasts from birth till somewhere between six to eighteen months, when the baby blob starts to distinguish between its body and everything else in the world. At this point the baby starts from having needs to having demands. Demands are not satisfiable with objects; a demand is always a demand for recognition from the other, for love from other. This process works like this: the baby starts to become aware that it is separate from the mother and that there are things that are not part of it. Thus, the idea of other is created, that awareness of separation or the fact of otherness creates an anxiety, a sense of loss. The baby demands a reunion, a return to that sense of original sense of fullness, for completeness of the other that will stop up the lack the baby is experiencing. For Lacan, the notion of otherness encountered in the imaginary phase comes before the sense of self which is built on the idea of otherness.

Lacan says these ideas of other and of lack and absences, of (mis)identification of self with other—are all worked out on an individual level, but they must form the basic structure of the symbolic order, of language which the child must enter in order to become an adult member of a culture: "It is the name of the father that we must recognize...which from the dawn of history identified his position with the figure of law" (Lacan, 1977: 67). The symbolic realm which is marked by the concept of desire is equivalent to adulthood; or more specifically for Lacan, the symbolic realm is the structure of language itself, which we have to enter into in order to become speaking subjects, in order to say 'I' or have 'I' designate something which appears to be stable.

The other is a structural position in the symbolic order; it is the place that everyone is trying to get to, to merge with, and in order to get rid of the separation between self and the other. It is in Derrida's sense, the centre of the system, of the symbolic and of language itself. But as the centre cannot be merged with, nothing can be in the centre with the other, even though everything in the system (people, etc.) wants to be. So the position of the other creates and sustains a never ending lack, which Lacan calls Desire. Desire is the desire to be the other. By definition, desire can never be fulfilled, it is not desire for some object (which would be need) or desire for love or another person's recognition of oneself (which would be demand) but desire to be the centre of system, the centre of language itself, that's what Lacan calls desire: the desire, which is never satisfied, because it can never be satisfied, to be the centre, to rule the system.

III

This paper limits itself to understand the trajectory of the subject from the imaginary to the symbolic order and to show

how once an individual enters the symbolic order he is caught in a whirl of never ending lack, loss and desire that keeps him/her on a relentless quest that is never fulfilled—a journey as Borges writes in his poem which never draws to a close. The novelistic genre is characterized by a sense of 'growth' and 'of becoming' and this facilitates the movement from the imaginary order to the symbolic order and back and forth. Coming back to *The Inheritance of Loss*, this analysis identifies the nature of the movement/growth/journey of three characters—Biju, Gyan and Sai.

To take up the case of Biju, the son of the cook who worked in the house of Jemu Patel, a retired judge aspires to go to America. For Biju and his father, the cook, America/angrez symbolically represent the centre towards which they want to advance. Biju goes to America to fulfill his 'Lack' to be in the position of power. Fanon has also pointed out that: "the white man is not only the other but also the master, whether real or imaginary" (Fanon, 1967: 138). To reach the land of dreams he will be fulfilled and get rid of a "feeling of nonexistence" (*ibid.*, 139). Whiteness gets equated with power and he aspires to be "angrez ke tarah" (Desai, 2006: 105). At the visa counter in the US embassy Biju dusted himself with exquisite manners of a cat: "I'm civilized, sir, ready for the US, I'm civilized man," he demands recognition from the other. America is a land of dreams and opportunities; "the green card, the green card" (99). Biju found that he is possessed of an awe of white people (77) but the symbolic order is traditional and the social world is hard. He realizes the snag of being in an alien culture which is not too kindly to him.

In America, Biju has to eke out an existence as an undocumented worker. Stumbling from one low paid restaurant job to another, living in seedy squalor with groups of other immigrant men. Spurred by his father, Biju had come to America to realize the American dream, but the actuality had something else in store for him. He recognizes that "it's a whole world of basement kitchens" and in exasperation dubs it "they call this first world??? Ekdum bekaar! (300).

Poor and lonely in New York Biju remembers his village. Lying on the basement shelf in sordid squalor he thought of his village where he had lived with his grandmother (102-03). The first phase of Biju's life from imaginary to symbolic order begins in childhood, the village where he lived was "buried in silver grasses that were taller than a man and made sound, shuu, shuuuu, shu, shuuu, as the wind turned them this way and that...Biju and his grandmother with her sari tucked up ...on diwali the holy man lit lamps and put them in the branches of the peepul tree and sent them down the river on rafts with marigolds—how beautiful the sight of those lights bobbing in that young dark...how peaceful our village is. How good the roti tastes there...fresh roti, fresh butter, fresh milk still warm fro buffalo..." (102-03). But the peaceful imaginary state is rudely ruptured as he enters the symbolic order—in the crass commercialism, rampant racism and rapacious ruin perpetuated by the neo-colonial exploitation. Biju comes back to India in the climatic scene of the novel robbed of his belongings (316) all his NRI dreams of "holding green cards and passports...dollars me kamaenge, pum pum pum" (298) comes to naught. But yet the reader finds a quaint satisfaction in the union of father and son in the backdrop of a disturbed Kalimpong. At last Biju feels safe and at peace compared to his lonely life as a waiter moving from one restaurant kitchen to another. Once again, if only for a short time the imaginary order prevails but the disturbed Kalimpong in the backdrop indicates, the brevity of this order which will break out and wholeness/completeness can never be arrived at.

Biju's desire for completeness through the materiality that America affords is unlike Sai's desire for completeness through her love for Gyan. Sai a teenage orphan, living with her grandfather gets romantically involved with her math's tutor, Gyan who is the descendent of a Nepali Gorkha mercenary. For both Sai and Gyan the imaginary order enters their lives in the form of their dumpling stage of love: "it had set them off on a tumble of endearments and nicknames...it connoted protection, affection (140). In their new found love for each other they behaved almost as sightseers even in their own town visiting places (140-41). Complete involvement and fulfillment in love makes Sai resent even simple intrusion from the cook (representing the symbolic order) as: "where were you? I have been waiting." She becomes conscious for the first time of the stickiness of family and friends when she had found freedom and space in love" (143). In their love, Sai and Gyan: "linked words, objects and affection in a recovery of childhood, a confirmation of wholeness, as at the beginning—arms, legs, heart" (126). This love creates an illusion or misperception of wholeness, interrelation and totality that surrounds and protects their fragmented selves. But the reality of the symbolic order intrudes soon. Their loves goes awry as their differences in social class, culture and their polarizing political principles become apparent. The progress of the human heart is clearly charted in Sai and Gyan—their yearning and passion for each other, their quarrels over their different social class and values. However, both emerge stronger after their movement from imaginary to the symbolic order. The nature of love as 'lack' is realized by Sai as she reminisces: "could fulfillment be felt as deeply as loss? Romantically she decided that love must surely reside in the gap between desire and fulfillment, in the lack, not the contentment, love was the ache, the anticipation, the retreat, everything around it but the emotion itself" (2-3).

Both Sai and Gyan negotiate movement from imaginary to symbolic order in their own ways. After recoiling from Sai's love Gyan falls in with the group of ethnic Nepalese insurgents. The symbolic order raises it head in the form of the chasm in class, culture and the demands of Gorkhaland movement that makes Gyan feel sullied by the romance (175). Gyan joins the ethnic nationalist movement of people who were fed up with being treated like the minority in a place where they were the majority, they wanted their own state, in which to manage their own affairs...they demanded a Gorkhaland...we are laborer on the tea plantations, coolies dragging heavy loads, soldiers. And are we allowed to become doctors and government workers, owners of tea plantations? No! We are kept at the level of servants (158). This demand for recognition/a place in the centre of the symbolic order will take Gyan to another journey.

The novel focuses on the fate of a few defenseless individuals who are insecure and unmoored and frequently struggling to survive in the modern world. A tragic note seems to hover in the air as one reaches the end of the novel, but this is not an unrelieved tragedy. The characters (Sai, Gyan and Biju) emerge stronger after their movement from the imaginary to the symbolic order. They have grown with the realization that they are ones who have come from far away and don't expect to arrive.

They strive to achieve a stable whole, unified self, they move from insufficiency to anticipation. Their move is from a fragmented body to an orthopedic vision of its totality, to a vision of itself as whole and integrated which is orthopedic because it serves as a crutch, a corrective instrument, an aid to help the subject achieve the status of wholeness. But of course this is impossible because lack, or absence, the sense of otherness, is the condition for self/subject functioning as a cultural being.

WORKS CITED

Desai, Kiran. 2006. *The Inheritance of Loss: A Novel.* New Delhi: Penguin Books.

Fanon, Frantz. 1967. *Black Skin, White Masks.* (tran.) Charles Lam Markmann. New York: Grove Press.

Lacan, Jacques. 1977. *Ecrits: A Selection.* New York: W.W. Norton and Company.

10

Kiran Desai's *The Inheritance of Loss*: A Study in Themes of Rootlessness, Alienation and Death

Gulrez Roshan Rehman

> Unreal city,
> Under the brown fog of a winter dawn,
> A crowd flowed over London Bridge, so many,
> I had not thought death had undone so many.
> Sighs, short and infrequent, were exhaled,
> And each man fixed his eyes before his feet.[1]

The all too practical, down to earth touchy kind of a tragic story in Kiran Desai's 2006—Man Booker Prize-winning novel, *The Inheritance of Loss* charismatically told through the deeply manoeuvred characters and by the off and on obtrusive intervention of the omniscient narrator, seems to somewhat echo what T.S. Eliot has been critically understood to mean in the above mentioned lines from the first section entitled "The Burial of the Dead" of his celebrated poem "The Waste Land"—"The attractiveness of death" or "The difficulty in rousing oneself from the death in life in which the people of the waste land live."[2]

The shade of unreality, however, in her novel seems to transcend all geographical boundaries—Kalimpong, Darjeeling, Sikkim, India, U.S.A., New York, etc. And the more picturesque and naturally scintillating it is the more unreal it becomes, and hence more easily surmountable. For instance, her remark about 'Sikkim the jewel-colored kingdom'—"The country had seemed unreal—so full of fairy tales of travelers seeking Shangri-la—it had proved all the easier to destroy" (p. 128)—holds true of Kalimpong et al. This unreality then seems to permeate the human relationship of her characters—The judge Jemuhhai and his wife Nimi, Sai's parents Mr. & Mrs. Mistry, Sai and her Nepali tutor Gyan, the cook and his son Biju, etc. The Indian diaspora is shown to live an emptied and rootless life of dissatisfaction or at best false satisfaction, at a very heavy cost of being alienated from their native social moorings.

Kiran Desai's *The Inheritance of Loss* has superbly dealt with the themes of rootlessness, alienation and death through the characters of her novel in a bewilderingly fascinating style of her own. She has profoundly unfolded the vicious and tragic shades of her themes in a captivating fashion. The title itself foreshadows the synaesthetic commingling of positives and negatives like 'Inheritance' and 'Loss.' But at a much profounder perception than the more superficial narrative of the story, one may unequivocally rather arithmetically, say that *The Inheritance of Loss* is equal to the disinheritance of gain—a life full of a strange 'emptiness' and 'solitude' of the sense of ultimately losing whatever one has, of the sense of alienation from society and self, perceived to be arising out of double-selves, veneers, rootlessness and death.

Even as the story begins, progresses and ends, the ambience of death—both literal and metaphorical—looms large all through. Particularly striking is the individual story of the retired judge, Jemubhai Popatlal Patel and his semi-rustic wife Bela rechristened Nimi Patel. Never ever the two are seen as husband-wife except once "when he had indeed liked her. He was twenty, she fourteen. The place was Piphit and they were on a bicycle, traversing gloriously down a slope through cow pats" (p. 308).

In fact, theirs is a pathetic price of alienation typically depicting the unwholesome manner of human species of Jemubhai's breed. The alienation of Gyan and Sai, the teacher-taught infatuated pair, in the backdrop of the Gorkha National

Liberation Front—led movement in Darjeeling during the mid-1980s, is a moving tale of the God-forsaken lonely little Sai, the granddaughter of Jemubhai, destroying her innocent soul beyond recognition. Panna Lal, the retired judge's cook and his son Biju, the typical green card chaser in United States, vividly depict the fantastic longings and ambition of the small, children of God, like them—a story terribly touching the human soul, a story of alienation from their roots and finally melting in the dust of nothingness. All the principal characters in her novel have their own sweet and sour dreams which blossom merrily and gently but ultimately get withered in time and space in a devastating fashion reminding one about the ultimate futility of human life.

The old misanthrope Jemubhai, with his sackless cheeks and artificial indentures, has been portrayed as living a dead life as it were: "The judge had fallen asleep and gravity acting upon the slack muscles, pulling on the line of his mouth dragging on his cheeks showed Sai exactly what he would look like if he were dead" (p. 2). Surely the game of chess which Jemubhai feigns to play solo appears to be merely a diversionary habitual stratagem of keeping himself away from the real human world of feelings and emotions of love, longing, piety and affection. In this regard, again, he resembles the party monger female protagonist of Eliot's movement in the second section "A Game of Chess" in *The Waste Land* whose only worry:

> What shall we do tomorrow?
> What shall we ever do?[3]

> is rhetorically addressed—

> The hot water at ten.
> And if it rains a closed car at four.
> And we shall play a game of chess,
> Pressing lidless eyes and waiting for a knock upon the door.[4]

Although in a somewhat different perspective, Desai quite symbolically portrays the otiose life of the once young and energetic ICS officer. The steel frame of the colonial civil service seemed to have so 'dehumanised,' Jemubhai that he seldom appears to be living a normal human existence, throughout the novel. He seems to have been co-opted by the British Empire to serve her colonial interests even as he ruthlessly rules over his own countrymen. Belonging to a poor Patel family in Gujarat, Jemubhai sort of found a treasure-trove in the fabulously rich merchant Bomanbhai Patel. Jemubhai's father arranged a calculated marriage of his son with Bela, later Nimi Patel, the most beautiful daughter of Bomanbhai in return for a huge dowry in cash and kind which enabled his son to sail over to England and become an ICS officer in five years. How one's ambitions could lead to self negation and to negation of one's close relations including a young, newly-wed wife is told by the judge's paradoxically married—'Brahmacharya' stage of life. The reader is not surprised at such strange things because one becomes excruciatingly conscious of Jemubhai's quintessential callousness and hypocrisy from the time of his marrying Bela as a stratagem of his colonial mindset to the final assault of wife Nimi because she has committed the 'crime' of venturing out of the gate of her residence in company of passionate congress women as "part of the Nehru welcoming committee at the Cantonment Railway Station" (p. 303). Right from the beginning, his approach towards her was one of a wolf searing at a dead body; even on the first night after the wedding and on the first night after his return from England. His was never an affable relationship with Mini and had always thought of her as "just a country bumpkin," "a liar," "incredibly stupid," whom he neither loved nor liked, but simply carried along. But now that she had caused him embarrassment at the hands of the commissioner—for he was too concerned for the false prestige of the entire Civil Service to have even cared for his married life—Jemubhai in a fit of rage brutally thrashed his wife and sent her away to Gujarat: "for the first time he hit her although he had wanted to before and fought the urge for some time. He emptied his glass on her head, sent a jug of water swinging into the face he no longer found beautiful, filled her ears with leaping soda water. Then, when this wasn't enough to assuage his rage, hammered down with his fists, raising his arms to bring them down on her again and again, rhythmically, until his own hands were exhausted and his shoulders next day were strained sore as if from chopping wood. He even limped a bit, his leg hurting from kicking her. "Stupid bitch, dirty bitch!" The more he swore, the harder he found he could hit" (pp. 304-05). The apparently civilised judge was actually a scheming misanthrope and a die-hard cynic, enough not to have been moved by the 'Blotchy bruises,' her quiet submission to his cruelty, and her pathetic plea 'I can't go.' He sent her away to Gujarat, only to have been informed six months later about "the arrival of a baby" to her. But when he did not come to take her back to Bonda, his father pleaded with him in vain for taking back Nimi and her baby-daughter. Disgustingly he gives Jemubhai up:

> It was a mistake to send you away; You have become like a stranger to us (p. 306). Surely, Jemubhai has been alienating himself from the peasant community of Piphit in Gujarat and in this process of alienation he lost his own identity both as a native Indian as well as a human being. He becomes a foreigner in his own country. Rightly remarks the novelist—"He had learned to take refuge in the third person and to keep everyone at bay, to keep even himself away from himself like the Queen." (p. 111)

Of him own choice, Jemubhai banishes not only Nimi, but humanity out of his life. Nimi dies of burns—"A woman had caught fire over a stove,"—reads another telegram. And now his alienation from her and from humanity becomes all the more absolute. The realities of his wretched tragedy are so bitter and self-inflicting that if he would not be or feign he would almost be dead. Jemubhai's alienation from the present in order to be steady on the past lies drawn upon thus: "The judge had considered the convent's request in the brief interlude of weakness he experienced after Bose's visit, when he was forced to confront the fact that he had tolerated certain artificial constructs to uphold his existence. When you build on lies, you build strong and solid. It was the truth that undid you. He couldn't knock down the lies or else the past would crumble, and therefore the present.... But he now acquiesced to something in the past that had survived, returned, that might without his paying too much 'attention,' redeem him" (pp. 209-10).

Precisely because of this reason he likes to be engrossed in the chessboard like a 'heron' not wanting to think of Nimi but in vain—"He returned to his chessboard and made his move, but it felt like an old move in an old game" (p. 89). He would teach the same lessons of loneliness and shame he had learned himself. In public, he never spoke to her or looked in her direction (p. 170). In his case, it was perhaps the burden of past guilts or "judgmental blunders that was proving too heavy for him to bear any longer, despite the knowledge that he had to for the sake of sanity—

> In this life, he remembered again, you must stop your thoughts if you wished to remain intact, or guilt and pity would take everything from you, even yourself from yourself....
>
> This was why he had retired. India was too messy for justice; it ended only in humiliation for the person in authority. (p. 264)

Jemubhai's company is symbolical reduced to his slave-like cook Panna Lal and his pet she-dog Mutt, and of course, later on, Sai "whom he didn't hate was perhaps the only miracle fate had thrown his way" (p. 210). In the post-colonial India, shorn of the ICS sheen, the retired judge, bereft of any power, has been very appropriately reprimanded, albeit passively, for his obsessive love for the lost Mutt, an animal, whereas he seems to have no love and affection for fellow human beings—be it the poor cook or the poor hungry begging couple at his door. The irony becomes much too clear. Hence, when he beats Panna Lal for not having been carefully looking after Mutt while it slipped away, Jemubhai's hatred of mankind reaches the climax. Although Mutt dies first in the judge's dream, before having gone missing. Here also the lapse was that of Jemubhai who did not give charity to the begging couple and turned them away twice who took revenge by stealing Mutt away in a sack for sale or breeding. Again the judge, in anger, wanted to kill the cook who was forced to feel a sense of guilt with regard to his servant class obligations to his master class the judge—

> The cook wondered if he had done something wrong and his guilt began to grow. Had he indeed been negligent? He had failed in his duty, hadn't he?... He should have been watching the dog the day she went missing.... (p. 313)

When the petty police officers at the police station in Kalimpong do not pay the desired respect to him, Jemubhai stands fully chastised—

> He remembered all of a sudden why he had gone to England and joined the ICS; it was clearer than ever why —but now that position of power was gone, frittered away in years of misanthropy and cynicism (p. 292). It was then that he realized his 'hamartia'—double self, veneer, false pride and callousness. He realised how he himself was squarely responsible for the deep alienation from his own self, from his wife and family, and at last from the nations of his birth and of adoption—Now Jemubhai wondered if he had killed his wife for the sake of false ideals. Stolen her dignity, shamed his family, shamed hers, turned her into the embodiment of their humiliation.... (p. 308)

The Wordsworthian remorse like—'And much it grieves my heart to think what man has made of man' gets echoed in Jemubhai's learning that "a human can be transformed into anything. It was possible to forget and sometimes essential to do so" (p. 308). The judge's alienation first from Nimi about whom he says—"She is unsuitable to be my wife" (p. 306), his father whom he calls "a village idiot" (p. 306), Mutt the she-dog, his community and nation, and more pathetically so, from his own self.

She has equally marvelously dealt about human instincts. The story of Mutt, the little she-dog of Jemubhai Patel is a subtle satire on human idiosyncrasies. This is clearly reflected in chapter forty-six of the novel:

> Sai looked out of her window and couldn't tell what all the noise was about.... She hadn't arrived by the time darkness settled in. (pp. 288-89)

Kiran Desai has very ingeniously unfolded the transformation of human mind and soul in chapter forty-nine of the novel. The following quote is quite illuminating—

> The judge got down on his knees, and he prayed to god, he, Jemubhai Popatlal the agnostic,... Was this faith that he had turned away, was it paying him back? For sins he had committed no court in the world could take on.... But who could be paying him back? He didn't believe in angered divinity, in a scale of balance. Of course not, the universe wasn't in the business of justice. That had simply been his own human conceit—until he learned better. Yet he thought of his family that he had abandoned. (pp. 301-02)

The judge's distancing from the human world and even from himself especially after Nimi's death is complete when he thrashes the old cook for not having been able to trace out the missing bitch Mutt. The cook who served him for such a long time could not endear himself to his master as much as a little useless dog could. Yet the judge, after losing his wife, daughter, son-in-law his ICS 'clout,' his love and affection, loses even Mutt and is denied even a dog's company by Nemesis so it seems. So when he sees the cook along with some soldiers hiding boxes of cigar in the bushes, he over looked it:

> The judge swore but continued on. He knew about this side business of the cook's and ignored it. It was his habit to be a master and the cook's to be a servant, but something had changed in their relationship within a system that kept servant and master both under an illusion of security. (p. 209)

But now even that 'illusion of security' was gone—no faith nor love, nor life, nor pain, nor happiness had touched him. Jemubhai had himself 'deconstructed' his world and this he realized when he had 'lost' everything and when this tragedy was irredeemable. More than a 'misanthrope' and a 'cynic,' he is 'metamorphosed into an ascetic quiet stoical of pain or pleasure'. Perhaps Nimi the 'Nemesis' "was paying him back."

All his labour that he put in to have become an ICS officer was turning its heat against him—his unwavering loyalty to the British crown, as opposed to the Indian national freedom struggle even at the tragic cost of abandoning his wife and daughter—had not paid-off well—but it was too late by that time for redemption. The judge, by the end of the novel leaves a legacy of losses only. The 'power' that he once wielded, transforms into an 'alien' power commanding a sway over him thereby making him feel powerless and alienated. He is an utter failure—both in his public as well as private life—as he could not do justice to his job as a judge because of the 'messy' situation here, or to his role as a husband/father/son-in-law. Almost in a Hardian vein, Kiran Desai, delineates, the tragic story of the 'romantic' coming together of Jemubhai and Nimi and their subsequent breaking away only to be partially united by the end of the novel. Here, of course, Jemubhai because like Henchard of Hardy's *The Mayor of Casterbridge* who also loses his young wife and baby girl in a gamble at the fair—the latter suffers a lot like Nimi and her daughter. Again, Henchard finally becomes the mayor of Casterbridge only to have met his now old wife and young daughter but they are not united with the worldly successful Henchard but a failure on the personal relationships front. Same is the case with Jemubhai who succeeds in becoming the first man in his community to have successfully competed at the ICS but who loses his wife Nimi by cruelly turning her away to 'death.' The only difference from the Hardian story is that the judge gets his granddaughter Nimi as a silver lining of sorts. But the mechanism of 'Fate' as being influenced by a mis-judgment as an act of great omission or commission, of the principal characters—runs as a common thread in both the works.

Kiran Desai's rendering of her novels theme of alienation, death and total loss is delineated quite aesthetically in almost every page of the book. None of the characters, whether minor or major, seem to gain anything but 'loss' or suffering and loneliness. Seeing as if through the inner, recesses of Sai's mind, the omniscient narrator rhetorically says at the very outset—

> "Could fulfillment ever be felt as deeply as loss?" (p. 2). Gaining in loss, appears to be a romantic notion, no doubt; but philosophically construed, one is made to interpret the line—"love must reside in the gap between desire and fulfillment, in the task, not the contentment" (pp. 2-3)—as to mean that life consists neither entirely in birth (desire) nor entirely in 'death' (fulfillment) but between the two. Life is, after all whatsoever and howsoever lined after birth till death—all rolled into one enigmatic whole, that is, the inheritance of 'Loss.' Jemubhai and Nimi lose each other; Sai's, parents lose each other, Sai and Gyan lose each other, the cook and his son Biju, Lola and Jaydeep, Father Booty—all of these characters portray one or the other kind of 'loss' which they invariably suffer. And the story is so brilliantly told that is become rather difficult to tell who has suffered more and why—the judge or Sai; the cook or his son; Nimi-Lola or Father Booty—or is it Nimi? No straightaway answer is possible, it seems.

Kiran Desai has emerged, with only two novels—first, *Hullaballoo in the Guava Orchard* and the second, *The Inheritance of Loss*, as an unparalleled 'terrific writer,' as Salman Rushdie calls her, of the new generation of English fiction writer of Indian origin. The central theme of alienation and death permeates throughout keeping the readers charmed and spell bound till the end. Biju is the symbol of the Indian diaspora in the post-colonial post-modern western world chasing a 'pipedream' as it were of becoming proverbially rich and un-Indian-like. Biju, as is shown in the hovel, is busy 'hopping' from one workplace to another and keeps a periodical connection with his father, Panna Lal the cook through letters and phone calls. A chronic green card-chaser in the US, Biju finally returns to India to meet his father with all his foreign acquisition packed in a trunk. But of his gain turns into 'loss' when he is robbed by the GNLF men in Siliguri and Biju is left only ruminating lamentably.

> He couldn't stop thinking of all that he'd bought and lost. Of the money he'd hidden under false soles in his shoes. Of his wallet. Suddenly, he felt an old throbbing of the knee that he had hurt slipping on Harish-Harry floor. (p. 318)

Ironically, and interestingly so, what he has inherited, in effect, from his American sojourn is not a wallet full of dollars, but an aching knee injury. In a sort of reversal of ironies, the cook's earlier pride on the American connection of his son becomes painfully funny by the end of the novel. The cook, after being rejected, metaphorically though, by the judge, stands to gain an impoverished America-return son—sans dollars, sans leather jacket and sans any sign of American possessions whatsoever. It is not for nothing that Biju too has met his nemesis. Arriving in New York and landing up "a full-time waiter position," Biju, "a naughty Boy" of the country side, perhaps unconsciously betrays his newly acquired hypocrisy when he takes pride in having only foreign food and master—"Angrezi Khana only, no Indian food, and the owner is not from India, he is from America itself" (p. 14). It is his psychological need for self-realization or self-actualization that he pursues an English or an American identity and prop—because he wants to feel superior to his poor co-nationals living in India contrarily a struggling sapless life. When the cook, too, explains the contents of his son's letter to the investigating policemen, he too seems to take pride on the American connection of his son Biju—"He works for the Americans" (p. 14). The cook—"was sure that since his son was cooking English food, he had a higher position than if he were cooking Indian" (p. 17). At best, it could be only a false pride on account of foreign achievements, being alienated and cut off from one's native roots. That very many places on earth, leave alone UK, USA and the Gulf, are being increasingly populated by the ever expanding Indian diaspora, has been graphically drawn out in the following catchechism between Biju and the Guyanese man—

> 'Where is Guatemala?' he had to ask
> 'Where is Guam'?

> 'Where is Madagascar?'
> 'Where is Guyana?'
> 'Don't you know?' the Guyanese man said.
> 'Indians everywhere in Guyana, man.'
> 'Indians in Guam. Everywhere you look, practically Indians.'
> ...
> Kenya, South Africa, Saudi Arabia, Fiji, New Zealand, Surinam....
> How had he learned nothing growing up? England he knew, and America, Dubai, Kuwait, but not much else. (pp. 21-22)

The satirical humour and intended irony is unmistakable here. Indians, in search of greener pastures or sources of livelihood for subsistence, are ever more than ready to take off to foreign land away from their homes and families, culture and tradition, society and nation, i.e. they perforce or willingly get uprooted from their soil of birth or what is affectionately, and more suitable so, called the motherland. This separation from the motherland, as felt or even suffered by the Indian diaspora reminds me of the sickening lines of Lady Macbeth in Shakespeare's tragedy *Macbeth*:

> I have given suck, and know
> How tender 'tis to love the babe that milks me—
> I would, whilst it was smiling in my face,
> Have pluck'd my nipple from his boneless gums,
> And dash'd the brains out, had I so sworn
> As you have done to this.[5]

Imagine the suckling mother as India and the babe as the Indians, the wilful or the compelling brain-drain or labour-drain emerges as too logical and hence the agony and pain and shamelessness often associated with departing from one's mother or mother-land. Yet the umbilical chord, though severed could not thoroughly alienate the NRIs and they at one time or other, feel the urge to visit their native land and remember this past associations with her. When Biju returns from America he is stranded at Siliguri, as there is no bus to Kalimpong because of the GNLF 'bandh.' However, negotiating the 'gauged bank' of 'The Teesta, an insane river in a jeep,' he realized—"Death was so close—he had forgotten this in his eternal existence in America—this constant proximity of one's nearest destination." Biju's father was ignorant, as Biju himself was, of the deep-rooted alienation and split-consciousness suffered by leaving one's native land for a foreign destination—"This way of leaving your family for work had condemned them over several generations to have their hearts always in other places, their mind thinking about people elsewhere, they could never be in a single existence at one time. How wonderful it was going to be to have things otherwise" (p. 311). Relevantly has it been said in the our traditional scriptures—

> "Janani Janambhumische swarga dapi gariari." That is mother and mother-earth are greater than heaven. Nevertheless, very ingeniously, the writer seems to be justifying this immigration of Indians to UK and USA particularly, as a reverse colonialism resorted to by the Indians and the Third world nationals—what Biju was to frequently hear in America: "Your father came to my country and took my bread and now I have come to your country to get my bread back" (p. 135). The clock seems to have begun moving anti-clockwise.

Even friendships do not hold good for long in a foreign land. Saeed and Biju were good friends in the States but when Saeed got employment at a Banana Republic, Biju loses his cherished jovial company and feels solitary:

> "The emptiness Biju felt returned to him over and over, until eventually he made sure not to let friendship sink deep anymore" (p. 102). Going back in his stream of consciousness, Biju realises the serenity, comfort and warmth of his native village life and transports himself from America to Kalimpong—"How good the 'roti' tastes here! It is because the atta is ground by hand, not by machine...and because it is made on a choolah, better than anything cooked on a gas or a kerorene stove..." (p. 103). Such native longings keep on troubling the conscience of Biju and his likes. Sai's jealousy of the

> cook's love for his son is a sort of counterfoil to heighten the lovelessness, loneliness and alienation of Sai's childhood and adolescent life.

Kiran Desai chooses to set the tone and tenor of somberness and the theme of ultimate submissiveness of man of Death, filtering through the reiteration of the terms 'dead,' 'dying,' 'death', etc. throughout the novel. The judge, in the very incipient pages of the novel, flashes off glimpses of "exactly what he would look like if he were dead" (p. 2). Life is consummated in death—'death' not necessarily being a cessation of life but an extension of it instead. People die only physically for themselves, but for their near and dear ones the dead live on in their remembrance becoming all the more loved and wanted than what they were when they were alive. Although Nimi did not live long enough in Jemubhai's company, but he was very cold, crude, cruel towards her during their very brief stay together as husband-wife in Bonda. But after casting her away to Gujarat he does not care to think about her till he gets news of her 'death by fire'—as if she was made to commit 'sati' for her living 'dead' husband. She, who had been "without enterprise, unable to entertain herself, made of nothing, yet with a disruptive presence" and "a Swaraji" for the ICS husband, "had fallen out of life altogether" (p. 172). The rancour and bitterness of their relationship had reached the nadir where both were estranged not only from each other but also from their respective world-views:

> By year's end the dread they had for each other was so severe it was as if they had tapped into a limitless bitterness carrying them beyond the parameters of what any individual is normally capable of feeling. They belonged of this emotion more than to themselves, experienced rage with enough muscle in it for entire nations coupled in hate. (p. 173)

Now, that Nimi was gone, "The judge was thinking of his hate" (p. 165), thinking how, he almost killed her before rejecting her repenting on his false pride and notions of standing upright in the eyes of his colonial masters, repenting his joining the colonial civil service—perhaps, repenting, not in so many words, at heart his greatest loss of Nimi. But the 'loss' was irredeemable—sparking off a series of loses in his life. So artistically ironic is the description of "a rumour of the judge's lost glory" fanned by the cook who too, "found himself telling lies" (p. 55), that a reader cannot tell the lie from the truth about Jemubhai's sorrow:

> A man so inspiring, but brought to his knees, to austerity and philosophy, by sorrow at his wife's death, the wife herself a martyred and religious mother of the kind that makes a Hindu weak in the knees, "that is why he sits by himself all day and every day."

He is very pertinently symbolized by "the car that never moved anywhere anymore" (p. 10). "It's the groaning journey made to Darjeeling for the judge to see his only friend Bose, long forgotten" (p. 12)—indicating his acute alienation not only from things and persons associated with his past but also, and more significantly so, from his own self.

It may not be entirely out of place, here, to refer to Karl Marx and Frederic Engels who pioneered the sociological concept of 'Alienation' of the workers in capitalist societies. A worker is a victim of exploitation at the hands of the bourgeoisie. Or we may transcribe it for our purposes here, to mean an Indian Jemubhai becoming a 'tool' in the hands of British colonial regime, a small cog in its machine of imperialism for exploitation of the Indians themselves. Just as labour produces the world of things, it also creates the devaluation of the world of men. This devaluation increases in direct proportion to the increase in the production of commodities, and hence to an increase in the margins of profit for the owners of the means of production, read colonial masters, here. To elaborate more, the following may serve the purpose:

> This fact expresses merely that the objects which labour produces—labours's product—confronts it as 'something alien' as a power independent of the producer the product of labour which has been congealed in an object, which has become material: it is the objectification of labour. Labour's realization is its

> objectifications. In the condition dealt with by political economy this realization of labour appears as 'loss of reality' for the workers; objectification as 'loss of the object' and 'object-bondage' appropriation as 'estrangement,' as 'alienation."[6]

In short, the worker appends his life and produces everything not for himself and his family, but for the 'powers' that manipulate him—the colonial empire or the bourgeoisie. And the more he produces the more he loses himself in the quagmire of the capitalist colonial exploitative system. What Marx says about 'alienation' in the following ancient inimitable words is of immediate relevance to our topic of discussion—"First the fact that labour is external to the worker, i.e. it does not belong to his essential being; that in his work, therefore, he does not affirm himself, but denies himself, does not feel content but unhappy...it is forced labour.... External labour, labour in which man alienates himself, is a labour of self-sacrifice, of mortification...that in it he belongs, not to himself, but to another...it is the loss of his self."[7]

Richard Schacht has succinctly explained the Marxian concept of 'alienation' as having two aspects—first, alienation from other men and second, self-alienation. For Marx, a man 'is self-alienated if his true human nature is something alien to him—if his life fails to manifest the characteristics of a truly human life such as individuality, society and cultivated sensibility. "Self-alienation, therefore, takes the form of dehuminization in his economic, social and sensuous spheres of life." He says: "The alienation of the worker in his product means...that the life which he has conferred on the object confronts him as something hostile and alien."[8]

Seen in the light of this explanation of 'alienation' of Pioneers of political economy, which does not seem a far-fetched comparison, Jemubhai's appears to be fittest case of alienation—as he sacrifices his social and personal life for best subserving the British colonial vested interests in India. His conscience screams that he is a 'foreigner,' yet he finally gets shorn of either Indianness or foreignness—hanging like a 'bat' between two identities. Even his, this alienation is infectious.

His cook's recriminations are a testimony, if any required, to this self-negation and self-abasement:

> My bones ache so badly, my joints hurt—I may as well be dead. If not for Biju.... (p. 3)

Although, he has spent a life-time serving the judge, the cook is never able to carve out a niche in heartless man's heart the more he has served him with sincerety, loyalty and diligence, the more he has fallen out of the judge's confidence. That is why, to keep his sanity he pins all his hopes on his son Biju who is also in the cooking business in America.

For instance, when on an excursion to the Darjeeling museum, Gyan cryptically says to Sai—"'He was the real hero, Tenzing,' Gyan had said, 'Hilary couldn't have made it without sherpas carrying his bags.' Everyone around had agreed. Tenzing was certainly first, or else he was made to wait with the bags so Hilary could take the first step on behalf of that colonial enterprise of sticking your flag on what was not yours" (p. 155).

Just as the antagonisms of class-conflict may sometimes involve violence in one or the other form, so we within peculiar ghastliness and ghoulish scenes during the waging of the Gorkhaland agitation in the novel:

> A beheaded body ran briefly down the street, blood fountaining from the neck, and they all saw the truth about living creatures—that after death, in final humiliation, the body defecates on itself (p. 276). Such is always the price for political-economic liberty and progress.

Symbolism, as thoroughly used by the writer of this novel, becomes a sort of linguistic force which unfolds the story of loss, alienation and death in all its lurid colours, even as it is intermeshed with delineation of such political issues as national freedom struggle, colonialism, neo-colonialism, balkanisation, casteism and communalism regionalism, globalization, economic inequality, fundamentalism, and terrorist violence. Despite being set in the mid-1980s and in the remotest north-eastern region of India, i.e. Darjeeling, Kalimpong and Siliguri,

Kiran Desai's novel manages to explore, with intimacy, insight and foresight, just about every international issues, as well as Indian ones. The Kalimpong house of Jemubhai is a symbol of retreat from the strain and stress of human existence—a self-created asylum of an old alienated bloke. His unusual expression of love and attention for Mutt, the she-dog is essentially a camouflage to conceal his complete alienation from his original roots, environment and people, especially his abandoned wife Nimi whom he neither loved nor despised.

Again, it is noteworthy that most of the characters of the novel, principal as well as minor ones perhaps seem to suffer from some form of solitude—more on the spiritual than physical side. All the peripheral characters of the novel appear to be innocent victims of alienation from their real selves. They excite feelings of pity and remorse for them whom time and space have crushed ruthlessly. Solitude, in fact, connects a state of mind and heart whereby one is more and more detached from the company of fellow-beings, friends and relatives as also from one's own self. We may even say that an individual's psyche is split into two halves—the individual proper and the self, the later at times keeps asking, mocking and torturing the former. How Jemubhai is later remorseful self curses his earlier individual proper which was stubborn, inconsiderate, haughty and cruel. "He retreated into a solitude that grew in weight day by day. The solitude became a habit, the habit became the man and it crushed him into a shadow" (p. 39). In an ironical reversal of roles, Jemubhai is "more lizard than human" and Mutt is "more human than dog" (p. 32). Even Father Booty, who had immeasurably contributed to the development of dairy-farming in Kalimpong, more than any Indian was issued notice by the administration to leave India within two weeks because he was a foreigner without valid visa:

> He knew he was a foreigner but he had best the notion that he was anything but an Indian foreigner. (p. 220). He, too, had to leave all his property—land, buildings, cattle, etc. alienating himself from his own cultivated possession, apart from his notions of acquired Indianness. His friend uncle Patty though assured him to

> look after the former's property till he gets back, and sitting along with Sai, they were listening to the Abida Parveen number "Allah hoo, Allah hoo, Allah hoo" perhaps signifying:
>
> "God was just wilderness and space," said the husky voice, careless with the loss of love (p. 222). The predominance of solitude is perhaps something which the author prefers to foretell in the few lines of Jorge Louis Burges entitled "Boast of Quietness" which she quotes by way of some kind of a foreword.
>
> Writings of light assault the darkness, more prodigious than meters.
>
> My humanity is in feeling we are all voices of the some poverty.
>
> Time is living me.
>
> More silent than my shadow.

Biju's typical aloofness and alienation in New York can be taken as symbolic of the whole Indian diasporas by extension—"Biju walked back to the Gandhi café, thinking he was emptying out. Year by year his life wasn't amounting to anything at all; in a space that should have included family, friends, he was the only one displacing the air, and yet, another part of him had expanded; his self-consciousness, his self-pity—oh the tediousness of it," the Indians living abroad, but still maintaining connections with their motherland, surely spend away the spring and summer of their lives on foreign soil, materially preparing for living their winter of their life back home. But they are not aware that such life is suspended animation and has no vision and satisfaction. They do not tend to openly castigate their country of adoption, rather they seek to put on the airs of the supposedly superior culture and civilization such as America and Britain. Biju, like any other NRI has put on a veneer, construed in order to conceal his sense of inferiority of humiliation, of pain in not belonging to one's native place though temporarily there could be but very few Swaraj Pauls, L.N. Mittals and Sunita Williams and Indira Nooyis. For the bulk of the Indian diaspora, as for Biju, the rhetorical question is—"Would he, life Harish Harry, manufacture a false version of himself and using what he had created as clues, understand himself backward? Life was not about life for him anymore, and death—what would even that mean to him? It would have nothing to do with death" (p. 268).

Perhaps, Shelley may be more effective in conveying this life-in-throns view of life: "Oh, lift me as a wave, a leaf, a cloud! I fall upon the thorns of life! I bleed!"[9] May be, the wisdom of our traditional scriptures, albeit in contravention of the modern nations of globalization and of 'reverse colonialism,' should drawn upon us, the sooner the better.

Janani janam bhumishche swargadapi gariyari:

That is, mother and mother-earth or motherland is greater than heaven. Life seemed to have come at a standstill Cho Oyu, not only with the slavic inertia and notional stupor of the judge, but also with the natural concomitants of alienation in action and stagnancy:

> Time might have died in the house that sat on the mountain ledge, its lines grown indistinct with moss, its roof loaded with ferns, but with each letter the cook trundled toward the further (p. 17). The judge was living here in this obnoxious 'shell' or even 'cell' "with the solace of being a foreigner in his own country, for this time he would not learn the language. He never went back to court." (p. 29)

Again coming back to the Kalimpong house of the retired judge, which "had long been a matter of curiosity in the bazaar" (p. 11) is aptly surveyed by the adolescent Gorkha insurgents as the one where the atmosphere, they noted, was of intense solitude" (p. 6). The ramshackle house of the judge, infested with hundreds of spiders—deceased and living, appeared to be in dire needs of repairs. This ambience of gloom and solitariness of the house is all the more reinforced by the pathetic sense of abandonment suffered by Jemubhai and his granddaughter Sai who lost her parents—Mr. and Mrs. Mistry, who were accidentally "crushed by the local bus wheels, weighted by thirty indomitable ladies from the provinces who had speeded two days to barter and sell their wares in the market" (p. 27). The cook's wife had also died an accidental death falling off a tree. The cook, realizing his guilt, surrenders to the furious judge who is repeatedly threatening to kill him "I'm a wicked man, a weak man. I'd better be dead than alive" (p. 320). Gyan is irritated by Sai's too much concern for the Christmas party, despite her being a Hindu. So her answer to Sai's question as to why he was yawning is "BECAUSE I'M BORED TO DEATH BY YOU, THAT'S WHY" (p. 163). The bold capitals more emphatic than usual. Gyan's forefathers too had died while serving in the British Indian army-martyred for foreign colonial interests as though. It was on 27th July of 1986, that a 'bandh' was organized by the GNLF in Kalimpong where amidst shouting of slogans "Jai Gorkha," "Jai Gorkhaland! Gorkhaland for Gorkhas!" something went amiss. The police brutally suppressed the mob violence by firing, which left many young boys dead. The macabre and gruesome violence engaged the police and the people—"...they jumped on one another, beating with sticks, bashing with rocks; began to slash with their sickles—a hand, a face, a nose, an ear.... This was how history moved, the show build, the quick burn...swallowing the young into old hate. The space between life and death, in the end, too small to measure" (pp. 275-76). Then the necrophiliac brooding as it were, of the author dominates in the novel. That we are all animals having a blood thirstiness characteristic of the carnivorous ones—"to triumph you must taste blood" otherwise we would be like "the deer, the cow" "the hunted" (p. 195)—is the age-old principle of the world. This hunter-hunted syndrome seems by extension, applicable to the colonialism neo-colonialism, post-industrial society and to all political struggles for independence and, or autonomy. Of particular significance is the GNLF's liberation movement in the novel which takes its own bloody toll. The unity and indomitable courage of the Gorkhas for 'Gorkhaland' did bring about results but it also took the toll of Sai-Gyan love. It is here that one sees the socio-political events intruding, and sometimes destroying, interpersonal relationship of friendship, trust, love and affection.

The author employs such symbols and images during her narration that create a magic of keeping the reader engrossed, almost what she remarks about Sai's reading habit seems equally relevant to her narrative skill: "She was beginning to read faster, more, until she was inside the narrative and the narrative inside her, the pages going by so fast, her heart in her chest—she couldn't stop" (pp. 68-69).

Of the two sisters Lola and Noni who teach Sai, Lola has lost her husband Jaydeep whom she, in a fit of anguish and frustration over losing their hard-earned land and house to the GNLF youngsters have grabbed their spacious vacant land, cruses—"Look at what you've done you bloody fool!!!... I don't even have my decency" (p. 245). But the greatest sacrifice at the altar of the GNLF led Gorkha Liberation Movement in Darjeeling during mid-1980s, is the love of Sai and Gyan. The novel has dramatically explored the budding romance between Gyan, the Nepali tutor and the innocent orphaned child Sai, whose parents embraced death in a violent accident. The theme of death of Sai's parents is very stunning and cruel.... It tears the human heart poignantly. The manner of alienation of Sai and Gyan typifies the fate of modern boy-meets-girl romance. Sai, "a lushed-lashed" maiden is no ordinary girl, it seems, in so far as "She could sense the swollen presence of the forest, hear the hollow-knuckled knocking of the bamboo, the sound of the jhora that ran deep in the décolleté of the mountain" (p. 34). A parallel may usefully be drawn between Wordsworth listening to "a long withdrawing roar" coming from behind the mountain while he is sailing in the boat in The Prelude in one hand, and Sai's premonition if downfall of Cho Oyu house:

> Suddenly, as if a secret door had opened in his hearing, she became aware of the sound of microscopic jaws slow-milling the house to saw-dust, a sound hard to detect for being so closely knit into the air, but once identified, it grew monumental. In this climate, she would learn, untreated wood would be chewed up in a season. (p. 34)

Sai and her Nepali tutor Gyan, came closer to each other in "the game of courtship, reaching, retreating, teasing, fleeing —

how delicious the pretense of objective study, miraculous how it could eat up the hours" (p. 125). Even as they roamed in their own hill-town with new found love and romance, the writings on the wall was clear—"We are stateless." "It is better to die than to live as slaves," "LIBERATION," "Gorakhaland for Gorkhas" (p. 126). And their romance grew in the background of this GNLF-led "insurgency" for carving a separate Gorkha state out of West Bengal. Meanwhile, their endearments and nicknames—giving went on—they were each other's "momo, mutton in dough, one thing plump and cozy within the other—it connoted protection affection" (p. 140). She was his "Kishmish" or raisin and he was her "Kaju" or cashew—both "Sweet, nutty and expensive" (p. 140). The edifice of their love-mansion was progressing in construction when suddenly Gyan was gathered up by a procession of young Gorkhas, many of his college friends included. Shouting the slogans of "Jai Gorkha" and "Victory to the Gorkha Liberation army," they all seem to have "melded into a single being" (p. 156). Perhaps, the immanent attraction of his ethnic movement for political autonomy was too much for him to resist and he was as if suddenly co-opted: "Then he shouted along with the crowd, and the every mingling of his voice with largeness and lustiness seemed to create a relevancy, an affirmation he'd felt before, and he was pulled back into the making of history" (p. 157). Gyan apparently forgot his "Kishmish" and "Momo" in a moment of political making which smacked of nothing less than our own Quit India Movement of 1942. Now he starts getting "BORED" by Sai and her anglicized-Christianised way of life. Deep inside his heart, he decided to 'sacrifice' his adolescent love with Sai for a much purer greater cause—"A feeling of martyrdom crept over him," as he sought justification for renunciating Sai in "the center of the Buddhist wheel of life clasped in a demon's fangs and talons to indicate the hell that traps us: rooster-snake-pig; lust-anger-foolishness; each chasing, each feeding on, each consumed by the other" (p. 175). And, there, Sai was also ruminating over her so easily giving herself away to him and was "contemplating desire, fury and stupidity" (p. 175).

The sham of politics devours Sai's love of Gyan, just as in the earlier generation Jemubhai had given up Nimi for the sake of false pride and sham constructs of colonialism, sham justice, pseudo loyalty, to Brtish imperial civil service in India. Although Gyan appears to know the true colours of all politics, which is nothing but ultimate betrayal of the faith of the masses, he helplessly gets drawn away from Sai to the insurgents—the routinization of charisma, the dwindling of socio-political movements into the political and bureaucratic trammels of red-tapism, corruption, favouritism, nepotism free from any moral bondage to history. The author seems to be making a very relevant political comment of universal application through the mouth of Gyan:

> Listen Momo, he said to a delighted Sai, 'Let's go to Australia.' Fly away, bye-bye ta-ta. Free from history. Free from family demands and the built-up debt of centuries. The patriotism was false, he suddenly felt as he marched; it was surely just frustration—the leaders harnessing the natural irritations and disdain of adolescence for cynical ends; for their own hope in attaining the same power as government officials held now, the same ability to award local business deals in exchange for bribes, for the ability to give jobs to their relatives, place to their children in schools, cooking gas connection.... (p. 157)

All this tomfoolery goes on because of the inadequacy and breakdown of the system of justice, which is lopsided in its leniency towards big crimes vis-à-vis smaller ones. Jemubhai, only after losing Nimi, gradually realises the emptiness and falsity of the judicial system. And here the following quote is illuminating:

> The fact was that one was left empty-handed. There was no system to soothe the unfairness of things; justice was without scope; it might snag the stealer of chickens, but great evasive crimes would have to be dismissed, of identified and netted, they would bring down the entire structure of so-called civilization.... There was no religion and no government that would relieve the hell

> (p. 200). Hence, he "stops going to court," alienated as he becomes from the very system of governance and dispensation of justice. Like Walter Pater, the chief advocate of the literary movement 'Art for Art's sake,' who lived out his principles to decay and death, both Jemubhai and Gyan, despite their knowledge and awareness about the inadequacy and duplicity of the systems of justice and politics, chose to take up cudgel on behalf of these sacrificing their loves Nimi and Sai respectively. Hence, their tragedies. Ironically enough, both also keep the sweet remembrances of their past alive in their streams of consciousness to which they off and on draw upon for solace. This is the eternal satisfaction of eternal repentance unlike the usual love which becomes too habitual and accustomed to have any excitement and love at all, and where merely "the façade" remains, like Cho Oyu being gauged by termites from within. (p. 233)

The house at the Cho Oyu has been, in my opinion the only mega symbol in the novel to which the author frequently ascribes various shades of symbolic meanings. One such insinuation is that our problems are due to our misperceptions and our struggles in chasing a chimera out of sheer chaos and blurred vision the novel recounts:

> At Cho Oyu, the judge and Sai sat out on the lawn. Mutt, catching sight of the shadow of her own tail, leapt and caught it, began to whiz around and around, confused as to whose tail it was. She would not let go, but her eyes expressed confusion and beseeching—how could she stop? What should she do?—She had caught a strange beast and didn't know it was herself. She went skittering about the garden. (p. 105)

So similar in misconceptions do they become that Mutt, the dog forms a trio with Jemubhai and Gyan. One cannot help but express the jaundiced and disjointed perception of the world which the novelist intends to symbolically expostulate, through the so celebrated lines of Mathew Arnold:

To lie before us like a land of dreams,
so various, so beautiful, so new,
Hath really neither joy, nor love, nor light,
her heart in her chest—she couldn't stop. (pp. 68-69)
Nor certitude, nor peace, nor help for pain;
And we have as on a darkling plain
Swept with confused alarms of struggle and flight.
Where ignorant armies clash by night.[10]

Obviously, *The Inheritance of Loss* is a modern masterpiece, having in its bones not only the pastness of its past and of its presence but also of its future. Written in a highly original style with use of mesmerizing language and of prose suffused with poetic fervour, the novel is at once topical and for all times. Barring description of foreign jaunts of Jemubhai and Biju, the novel is, for the most part riveted on Kalimpong, a small town near Darjeeling, yet its compass is extraordinarily expansive, alluring, illuminating but essentially devastatingly nostalgiac. Richly interspersed with some brilliant passages or lines of life's philosophy inhering in meanings of rootlessness, alienation and death, the novel ends on as optimistic note enkindling in the humanity a large-hearted bravado to look beyond all despairs, to look beyond past—into the future while standing steady on the present. Quite cryptically the novelist throws up a silver-lining—Biju's meeting his 'Pitaji' nowhere else than at the gate of the self-same jinxed, crumbling, isolated house at the foot of Mount Kanchenjunga. Similarly there is hope for the embittered judge and for Sai and Gyan; for Lola and Noni and for father Booty—for the redemption of whole humanity from pain and suffering of squalor, solitude, disease, decay, death and alienation. Just as there is hope for the nations of the world rocked by terrorist violence; India included for Gorkhaland and for all such regions of India disturbed by insurgency and separatist violence like Purvanchal and Harit Pradesh in Uttar Pradesh, Telangana in Andhra Pradesh, and Vidarbha in Maharashtra.

Particularly in case of Gorkhaland, if Gihising of GNLF has decayed and out-lived his utility, how in 2008, the hope of the subaltern in the hills lies in Bimal Gurung of Gorkha Janamukti Morcha (GJM) such in the course of history. Individuals do not matter much as they are welded into a holistic identity. If only Gyan could fathom the warmth and intensity of Sai's emotions of love, and forsake the path of political agitation. Gorkhaland Liberation Movement then could have invested so many other Gyans to carry on the agitation. The novel then concludes on these significant notes:

> The five peaks of Kanchenjenga turned golden with the kind of luminous light that made you feel, if briefly, that truth was apparent. All you needed to do was to reach out and pluck it. (p. 324)

The message, if at all there is one, loud and clear in the following biblical saying—"Know thyself. For the kingdom of Heaven is within you."

NOTES

1. T.S. Eliot, "The Burial of the Dead," *The Waste Land*, ll. 60-64 (Oxford University Press, New Delhi, 1987).
2. Cleanth Brooks, "*The Waste Land*: Critique of the Myth," *A Collection of Critical Essays*, ed. J. Martin (1968), p. 61.
3. T.S. Eliot, *op. cit*, "A Game of Chess," ll. 133-34.
4. *Ibid.*, ll. 135-38.
5. William Shakespeare, *Macbeth*, Act I, Scene vi, ll. 54-59.
6. Marx and Engels. "On Alienation," C. Wright Mills ed. *Images of Man* (New York, George Braziller, 1960), pp. 498, 500.
7. Karl Marx, *Early Writings* (New York, McGraw-Hill, 1964), p. 110.
8. As quoted by Richard Schacht, in *Alienation* (Garden city, Doubleday, 1970), p. 95.
9. P.B. Shelley, "Ode to the West Wind," *Palgrave's Golden Treasury*, Oxford University Press, Calcutta (1968), p. 296.
10. Arnold Matthew, "Dover Beach," *Palgrave's Golden Treasury*, Oxford University Press, Calcutta (1968), p. 365.

All the textual references are from *The Inheritance of Loss*, Penguin Books, India, 2006.

11

Kiran Desai's *The Inheritance of Loss*: The Politics of Being "A Drab Immigrant"

Kripanath Mishra

The humble aim of this paper is to introduce briefly Kiran Desai's second novel, *The Inheritance of Loss*, which has won for the writer the most enviable Man Booker Prize for 2006. The paper intends to take a close look at the text, examine its thematic dimensions and understand the novelist's mind and art. This magnificent novel, we know, has received international acclaim and drawn the attention of the entire world of academics for its exciting story as well as remarkable insight into the contemporary issues such as the postcolonial discourse, the postmodern predicament, the pain of immigration, history, nationality, politics, subalternism and the impact of the forces of globalization on the current economy and culture. In addition, the narrative sensitively depicts the individual's dilemma and passions, nostalgia and disillusionment, cross-border experience and sense of inequality, chaos and despair so beautifully.

Situated in 1980s of India, *The Inheritance of Loss* recounts an intensely absorbing story. At its centre we have a family of a retired judge and widower, Jemubhai Popatlal Patel. In Kalimpong, a small town of the eastern region of India, the judge, who was once a student of the Cambridge University presently lives with his 16 year-old granddaughter, Sai Mistry. In a painful incident Sai's parents died in Moscow when she was only five. Jemubhai lives in Cho Oyu, a large dilapidated house built by a Scotsman but now owned by him, with his chatty cook, whose only son Biju works in restaurants of New York. It is really interesting that while the cook always thinks proudly of his son doing job in New York, a metropolis in America, the son more often remembers, sadly, his father as well as his childhood days in a village in India. The tension between these two kinds of feelings provide energy to the work. As to Sai, she passionately falls in love with her mathematics tutor, Gyan, a Nepali Gorkha. But then, Gyan gets involved in the violent Nepali insurgency for the autonomy of Gorkhaland and is forced to back out from his commitment to love. After undergoing an agonising experience in New York restaurants as "a drab immigrant," Biju eventually decides to return to his father in India with the humble dream of buying a taxi and home of his own. Nonetheless, on his way home from Calcutta, somewhere between Siliguri and Kalimpong actually, he undergoes a harrowing experience of inhumanity. The Gorkha National Liberation Front (GNLF) militants rob him off his all belongings including his savings, wallet, shoes, clothes and belts and he is forced to run home without clothes. Though Biju is united to his father at the end, the novel leaves a deep poignant impact on the readers' mind.

We know that the fictional world of expatriate Indian writers reflects a wide and varied range. Alienation from the roots, anxiety to achieve the intended goals—economic or something else, cultural dislocation, problems of identity in the adopted land, conflicts between the values of the motherland and those of the western society, tensions of assimilation in an alien society, nostalgic memories, racial differences and the sense of being a marginalized community in the adopted homeland are the dominant issues in the novels of Indian immigrants, such as Salman Rushdie, Vikram Seth, Vikram Chandra, Meena Alexander, Shoma Ramaya, Bharati Mukherjee, Rohinston Mistry, Saros Cowasjee, Shashi Tharoor, Bharti Kirchner, Amitav Ghosh, Kiran Narayan, Chitra Bannerjee Divakaruni and Jhumpa Lahiri, to quote a few best-known names. *The Inheritance of Loss* appears informed with perspectives on all these themes.

The Inheritance of Loss can rightly be described as an excellent postcolonial novel. The above mentioned outline of the plot suggests how as a postcolonial product it deals with the relationship between the west and the non-west, between the colonizing and the colonized. Moreover, it reflects the postcolonial India—its life and culture—realistically and sensitively. The incidents and situations described in it cover up the transitional period of Indian history from 1920s to 1980s, i.e. a period of about fifty years of emerging India. Obviously, a part of this period deals with a time of British occupation and the rest narrates the phase after India got independence in 1947. The work thus remarkably exhibits the contemporary political, social, economic, cultural and moral fabrics as well as issues, essential mood and conditions. Oppression on women has also been deftly integrated into the novel.

There is no denying the fact that migration is a global phenomenon of the contemporary time. Crossing national boundaries has been a recurrent issue for the writers of postmodern literature. In his essay, "The Diaspora in Indian Culture," Amitav Ghosh, the noted writer, has rightly observed:

> The modern Indian diaspora—the huge migration from the subcontinent that began in the mid-nine tenth century—is not merely one of the most important demographic dislocations of modern times: it now represents important force in world-culture.[1]

C. Vijayashree, too pithily sums up the features of this trend of postcolonial expatriation in his essay, "The Politics and Poetics of Expatriation: The Indian Version(s)":

> The phenomena of emigration and expatriation are by no means new but their scale in the present times is dramatic. The growing incidence of expatriation, particularly in the post-colonial societies in the second half of the twentieth century, and the psychic states attendant upon the awareness of connections and disconnections it effects, however, constitutes a

> contemporary phenomenon. This experience of inhabiting two geographical and cultural spaces simultaneously is wrought with subtle and involuted tensions which get polarized into patterns such as dislocation vs. relocation, domicile vs. diasporic consciousness, dispossession vs. integration, heritage vs. hybridity and exile vs. involvement. Such tension, however, has proved to be an active source of creative energy and resulted in the emergence of a powerful and impressive body of expatriate writing.[2]

In one interview after she was given the Booker, Kiran Desai told that her novel tries to capture what it means to live between East and West and what it means to be an immigrant. The book as such weaves into her narrative the realities and myths, truths and illusions of this phenomenon of the contemporary exodus. The story of *The Inheritance of Loss* predominantly moves between Kalimpong in India and New York in America. Like many of the present writers perhaps the novelist also believes that no culture is self-contained. Nor can any nation exist in isolation. The thoughts, actions, aspirations, dreams, memories and sufferings of the two main protagonists, Jemubhai and Biju, as migrants in London and New York respectively, represent the expatriate consciousness as well as perspectives of the work in this context. The selection of Kalimpong as the backdrop for the narrative reflects the novelist's implications since the place have populations of Tibetan refugees and large populations are Nepalis who were brought there long ago by the British power to work on tea plantations. Besides, the plateau is surrounded by Bhutan, China, Tibet and Nepal. Evidently borders of these countries are connected and overlapping here:

> Here, where India blurred into Bhutan and Sikkim, and army pull-ups and push-ups, maintaining their tanks with khaki paint in case the Chinese grew hungry for more territory than Tibet, it had always been a messy map. The papers sounded resigned. A great amount of warring, betraying, bartering had occurred; between Nepal, England, Tibet, India, Sikkim, Bhutan;

> Darjeeling, stolen from here. Kalimpong plucked from there—despite, ah, despite the mist charging down like a dragon, dissolving, undoing, making ridiculous the drawing of borders.[3]

Jemubhai originally belongs to the famous Patel family in Gujarat. His ancestral home was in Piphit, a village somewhere near Ahmedabad or Baroda. He was a brilliant student in school and got scholarship in college. After the completion of his graduation Jemu, the only son of his father, was sent to England for higher education. One day the judge recalls how,

> He had first left home at the age of twenty, with a black tin trunk just like the one Sai had arrived with, on which white letters read "Mr J P Patel, S S Strathnaver." The year was 1939. The town he had left was his ancestral home of Piphit. From there he had journeyed to Bombay dock and then sailed to Liverpool and from Liverpool he had gone to Cambridge. (p. 35)

Jemu's father did not have enough money for sending his son to England. So he took loan at a high interest rate. The judge is accompanied by his father to Victoria Terminus Sea-port to say good-bye. However, the judge's mother becomes too emotional at home. Her motherly feelings surge up at the thought of his son going to Europe. The novelist in her has painted the typical Indian mother with lots of traditional and cultural traits. Jemu is given the desi cuisine, choorva, to be eaten on way and a coconut to be submitted into the seawater for his safety and god's blessing abroad,

> Her little son with his frail and comical moustache, with his love for her special choorva that he would never get in England and his hatred of cold that he would get too much of; with his sweater that she had knit in a fanciful enough to express the extravagance of her affection; with his new Oxford English Dictionary and his decorated coconut to be tossed as an offering into the waves, so his journey might be blessed by gods. (p. 36)

In London, Jemu starts living in the house of one Mrs Rice on Thornton Road but feels acutely lonely and sad. In completely an alien West world he feels hesitant and timid to go out and talk and deal with people comfortably. He virtually withdraws himself—

> He worked twelve hours at a stretch, late into the night, and in thus withdrawing, he failed to make a courageous gesture at a crucial moment and found, instead, that his pusillanimity and his loneliness had found fertile soil. He retreated into a solitude that grew in weight day by day. The solitude became a habit, the habit became the man, and it crushed him into a shadow. (p. 39)

This shows the consequences but the reasons are presented soon after this. Jemu actually remains conscious of his Indian brown colour, accents, pronunciation and, above all, the despising as well as discriminatory racial looks of the whites. In him, the writer has very precisely portrayed the suppressed psyche of a young Indian among the white Britishers:

> For the entire days nobody spoke to him at all, his throat jammed with words unuttered, his heart and mind turned in to blunt aching things, and elderly ladies, even the hapless—blue-haired, spotted, faces like collapsing pumpkins—moved over when he sat next to them in the bus, so he knew that whatever they had, they were secure in their conviction that it wasn't even remotely bad as what he had. The young and beautiful were no kinder; girls held their noses and giggled, "phew, he stinks of curry!" (p. 39)

The dehumanizing as well as agonizing impact of this kind of ill treatment exposes the realities of the so-called civilized and developed west:

> Eventually he felt barely human at all, leaped when touched on the arm as if from an unbearable intimacy, dreaded and agonized over even a "How-do-you-do-lovely-day" with the fat woman dressed in friendly pinks who ran the corner store. (p. 40)

Globalization, precisely speaking, is characterized by flows of people, trade, capital, information, technology and opportunities across borders. It has taken into its ambit cultural, political and environmental issues too. The general aims have been to expand economic freedom, provide equality of opportunities, better education, good health and, above all, to reduce poverty globally. Biju's migration to New York for better opportunity, living standards and wealth shows the impact of this system of globalization. In him Kiran Desai appears to have portrayed, primarily, the impact of the politics of globalization and post colonialism on the economic structure of the once colonized nation. When the advertisement is made in local paper for drudge staffs in America, Biju applies, goes through an interview in Kathmandu, Nepal, and finally gets selected. However, while standing in queue for visa processing at the US embassy, he observes the pitiable conditions of the applicants and undergoes feelings of disgrace and humiliations. The author has incredibly described the tension of Biju's mind, between his aspirations and his helplessness resulting from fear of losing the chance of going to the US:

> Standing there, feeling the enormous measure of just how despised he was, he would have to reply in a smart yet humble manner. If he mumbled, tried too hard, seemed too cocky, became confused, if they didn't get what they wanted quickly and easily, he would be out. In this room it was a fact accepted by all that Indians were willing to undergo any kind of humiliation to get into the States. You could heap rubbish on their heads and yet they would be begging to come crawling.... (p. 184)

Anyway, after all formalities of obtaining visa, Biju goes to New York where he works in different restaurants as an illegal immigrant and thus encounters unhappy social as well as cultural experiences in the West. He has to live, with so many other immigrants, miserably in a shabby and inhuman condition of the basement of a building,

> Biju joined a shifting population of men camping out near the fuse box, behind the boiler, in the cubby holes, and in odd-shaped corners that once were pantries, maid's room, laundry rooms, and storage rooms at the bottom of what had been a single-family home, the

> entrance still adorned with a scrap of colored mosaic in the shape of a star. The men shared a yellow toilet; the sink was a tin laundry trough. (pp. 51-52)

The episode where Biju skids on rotten spinach in the kitchen of Gandhi Café is really one of the remarkably drawn pictures in the novel. Biju gets injured and requests Harish-Harry, the representative of the agency which hires Biju and other workers from the post-colonial world, to send for a doctor. Harish-Harry immediately and cruelly rejects the idea telling it is too costly to bear the medical expenses in America. Biju's reactions then gives us idea about the hard living of the poor people and thus exposes the consumer culture as well as immoral business competition in the developed world. The following words show Biju's anguish and resentment:

> "Without us living like pigs," said Biju, "what business would you have? This is how you make your money, paying us nothing because you know we can't do anything, making us work day and night because we are illegal. Why don't you sponsor us our green cards?" (p. 188)

Thus, Biju and people like him are exploited. They suffer actually a postmodern form of subjugation. Biju's struggle for survival while working in the grimy restaurants of New York and final retreat from America reveal the abject failure of the economic globalization and the forces of modernization. His journey can be called a saga of disappointment and disillusionment. His failure is the failure of the downtrodden in the land of plenty. He goes to New York with all dreams of economic freedom and opportunities but his hopes are belied. He passes through intense and agonizing self-exploration and chooses to come back to his country to identify himself:

> Biju walked back to the Gandhi Café, thinking he was emptying out, year by year, his life wasn't amounting to anything at all; in a space which should have included family, friends, he was the only one displacing the air. And yet, another part of him had expanded: his self-consciousness, his self-pity—oh the tediousness of it. Clumsy in America, a giant-sized midget, a bigfat-sized

> helping of small.... Shouldn't he return to a life where he might slice down his own importance, to where he might relinquish this overrated control over his own destiny and perhaps be subtracted from its determination altogether? He might also experience of not noticing himself at all. (p. 268)

Kiran Desai portrays not only how Americans look at the people from Third World countries but also how the immigrants view the Americans. Racial situations and reactions have come up at many places in the narrative. Biju has inherited feelings of nationality and hatred for the subjugating white world as such:

> This habit of hate had accompanied Biju, and he found that he possessed an awe of white people, who arguably had done India great harm, and a lack of generosity regarding almost everyone else, who had never done a single harmful thing to India. (p. 77)

In addition, to depict political unrest, violence, hypocrisy and corruption are yet other focal points of the novel. Even though India has got sovereignty, its people are not satisfied. Militancy, sectarianism and regionalism are rampant. The novel begins and ends with the descriptions of agitation, chaos, loot, snatching and violence. Lola's following utterance sums up the idea:

> Because on that basis they can start statehood demands. Separatist movement here, separatist movement there, terrorists, guerillas, insurgents, rebels, agitators, instigators, and they all learn from one another, of course—the Neps have been encouraged by the Sikhs and their Khalistan, by ULFA, NEFA, PLA; Jharkhand, Bodoland, Gorkhaland; Tripura, Mizoram, Manipur, Punjab, Assam.... (pp. 128-29)

The point to note is that this phenomenon is universal. The whole world is suffering from this disease of political and social chaos: Africa, America and Pakistan, Bhutan and Nepal, for example.

In sum, the novelist's vision captures here a vast landscape of the modern human life. Subjugation, inequality and victimization of women by men in the Indian society seem other important aspects of the dynamics of the novel. The innocent Nimi, Jemu's wife, is trapped by the hypocritical and vile politician, Mrs Mohan, who belongs to the Congress Party, and becomes a scapegoat of her immoral trick. She requests the judge's wife to go with her and her supporters to the Cantonment Railway Station to welcome Mr Nehru. She becomes a part of the procession and for this act the judge is summoned by the district commissioner and reprimanded. The judge, in retaliation of his embarrassment, humiliation and demotion, returns home, abuses his wife badly and hits her brutally. Not only this, she is sent back to her father's house where after unbearable ordeal at the hands of her relatives, she succumbs to death. The novel, we can say, represents an amazing story of our time with perennial human interest.

NOTES

1. Amitav Ghosh, "The Diaspora in Indian Culture." *The Imam and the Indian: Prose Pieces*. Delhi: Ravi Dayal/Permanent Black, 2002, p. 243.
2. C. Vijayasree, "The Politics and Poetics of Expatration: The Indian Version(s)", eds. Harish Trivedi and Meenakshi Mukherjee. *Interrogating Post-Colonialism: Theory, Text and Context*. Simla: Indian Institute of Advanced Study, 1996, p. 221.
3. Kiran Desai, *The Inheritance of Loss*. New Delhi: Penguin Books, 2006, p. 9.

   All the textual references are from *The Inheritance of Loss* with page number in parentheses.

12

Conflicts of Globalization, Multiculturalism and Economic Inequality in Kiran Desai's *The Inheritance of Loss*

Srutimala Duara

The Inheritance of Loss, published by Atlantic Monthly Press, is set in a remote corner of India against the backdrop of growing Nepalese unrest, and in the hard streets of Manhattan, where illegal immigrants try to make a living while eluding the authorities. Kiran Desai's second book concerns itself with what she calls "the enormous anxiety of being a foreigner."

Kiran Desai's extraordinary new novel *The Inheritance of Loss* manages to explore, with intimacy and insight, just about every contemporary international issue: globalization, multiculturalism, economic inequality, fundamentalism and terrorist violence. The novel heralds Kiran Desai as one of the most perceptive novelists. Her novel moves between several worlds at an almost breathtaking speed—from the mist-filled world of Kalimpong to the dingy basements of New York, where she depicts with candour and sympathy the hidden world of stowaways and illegal labour. It includes several periods as well, while being set in the 1980s, it also tells a story of life under the shadow of colonial rule. It is also about how people live in the same milieu, bound by good relations and ill feeling; the book speaks in the same breath of estrangement and togetherness. She illuminates the pain of exile and the ambiguities of post-colonialism with a tapestry of colorful characters: an embittered old judge; Sai, his sixteen-year-old orphaned granddaughter; a chatty cook; and the cook's son, Biju, who is hop-scotching from one miserable New York restaurant to another, trying to stay a step ahead of the INS. The Booker went to Kiran Desai for a novel about the 'anxiety of being a foreigner'.

The judge's world is a lonely one, with his tragic marriage, and his inability to belong anywhere, whether in England or later as a colonial official, where his anglicised brownness sets him apart—from his own countrymen and his fellow British officers. Born into a middle-class Patel family, judge Jemubhai sails for England in 1939. Feeling lost, and scorned for his skin, color, smell, feeling totally isolated and very foreign, he returns as an ICS officer serving the British. As a student, isolated in racist England, the future judge feels "barely human at all" and leaps "when touched on the arm as if from an unbearable intimacy." Yet on his return to India, he finds himself despising his apparently backward Indian wife. He found his wife too 'Indian' and sent her back to her parents, where six months later she produced a daughter. Full of self-hate as well as hate for his family, community, and anyone for not being British, which includes his wife, the judge settles in Kalimpong in a crumbling old relic of a mansion from the colonial era. The novel depicts very well in Jemubhai the dilemmas of post colonialism. The judge Jemubhai's perfect manners and demeanor is very much British but he cannot get himself free from the shackles of traditional Gujarati and Indian mentality. He feels guilty of ill-treating his wife Nimmi, of shoving away the "holy coconut throwing in the water custom."

Thus, Jemubhai's mind has begun to distort; he grew stranger to himself than he was to those around him, found his own skin odd-colored, his own accent peculiar. He forgot how to laugh, could barely manage to lift his lips in a smile, and if he ever did, he held his hand over his mouth, because he couldn't bear anyone to see his gums, his teeth. They seemed too private. In fact he could barely let any of himself peep out of his clothes for fear of giving offence. He began to wash obsessively.... To the end of his life, he would never be seen without socks and shoes and would prefer shadow to light, faded days to sunny, for he was suspicious that sunlight might reveal him, in his hideousness, all too clearly.

With a keen eye for telling detail and profound wisdom, Desai weaves the weight of colonial history with its slow burn of humiliation, and creates a rich tapestry of characters that live with questions of identity and alienation, exiles at home as well as abroad.

The main story is about the kinds of losses the characters endure. Sai, the orphaned granddaughter of the judge is returned to his care from the convent school. Hiding from his own life and at a loss to provide the love and warmth she yearns for, the judge turns her care over to the cook. The cook witnesses India's hierarchy being overturned and discarded. Infected by the desire to leave home among the people he sees around him, the cook, who has lost his wife, also sends his son Biju off to work on a cruise ship which deposits him in New York. All his hopes are on his son Biju, who had the good fortune to get a tourist visa for the USA and left to make his fortune. Instead he found only illegal, underpaid work in the kitchens of a succession of New York restaurants. Biju struggles to buy into the American immigrant dream and is confused by the 'made good' Indian Hindu business men eating 'rare' steaks in one of the restaurants where he worked.

Back in Kalimpong, the judge hired two elderly ladies—Lola and Noni—to tutor his granddaughter. These old girls clung to the old ways—with their M&S undies and pride in Pixie, Lola's daughter who works for the BBC. They soon found they couldn't cope with Sai's maths and physics tutoring and drafted in the help of a local Nepali man, Gyan, who became gently but romantically involved with Sai.

Soon Kalimpong becomes the hub of activities. The Nepali's struggle to get their own rights and land slowly creeps into the lives of the characters, the cook, the judge, Sai, Noni, Lola and gnaws and questions their very being. The characters like Father Booty and Uncle Potty who have been living here for years and never bothered to ponder upon their rights to live in this land, are very much caught in the dark just like the middle aged sisters Lola and Noni, who, polished with an education, books and English literature get a rude shock when the GNLF leader molests Lola with his vulgar words and mocks at her middle agedness. The Nepalese insurgency threatens Sai's new-sprung romance with her handsome tutor, their lives descend into chaos. Gyan is lost to her when he is absorbed into the 1986 Gorkha insurgency. He joins the movement not as much for the cause but as an outlet to vent his own rage and alienation. The movement does not even spare Biju, the cook's son in America who comes back only to be robbed of all his money and belongings. But yet the reader finds a quaint satisfaction in the union of father and son in the backdrop of a disturbed land of Kalimpong. At least Biju feels safe and at peace compared to his lonely life as a waiter thrown from one restaurant kitchen to another.

Other minor characters who teach in some way share the sense of 'loss' alluded to in the title include Father Booty (a Swiss priest who runs an unlicensed dairy) and Uncle Potty. Everyone is in some way alienated by their environments and experiences, clinging on to aspects of the colonial past whilst not belonging entirely to the 'old ways' and not fitting in with the new.

With great tenderness and humor, Desai has populated her book with vibrant characters such as the anglophile sisters Lola and Noni; the refugee Afghani princesses; the Swiss priest Father Potty who had thought his home India, but is deported with dispatch when the Gorkha separatist movement breaks out; the most memorable Saeed Saeed who teaches Biju everything he knows. Not the least are Mustafa the cat, Mutt the judge's purebred pet dog—who is lost—and other various animals, alive and dead, who make command appearances in the story.

In both places, New York and Kalimpong, Indians live parallel lives, conflicted by class and nationality. Untouched by globalization and the prosperity it has brought into one class of Indians, people like the cook and Gyan find the vestiges of colonialism in their unchanging poverty, in the unbreachable power imbalance. With a narrative voice that sparkles with compassion at this imbalance, Desai leads the reader into the inner lives of the poor, and the shadow lives they live within the country where they are born. Sai's first glimpse of the cook:

> It seemed a long while before they heard a whistle blowing and saw a lantern approaching, and there had come the cook, bandy-legged up the path, looking as leather-visaged, as weathered and soiled, as he did now, and as he would ten years later. A poverty stricken man growing into an ancient as fast-forward. Compressed childhood, lingering old age. A generation between him and the judge, but you wouldn't know it to look at them. There was age in his temperament, his kettle, his clothes, his kitchen, his voice, his face, in the undisturbed dirt, the undisturbed settled smell of a lifetime of cooking, smoke, and kerosene.

She rarely came into the cook's hut, and when she did come searching for him and enter, he was ill at ease and so was she, something about their closeness being exposed in the end as fake, their friendship composed of shallow things conducted in a broken language, for she was an English-speaker and he was a Hindi-speaker. The brokeness made it easier to never go deep, never to go into anything that required an intricate vocabulary, yet she always felt tender on seeing his crotchety face, on hearing him haggle at the market, felt pride that she lived with such a difficult man who nonetheless spoke to her with affection, calling her Babyji or Saibaby.

Slogging for the meanest wages in the kitchens of the fancy restaurants of New York City, Biju is learning:

> From other kitchens, he was learning what the world thought of Indians:
>
> In Tanzania, if they could, they would throw them out like they did in Uganda.
>
> In Madagascar, if they could, they would throw them out.
>
> In Nigeria, if they could, they would throw them out.
>
> In Fiji, if they could, they would throw them out.

In China, they hate them.
In Hong Kong.
In Germany.
In Italy.
In Japan.
In Guam.
In Singapore.
Burma.
South Africa.
They don't like them.
In Guadeloupe—they love us there?
No.

Unlike the class of Indians who are now celebrated for their economic success in America, people like Biju hop from one bad job to another, always staying just a half-step ahead of the INS, in despair for the, "Oh the green card, the green card, the...."

On TV:

> A taxi driver appeared on the screen: watching bootleg copies of American movies he had been inspired to come to America, but how to move into the mainstream? He was illegal, his taxi was illegal, the yellow paint was illegal, his whole family was here, and all the men from his village were here, perfectly infiltrated and working within the cab system of the city. But how to get their papers? Would any viewer out there wish to marry him? Even a disabled or mentally retarded green card holder would be fine.

Packed into rat infested apartments in Harlem, Biju's life is a juggling act and not at all far from the poverty his father believed he has escaped. In addition he bears the weight of terrible loneliness and does not know how to relive alienation:

> He had been abandoned among foreigners: Jacinto the superintendent, the homeless man, a stiff bow-legged coke runner.... (In the summer) women of great weight and heft appeared in shorts with shaven legs, stippled with tiny black dots, and groups of deflated men sat at cards on boards balanced atop garbage cans.... They

> nodded kindly at him, sometimes they even offered him a beer, but Biju did not know what to say to them, even his tiny brief "Hello" came out wrong; too softly, so they did not hear, or just as they turned away.

Biju, homesick and missing his father, returns to a Kalimpong that the violent insurgency, lasting two years, had left in total ruin and anarchy. Without a green card, he is uncertain of his future.

Desai bears witness to the suffering of the poor and the powerless by holding up an unflinching mirror to their lives. And like him, she infuses their bitter lives with the kind of humour that only the refugees can deliver. The people she writes about may be bent but they are not broken. Setting the story in Kalimpong and Sikkim, with keen and perceptive visual and aural details, Desai describes the beauty of the Indian landscape which ultimately saves them from their losses. She writes of Biju in his lonely Harlem basement bed:

> He thought of his village where he had lived with his grandmother on the money his father sent each month. The village was buried in silver grasses that were taller than a man and made a sound, shuu shuuuu, shu shuuu, as the wind turned them this way and that.... Fishing eagles hovered above the water, changed their horizontal glide within a single moment, plunged, rose sometimes with a thrashing muscle of silver. A hermit also lived on this bank, positioned like a stork, waiting, oh waiting, for the glint of another, an elusive mystical fish: when it surfaces he must pounce lest it is lost again and never return.... When he had visited his father in Kalimpong, they had sat outside in the evenings and his father had reminisced: "How peaceful our village is. How good the roti tastes there! It is because the atta is ground by hand, not by machine...and because it is made on a choolah, better than anything cooked on a gas or kerosene stove,... Fresh roti, fresh butter, fresh milk still warm from the buffalo...." They had stayed up late. They had not noticed Sai...staring from bedroom window, jealous of the cook's love for his son, Small-mouthed bats

drinking water from the jhora had swept over again and again in a witch flap of black wings.

The novel raises several large, important questions. What about the dividends from globalization? What about the celebration of hybridity, the global citizen, and the spawning of new ideas? At what point does colonialism become an excuse for corrupt government? Desai answers them in a quiet voice and not all answers are complete. But they don't have to be because they force the reader to think of the answers she does give for a long time.

Kiran Desai was born in Delhi and lived in India until she was 14 when her family moved first to the UK and then a year later to the USA. Like her female lead character she was convent-educated and like one of her characters, she experienced hostility and alienation when moving to a new country. Much has been made of the parallels between the book and Desai's family history but it is not an autobiography. Desai herself has said that in places it's about experiences within her family—such as the experience of immigration and going back to India.

Eastern and Western values clash as well as individual destinies clashing with the march of history in this thought provoking addition to the rich collection of Indian fiction. What bind these seemingly disparate characters are a shared historical legacy and a common experience of impotence and humiliation. "Certain moves made long ago had produced all of them," Desai writes, referring to centuries of subjection by the economic and cultural power of the West. But the beginnings of an apparently leveled field in a late 20th century global economy serve merely to scratch those wounds rather than heal them. Almost all of Desai's characters have been stunted by their encounters with the West. In fact, Desai's novel seems to argue that such multiculturalism, confined to the Western metropolis and academe, doesn't begin to address the causes of extremism and violence in the modern world. Nor, it suggests, can economic globalization become a route to prosperity for the downtrodden. "Profit," Desai observes at one point, "could only be harvested in the gap between nations, working one against the other." This leaves most people in the postcolonial world with only the promise of a shabby modernity—modernity, as Desai puts it, "in its meanest form, brand-new one day, in ruin the next."

REFERENCES

KIRAN DESAI: Exclusive interview. *Perspective*.

Maisonneuve Magazine An Interview by Valerie Howes.

Review by Champa Bilwakesh: *In Guadeloupe—they love us there*? Atlantic Monthly Press, 2006.

Review: *The Inheritance of Loss*, by Fiona Pryor, *Entertainment Reporter*, BBC News website.

'Wounded by the West,' *New York Times* Book Review by Pankaj Mishra Published: February 12, 2006.

www.groveatlantic.com

13

The Inheritance of Loss: A Reading of the Ending

Purnendu Chatterjee

> ...the novel shall not be natural history...it shall not be a mere transcript of life...it shall be something exhibited for our contemplation which is not merely "like life," but "true to life"—no "wax work figure," but the expression of a vision which has *embraced the commonness of reality, without being made common by it.*[1] [R.A. Scott-James]

This assertion of the eminent scholar implies that a novel must touch life, sometimes tangentially, sometimes profoundly at various points and, yet, retain an artistic grace and an appeal that would stir the sensibilities of the readers. Probing life at several points, the novel is bound to elicit multiple responses from its readers for the simple reason that all readers would not have the same ideologies and points of view about life. In fact, a novel par excellence is bound to educe different reactions from one particular, sensitive, reader as he/she traverses through the various phases of life. The varied experience that life inevitably casts along his/her life's course colours his/her vision about life. Obviously, with each change in life's domain he/she will look at the same novel in a different perspective. The shift in his/her vision of life brings in its trail changes in his/her response to the novel. However, the fact that the novel continues to appeal, in protean manner, is an indicator of its artistic dimension.

This abiding appeal of the novel makes it a literary genre. The perennial appeal of literature—and this is equally applicable to the novel—is that it refuses to straitjacket itself into a single and finite concept. This is what distinguishes literature from philosophy or history. As Stanley Fish, partially echoing Sidney's *Defence of Poesy*, puts forward:

> Something must always be left over, unaccounted for, open to still another turn of interpretive screw; were this not so, the work could be said to have engaged in totalizing—in telling (or claiming to tell) the truth about the world at once and for all—and thereby forfeited its right to be called 'literary.' To be sure, literary works are full of propositions of the kind one finds in philosophy or history ('This is so' or 'This is what happened) but in a literary performance...propositions and accounts of facts do not come into primary focus; rather they provide the material, or 'stuff,' on which the literary impulse—the impulse to probe ever deeper the incorrigible duplicity of assertion even as it presents itself as univocal and single—can be exercised.[2]

The plurality of viewpoints that a novel lends itself is at once an indicator of the novel's literary scope as well as the genius of the writer. It is not easy to put the multiple themes into an artistic whole, as a novelist ought to achieve.

Kiran Desai performs this difficult task with élan in her Man Booker Prize winning novel *The Inheritance of Loss*. Desai has spent, as she herself affirmed, seven long years—her first novel *Hullabaloo in the Guava Orchard* was published in 1998—in the throes of this novel:

> At one point I had something like 1,500 pages of notes, and it was a real struggle to hold it all together and then pare it down.[3]

The Inheritance of Loss reflects the gratifying toil that its maker had undergone in the process of weaving the novel. The novel, like all excellent novels, does not restrict itself to a single, finite concept but, lends itself to various viewpoints. *The Inheritance of Loss* may be studied, along with the works of Jhumpa Lahiri and Amy Tan among others, as an example of Asian Diaspora in America; it may be read along post-colonial lines; the novel may also be interpreted in eco-feminist terms; it may be studied as well in the lights of multi-culturism, the predicament of immigrants, to name only a few.

In this paper, however, I propose not to study *The Inheritance of Loss* in the light, though the temptations are potent, of any of these critical theories. I shall study the ending —I mean the last chapter—of the novel and reflect how it gathers, in a sort of collage, the various major characters that have loomed large across the plot of the novel. The present study shall also reflect that the novel does not end in a final and finite vision but, in a slow cadence, creates a situation that is not delimited by the dimensions of time and space and may be variously interpreted. However, before taking up the proposed study, I shall make some general, but relevant, observations about the implications of the ending of a novel.

I

The ending of a novel is significantly important because from a terrible beginning, a novel may recover; the ending is what it leaves a reader with. A brilliant beginning may be affected by a sudden explosion of imagination, but a superb close implies a sustained vision of the author. The deepest rooted of endings is the childhood one: "And they all lived happily ever after." Unlike the beginning of such stories, "Once upon a time, it is not just a formula. It is a hope that the result the story has achieved will remain in place even now the story-telling has finished."[4] But more than that, it acknowledges what the story was about all along. Folk tales that conclude like that have, all along, been about happiness and challenges to it; the subject of the story is there in its last line.

Stories that most of us would call traditional usually feature plots that promote a definite and satisfying conclusion. Within the strictures of a traditional plot, character functions to fit the demands of the form and to satisfy the reader's psychological need for closure. Nevertheless, because lives do not follow conventional plots, novels that attempt genuinely to probe the lives of characters often end with an arbitrary turn of events that seems to flout tradition. Saul Bellow's Augie March ends his career with an avowal that looks toward the future, as if it were impossible to conceive an ending that would both resolve the issues raised and at the same time be consistent with the character's potential. Frank Kermode describes the situation as:

> ...the paradigms will correspond, the more fully as one approaches a condition of absolute simplicity, to some basic human 'set,' biological or psychological. Right down at the root they must correspond to a basic human need, they must make sense, give comfort.... At some very low level we all share certain fictions about time, and they testify to the continuity of what is called human nature.[5]

One of the things which is important about literature, then, is that it imposes a consciously false concept on time, that it is indeed about time. In a crucial passage of the book this view is given very laconic expression:

> The clock's 'tick-tock' I take to be a model of what we call a plot, an organisation which humanises time by giving it a form; and the interval between 'tock' and 'tick' represents purely successive, disorganised time of the sort we need to humanise.[6]

The closer a writer gets to reality in his characters, the further he must depart from the strictures traditional plots lay upon character. And the converse is also true: a traditional plot requires characters less than true to life.

The nearer a writer comes to life, the wider his/her art becomes. Life is full of flux and the author portrays not only the changeability, but also the stasis that lies beyond the flux. In making such an effort, the novelist tends to break down the boundaries of time and space. It is through the temporal that the writer tries to embody the apocalyptic. Such an attempt itself implies that a novel which is true to life must move onward and outward without being limited by the here-now/there-then continuum. So the ending of novel attempting to recapture life does not end in a decisiveness of vision. The novelist of such a novel does not announce at the end, 'This is all that is to be said;' the author rather tentatively posits an ending that seems to say, 'This is how life stands at present.'

II

Set in the mid-1980s in Kalimpong, high in the northeastern Himalayas, *The Inheritance of Loss* centres on three people and one dog living together in an ancient house named Cho Oyu. There is the frustrated, reptilian judge, Jemubhai Patel, lost in his chessboard and in his memories: of a youth spent at Cambridge many decades earlier; of humiliation in a foreign land. Staying with are his beloved dog Mutt and his 17-year-old granddaughter Sai, who was orphaned as a child. The judge's cook, who manages the household, and a few neighbours scattered around the area, round off the cast. As the story unfolds, insurgency is growing in the region: the Indian Nepalese want their own country or state, a Gorkhaland where they will not be treated as servants; young boys, trying to be men, roam the mountainside looting houses, collecting ammunition. Their predicament is contrasted against that of Indians settled abroad, the cook's son Biju, stumbling from one job to the next in the US, in a grimly humorous parallel narrative. Reading *The Inheritance of Loss*, one initially feels it could have been shorter-with many characters, and a narrative that leaps around in time and space, it occasionally gets unfocussed. However, Desai's descriptions of the things she had to leave out (the back-stories of characters who seem shadowy in the final draft, for instance) are so vivid, it is possible to wonder instead if a longer version of the book might have been more effective.

The last chapter of *The Inheritance of Loss*,[7] like most of its earlier chapters, is written in the form of a collage. An attempt to summarize the events of the closing chapter may stand like this: the cook, in a fit of drunkenness, admits to Jemubhai Patel that he had cheated his master in several ways and was responsible for the loss of Mutt; the judge beats the cook frantically; Sai is disgusted of the whole chaos; Lola, Noni, Mrs. Sen and Uncle Potty abide in their crumbling world while Biju, ransacked by the Gorkhaland activists, returns to Cho Oyu and meets his father.

The actions of the judge and the cook need to be decoded in order to comprehend the implications of the closing chapter. A major portion of the narrative is taken up by Jemubhai's past, his journey from a small village in Gujarat to England and his subsequent return as an ICS officer of the Raj. The journey has had the most profound effect and his experiences in England, the humiliations—whether real or perceived—have seared into his soul, changing him forever. So, as Jemubhai climbs the ladder of material success, his soul plummets to new depths. As his creator points out:

> I think transporting a man from a poor family into a supremely wealthy society must really have an impact... must result in some kind of mental deterioration. In most cases, it is those back home who take the brunt as the power balance changes. Jemubhai's case is an extreme. I call him an ogre and believe me, there are ogres in existence.

It may appear surprising that a man who could not love his wife, his daughter and his granddaughter, who had borne the brunt of a dichotomy that colonization often, brought in its trail:

> He envied the English. He loathed Indians. He worked at being English with the passion of hatred and for what he would become, he would be despised by absolutely everyone, English and Indians, both, almost all his life and who had developed a "misanthropy and cynicism" over the years could love a dog to such an extent that he would move the police to search it and beat his cook frantically for being responsible for its loss. His love for the dog and his frenzied beating of the cook are suitable indicators of his psychic status.

His relationship with Mutt is not a common relation of a man with his pet dog, nor has he an extraordinary alliance with Mutt as Jim Corbett had with Robin. A cynic as the judge is, his cynicism is further intensified as the Nepalese activists tweak his nose. He came to the realization that an animal is better than a man is. An unconscious inversion of Tennyson's concept of man as, presented in *The Lotos Eaters* the "roof and crown of things"!

> He couldn't conceive of punishment great enough for humanity. A man wasn't equal to an animal, not one particle of him. Human life was stinking, corrupt, and meanwhile there were beautiful creatures who [sic] lived with delicacy on the earth without doing anyone any harm.

Receding from humanity, he strikes up a close relation with a lower animal—a definite reversal of values. Hence, he beats up the cook. The manner in which he tortures the cook is significant:

> The judge was beating with all the force of his sagging, puckering flesh, flecks of saliva flying from his slack muscled mouth, and his chin wobbled uncontrollably. Yet that arm, from which the flesh hung already dead, came down, bringing the slipper upon the cook's head.

The savagery of the judge coupled with his physical weakness creates a grimly grotesque figure that deserves, surely as the author wishes, the readers' derision than their sympathy.

The cook's sudden confession of his past crimes is not without a cause. Moreover, he was not responsible for the loss of Mutt. The wife and father of the man who was blinded by the police stole the dog. They had repeatedly requested the judge to help them but, obviously, to no avail. They stole the dog—not in vengeance—so that they could earn some money, which would hold their body and soul together, by selling it to some fashionable people.

The cook's behaviour is apparently puzzling, but the reasons for his, may I say, almost suicidal actions lie in his mental praxis. The cook is significantly given no name, just as Katherine Mansfield does not give a name to the Boss in her short story *The Fly*. Of course, unlike Mansfield psychological treatment of the Boss's character, Desai does not use profound psychological insights to develop the character of the cook. Both the Boss and the cook represent impoverished specimens of humanity: the former standing for a type of people in whom decadent materialism has displaced the heart from its right place; the latter representing spineless, weak, and cringing individuals who enjoy a shadowy existence.

The cook's whole life centres round his son Biju who lives as an illegal immigrant in America. Once the sanguine claws of terrorism cut through the world of the hills and the entire idyllic atmosphere turns topsy-turvy, the cook grows anxious. In this predicament, he loses contact with Biju. The obvious corollary is that he is shaken to his nerves. He feels, and even starts believing, that Biju had never existed and that he had only been like a dream.

> The cook didn't mention his son...he had none...he'd never had one...it was just his hope writing to him...Biju was nonexistent....

Once, in his psyche, Biju becomes "nonexistent" the entire world breaks down for him. He feels that he has nothing to live for. Being weak by nature, he does not have the mental strength to tide him over the pessimistic thoughts, nor does he possess the mental strength—which is, of course, perverted—to lay hands on himself. He ruminates

> I'd be better dead than alive.

In his muddled brain, which is caused by an overdose of alcohol at Thapa's Canteen and a copious dose of chhang prepared by him, he makes a plan that would release him from the pains of life. So, he admits all his faults to his master hoping that the judge would beat him to death. The cook's repeated request to the judge, "Kill me," evinces a passive effort on his part to end his existence.

The chaotic situation at Cho Oyu, the judge beating the cook, disturbs Sai. Sai is the central character in the novel. Her love spats with Gyan is over and, in the middle of the closing chapter, she has "her heart lying in pieces." It is through Sai that the author builds up a fatalistic view of life that challenges comparison with Hardy's vision:

> Never again could she think there was but one narrative and that this narrative belonged only to herself, that she

> might create her own tiny happiness and live safely within it.

The "narrative," of course, is a metaphor for life and through Sai's ultimate epiphany Desai has thoroughly driven home that there's nothing Sai can do to change her fate. Sai accomplished to wake up to the same awareness that the rest of the book's characters have been struggling with: her life does not belong to herself.

Sai, however, is not completely bogged down by this gloomy fatalistic realization. She thinks of the world that lies beyond the Cho Oyu and draws strength to transcend beyond the gloomy fatalism.

> She thought of her father and the space program. She thought of all the National Geographics and books she had read. Of the judge's journey, of the cook's journey, of Biju's. Of the globe twirling on its axis.
>
> And she felt a glimmer of strength. Of resolve. She must leave.

Sai's thoughts stretch beyond Cho Oyu and, in one grand sweep, embraces the world and the probing into the universe. This psychic journey gives her a sense of relief from the claustrophobia of Cho Oyu—created by the judge and the cook—and helps her overcome her recent disillusionment from love. Once she enjoys, however momentarily, this sense of relief her adolescent heart gathers up a determination to leave Cho Oyu and face the world with much happier results than the judge, the cook and cook's son have managed. It is in this point that Sai is different from the other characters in the novel.

As Sai decides to move out of the narrow confines, Mrs. Sen, Lola and Noni continue a decadent existence holding desperately to the first world that refuses to acknowledge such slips of humanity. In spite of being minor characters in the novel, they help the author in driving home the phenomenon of post-colonial neurosis. Mrs. Sen in weaving a sweater, that she never completes, for Rajiv Gandhi—her weaving lacks the vitality of Madame Defarge's knitting in Dickens' *A Tale of*

Two Cities—is stuck in time. She appears to be a close kin, sans ghastliness, of Miss Havisham in Dickens' *Great Expectations*. She vainly prides herself on her daughter for she works with the CNN and becomes a rival to the two sisters, Lola and Noni, because Lola's daughter works with the BBC. But all these first world associations cannot save them from being ruthlessly treated by the Gorkhaland activists. They are pathetic characters who are haplessly and helplessly stranded in a time that is out of joints.

A similar pathetic character is Uncle Potty. He is an alcoholic, harmless human being who cares for Sai and is worried that the "rowdies," i.e. the Nepalese activists, would harm her. He is so vulnerable and feeble—the effects of alcohol not to be slighted—that

> When Uncle Potty woke, he would realize he'd signed away his property and father Booty's, as well, to new owners....

The word "woke" is metaphor for realizing. It is evident, that though he would comprehend his loss at a certain point of time, he would have no power to recover his loss.

A close reading of the last chapter of *The Inheritance of Loss* reveals that, except Sai, all the characters—the judge, the cook, Mrs. Sen, Lola, Noni and Uncle Potty—are suffering from psychic paralysis. It is only Sai who has enough mental strength to propel herself away from her present predicament. So, it is poetically just that she is given a vision of the "truth," however tentatively, at the end of the novel. Before she obtains the vision of "truth," she watches the arrival of Biju.

Biju comes to meet his father at Cho Oyu wearing a woman's nightgown that he had been given (so thoughtfully!) to him by the anti-socials after ransacking him. Biju's dress signifies the upheaval in the social world of the hills. Dress is a social construct. A man wearing a woman's nightgown is quite grotesque in normal times. But the manner in which Desai presents Biju in the woman's nightgown has nothing of the bizarre in it. Biju's dress implies that in a world that has lost its fundamental humanity, what, indeed, is gender?

The filial feeling of the cook, however, is not deterred by his son's uncouth dress. He is wild with joy at getting his son back. The author describes the meeting between father and son without any slips of prolixity:

> Sai looked out and saw two figures leaping at each other as the gate swung open.

The verb "leaping" reflects the intense emotion that underlines the meeting. Now, the cook will wish to live again, for the very sustenance of his life, whom he had thought as imaginary, was near him again, throbbing and pulsating—in spite of his wretched condition—with life. Biju, on the other hand, will bury not only all the ignominy of being an illegal third world immigrant to a first world civilization, but also the last insult that he had in the hands of the local rowdies.

As the father and the son are locked in embrace, Sai is blessed with a glorious spectacle of nature:

> The five peaks of Kanchenjenga turned golden with the kind of luminous light that made you feel, if briefly, that truth was apparent.
>
> All you need to do was to reach out and pluck it.

Desai, tellingly brings out the splendour of the snowy peaks of Kanchenjenga irradiated by the first rays of the sun. It is to her credit that she paints a picture out of words. However, Desai does not stop here. In this brilliant and tangible description of nature that she relates to her readers, implied by the second person pronoun, she refers to the abstract concept of truth. What "truth" is Desai referring here? It, perhaps, may be the truth of genuine human relationship that stands tall in the face of all odds. Sai would have her faith restored in human relationship, after her disastrous affair with Gyan, and look into the future with a firm confidence and conviction. The "truth" may also imply the fact that irrespective of what happens to the world of man, nature remains unalloyed. Man is infinitesimally smaller and far less potent as compared to nature.

> Slowly, painstakingly, like ants, men would make their paths and civilization and their wars once again, only to have it wash away again....

The notion of "truth" that Desai sets up, thus, lies beyond a single, unitary and finite concept. It teases the readers out of thought as they close the novel, only to return to it again and again.

NOTES

1. R.A. Scott-James. *The Making of Literature*, Allied Publishers Ltd. New Delhi, 1989, p. 373.
2. Stanley Fish. "Political Consciousness in Philip Rice and Patricia Waugh" (eds.) *Modern Literary Theory* (4th Edition) O.U.P. New York, 2001, p. 435.
3. Maitreyee S. Ganapathy. "Never-ending Narratives," *The Hindu*, Online Edition, Sunday, Feb 05, 2006.
4. "The End. At Last." *The Telegraph*, Online Edition, Wednesday, Feb. 20, 2008.
5. Frank Kermode, *The Sense of an Ending*, Oxford, 1968, pp. 43-44.
6. *Ibid.*, p. 45.
7. All quotations of *The Inheritance of Loss* are from Penguin Books, New Delhi, 2006.

14

Kiran Desai's *The Inheritance of Loss*: A Study in Insurgency

Sharada Iyer

Kiran Desai created literary history by becoming the youngest woman to win the Man Booker Prize 2006. At 35, Desai walked away with the most prestigious award for English fiction. Her father Ashwin Desai had predicted way back in January when the first publication of *The Inheritance of Loss* was out "I predict this book will win the Booker Prize. I have read the works of most of the Booker prize winners through the years and this has everything for a Booker Prize." Described as "a radiant, funny moving family saga" it is a sprawling novel that runs from the Himalayas to New York City, taking in Marks Spencer knickers, Grand Marnier and Nepalese insurgents and offers an insightful and often humorous commentary on multiculturalism and postcolonial society.

Before Kiran Desai won the Man Booker Prize, her first novel *Hullaballo in the Guava Orchard* (1999) had won the Betty Trask award for a first novel. It received an enthusiastic commendation from India's first Booker winner Salman Rushdie for "the first dynasty of modern Indian fiction" with an excerpt finding its way in Rushdie's *Anthology of Indian Writing*, *Mirror Work* and the New Yorkers Fiction issue, though the novel did not really make waves.

The second novel *The Inheritance of Loss* comes after a painful seven years apprenticeship, living in Brooklyn, often going off to visit her mother, Anita Desai in upstate New York or travel with her and writing part of it in Kalimpong. Hermione Lee, the chairman of the judges, explained the reason for picking up *Inheritance of Loss* from a list of substantial novel by big names he explained the philosophy behind this unusual but, interesting short list "A distinctive original voice, an audacious imagination that takes reader to undiscovered countries of the mind, a strong power of story telling and a historical truthfulness. A magnificent novel of human breath and wisdom, comic tenderness and powerful political acuteness" the epigraph from Jorge Luis Borger sets the tone for a novel concerned with the struggles of little people, a novel of troubled times. "They speak of humanity/ my humanity is in feeling we are all voices of that same poverty."

The novel opens with a teenager, Sai, the child of a Gujarati mother and Zoroastrian father who is part of Indo-Russian space collaboration in the last days of the old Soviet State; they are killed in an accident, leaving Sai an orphan. She comes to live with her Cambridge Anglophile grandfather, a retired judge in Kalimpong, on the Indian side of the Himalayas. When Sai comes to live with her embittered grandfather, it is the cook who gives her the warmth that he is unable to give his son, Biju. Biju the cook's son is an illegal immigrant far away in New York, drifting from one temporary job to another in the underworld of restaurant kitchen.

Back in Kalimpong, Sai is romantically involved with her maths tutor, Gyan, the descendant of a Nepali Gurkha mercenary but he eventually recoils from her obvious privilege and falls in with a group of ethnic Nepalese insurgents. Meanwhile in the world outside Cho Oye, a growing insurgency is threatening to explode across the hill.

The novel explores with intimacy and insight, about every contemporary international issues—globalization, multiculturalism, economic inequality, fundamentalism and terrorist violence. It is about the many faces of oppression, the paradoxes of growth and injustices and communities struggling with the violence and pain of change. Though intercut with many overlapping themes the most arresting one is the Gorkhaland movement. Kiran Desai distinguishes herself as one of the few novelists, or perhaps the only one to have deeply and sensitively explored this problem as a theme in Indian English Writing, hence this deserves to be treated exclusively as a distinct feature of the novel. A movement which started as a request to be recognized as a minority, along with the others, like—the Anglo-Indians degenerated into a demand for a separate state of Gorkhaland. Its origin, which gradually shaped into a dangerous, disintegrating virulent, violent nightmarish terrorist movements, akin to the Naxalbari, and how Kiran Desai has successfully woven it into the texture of the novel as an integral part of it makes an interesting study.

The Gorkhaland movement has its roots in the demand of Gorkhas living in Darjeeling district and Duars of West Bengal and the Gorkhas in India and abroad, though they see India as their motherland, want a separate state for themselves within the constitutional framework of India. The ethnic identity Gorkha comes from the district of Gorkha within Nepal which was the Kingdom of the "hilly billy Napoleon" Prithvi Narayan Shah. The Gorkhaland National Liberation Front (GNLF) which led the movement disrupted the district with massive violence between 1986-89. The Gorkhaland movements distinguished Darjeeling Gorkhas from Nepalis residing in India from Nepali speaking Indian citizen from other parts of the country and Sikkim. Gorkhaland supporters therefore preferred to call the Gorkha language as Gorkhali rather than Nepali. The 1981 census of India, respecting their sentiments called the language Gorkhali/Nepali. However, when the Eighth Schedule of the Constitution was amended in 1992, to make it a Scheduled Language, the terms Nepali alone was used. In 1986 the GNFL, having failed to obtain a separate administrative identity from the Parliament, again demanded a separate state of Gorkhaland. The party's leader Subash Ghising headed a demonstration that turned violent, which was sternly repressed by the state government. The disturbance almost shut down the districts mainstay of tea, tourism and timber. After two years of fighting and the loss of more than thousand lives, the government of West Bengal and the Centre finally agreed on an autonomous hill district in July 1988. GNFL gave up the demand for a separate state and in August the Darjeeling Gorkha Hill Council came into being with Ghising as chairman. The Council had authority over economic development programs, education and culture.

However, difficulties arose over the panchayat election. Ghising wanted the Hill Council excluded from the national law on panchayat election. The then Prime Minister Rajiv Gandhi, heeding to this request introduced a constitutional amendment in 1989 to exclude Darjeeling Gorkha Hill Council along with several other north-east hill states and region—Nagaland, Mizoram, and the hill regions of Manipur but it was not passed. However, in 1992, Parliament passed the Seventy-third Amendments which showed a serious commitment to the idea of local self-government—by panchayat, the amendment excluded all the hill areas except Darjeeling. Ghising felt this was the doing of West Bengal and threatened to revive militant agitation for a Gorakhland State he also said that GNLF would boycott the village panchayat election. A large portion of his party, refused to accept the boycott and split off under the leadership of Madan Tamang to form the All India Gorkha League which won a sizable number of panchayat seats. In August 1995 Sherpa complained to the state government that Ghising had misused hill council fund and West Bengal Chief Minister Jyoti Basu promised to investigate. In May 2005, the organization organized a huge rally to revive the dormant demand for a separate state but failed to go forward on the issue since then.

The Inheritance of Loss opens with a newspaper reporting of February 1986, which sets the tone of the novel.

> In Kalimpong high in the North Eastern Himalayas—where they lived the retired Judge and his cook, Sai and Mutt (the Dog) there was a report of new dissatisfaction in the hills, gathering insurgency, men and guns. It was the Indian Nepalese this time, fed up with being treated like the minority in a place where they were in a

> majority. They wanted their own country or at least their own state in which to manage their own affairs.... (p. 9)

A group of young boys under twenty had entered the judge's house. They had come through the forest on foot. Dressed in a universal guerilla fashion—leather jacket, khaki pant, bandana and a gun, they were looking for anything they could find for an impoverished movement with a raging army, Kukri, sickles, axes, kitchen, knives, spade, any kind of firearm. They had come for the judge's hunting rifles. But took every thing that they could lay hand on—drinks cigarettes, ordered tea and snacks, defecated in the toilets, left it stinking and forced the judge and other to say "Jai Gorakha", "Gorkhaland for Gorkhas".

In the beginning, nobody had paid much attention to the events in the hill side. The new posters in the market were referring to old discontent the slogans scratched and painted on the side of government offices and shops. "We are stateless", "It is better to die than live like slaves", "We are constitutionally tortured. Return our land from Bengal" (p. 126). The call was repeated along the road at the top of Ringkingpong Hill one saw LIBERATION scrawled across the water works.

For a while nobody knew which way it would go, it was dismissed as nothing more serious than the usual handful of student agitators but then one day fifty member of the youth wing of GNLF gathered to swear an oath at Mahakaldara to fight to death for the formation of a homeland—Gorkhaland. They marched down the streets of Darjeeling, look a turn round the market and the mall. They shouted "Gorkhaland for Gorkhas we are the Liberation Army" they waved their unsheathed kukris, sliced the fierce blades, though the tender mist under the watery sun Quiet suddenly; everyone was using the word INSURGENCY.

There were some like Noni (Nomita) who lived with her sister Lola (Lolita) in a rose covered cottage named 'Mon Ami.' When Lola's husband died, Noni who was spinster came to live with her sister. Noni felt the Nepalese had a point "First they were thrown out of Assam and then Meghalaya, and then there's the King of Bhutan growling against...." They have been here, most of them, several generations why shouldn't Nepali be taught in schools.

> Lola: Because on that basis they can start statehood demands...the Neps have been encouraged by the Sikhs and their Khalistan, by ULFA, NEFA, PLA, Jharkhand, Bodoland Gorkhaland, Tripura, Mizoram, Manipal, Kashmir, Punjab, Assam..... You saw the letter they sent to the Queen of England, Gorbachev and Reagan? Apartheid genocide colonial subjugation, vivisected Nepal...when did Darjeeling and Kalimpong belong to Nepal. Darjeeling, in fact, was annexed from Sikkim and Kalimpong from Bhutan. (pp. 128-29)

Historically, Darjeeling and its surrounding terai areas formed a part of then Kirat Kingdom called Bijaypur, after the disintegration of Bijaypur kingdom it fell to Sikkim and Bhutan. From 1790-1816, Darjeeling and its immediate contiguous area were overrun by the Gorkhas of Nepal. After the Anglo-Nepalese War (1814-15) the Treaty of Sigauli was signed between the Gorkhas and the East India Company, Darjeeling was wrestled back from the Gorkhas of Nepal by the Britishers and handed back to Sikkim, after the Treaty of Tataliya. Col. Llyod became the representative of the East India Company to Darjeeling, during his time Darjeeling was annexed into the British India Empire. The map of Darjeeling came into existence after the induction of Kalimpong and Duars area after the Anglo-Bhutanese War 1864. And Indira Gandhi as Noni says had maneuvered a plebiscite and all the Nepalese who had flooded Sikkim voted against the king. India had swallowed the jewel colored kingdom.

Noni, Lola and Mr. Sen feel it was all due to Nehru, the biggest mistake he made was "this state making". Under this rule any group of idiots could stand up demanding a new state and get it. "Mrs. Sen to whom Pakistan and Muslim were favorites topics continued" Pakistan, there is the problem first heart attack to our county, no, that has never been healed."

> Lola: Illegal immigration it's an issue of a porous border is what you can't tell one from the other. Indian Nepali from Nepal Nepali, and then the way these Neps multiply.
>
> Mrs. Sen: Like Muslims. (p. 129)

Meanwhile, Gyan and Sai's romance flourished and the political trouble continued to remain in the background for them. Gyan asked Sai about her family, but she felt uncertain about what she should say, because she thought if she told him about the Space Program, he might feel inferior and ashamed hence she said, my parents eloped and nobody spoke to, then again they died in Russia where my father was a scientist (p. 141). But his own family story also led overseas, he told Sai quite proudly. They had more in common than they thought.

In 1800, Gyan's ancestors had left their village in Nepal and arrived in Darjeeling, lured by promises of a work in a tea plantation. By and by came the Imperial Army measuring potential soldiers in village all over the hills. Gyan's great grandfather had been chosen, they were attracted by the comfort and money provided by the army. So they swore allegiance to the crown, and off he went the beginning of over a hundred year of family commitment to the wars of the English.

The family had since invested their money in school teaching and Gyan's father taught in a tea plantation school beyond Darjeeling but for all they had done, what did they get?

In 1947, when the British left granting India her freedom, granting the Muslims Pakistan, granting special provisions for the scheduled castes and tribes leaving everything taken care of, brothers and sisters except us—

> EXCEPT US—The Nepalese of India, we are laborers on the tea plantation, coolies dragging heavy loads, soldiers. Are we allowed to become doctors and government workers, owners of the tea plantation? No! We are kept at the level of servants we fought on behalf of the British for two hundred years. We fought in World War I we went to East Africa to Egypt to the Persian Gulf. We

> were moved from here to there as it suited them. We fought in the World War II in Europe, Syria Persia, Malaya, and Burma. Where would they be without the courage of our people? We are still fighting for them...we are soldiers, loyal, brave. India or England they never had caused to doubt our loyalty. In the war with Pakistan we fought our former comrades on other side of the border. How our spirits cried. But we are Gorkhas. We are soldiers.... And have we been rewarded? Have we been given compensation? Are we given respect? No. They spit on us.
>
> In our country, the country we fight for, we are treated like slaves. Everyday the lorries' leave bearing away our forests sold by foreigners to fill the pocket of foreigners. Our stones are carried to build their houses and cities. We are laborers, working barefoot in all weather, thin as sticks, as they sit fat in the manager's houses with their fat wives, with their fat bank account, and their fat children going abroad we must fight brothers and sisters to manage our own affairs. We must unite under the banner of the GNLF GORKHA NATIONAL LIBERATION FRONT.... This is our motherland where we were born, where our parents were born. We will run our own affairs in our own language. If necessary, we will wash our bloody kukris in the mother waters of the Teesta. Jai Gorkhas some drew blood from their thumb with their kukris to write a poster demanding Gorkhaland in blood. Brave Gorkha soldiers protecting Indian please quit the army at once. For when you retire you will be treated as a foreigner. (pp. 159-60)

The men were shouting they meant what they were saying; they felt a lack of justice. Gyan who had listened to it felt a moment of shame remembering his tea parties with Sai, the cheese toast, queen cakes from the baker. He voiced an adamant opinion that the Gorkha movement takes the harshest possible route. So in the excitement of the moment, he told of the guns, the well stocked kitchen, the liquors in the cabinet, the lack of phone and there being nobody to call for help, all about the judge's house Cho Oyu.

A few weeks after the robbery at Cho Oyu, a program of action was drawn.

> Road blocks to bring economic activities to a standstill and to prevent the trees of the hills, the boulders of the rivers valley's from leaving the plains. All vehicles would be stopped.
>
> Black Flag day on April 13.
>
> A seventy two hours strike in May. No national celebration. No Republic Day. Independence Day or Gandhi's Birthday.
>
> Boycott election with the slogan. "We will not stay in other people's state of West Bengal."
>
> Burning of Indo-Nepal treaty of 1950.
>
> Nepali or not, everyone was required to contribute funds, to purchase calendars and cassettes tapes of speeches made by Ghising, the top GNLF in Darjeeling and Pradhan the top man in Kalimpong. It was requested that every family send a representative to every procession and also to show up at the burning of the Indo-Nepal Treaty. If they did not they would know.... (pp. 191-93)
>
> The Gymkhana club taken over by the GNLF who camped in the ballroom and the skating rink.

As Lola, Noni, Father Booty, Uncle Potty was leaving Glenary after a lunch, they met the procession, and in it they saw Gyan, who refused to recognize Sai.

During their visit to the Teesta Valley renowned for its butterflies Father Booty caught a snap of butterfly on a cable of bridge but since photography was strictly prohibited on the bridge and Father Booty was caught by the guard. The police did not take his words of butterfly; he was taken to task, booked. He was found to be residing in India illegally, his property snatched, and he was asked to leave Kalimpong where he had lived for 45 years.

A series of strike kept business closed, everyone were terrorized to keep their shutters down. The conditions were worsening. No tourist arrived from Calcutta, no visitor with their riches, nobody came to the hotels, nor the company guest houses, children were withdrawn from boarding schools as parents read with horror of the hills being disturbed by separatist rebels and guerilla tactics. No gas, or kerosene, no water, no electricity because the electricity department had been burned down.

Apart from looting, the worse was yet to come, forcibly occupying the land as Lola's and Noni's—going to the Pradhan was useless, because you would only be ridiculed and humiliated as Lola was. It made her feel that Gorkha's were not good people, were mercenaries that's what they were. Pay them and they are loyal to whatever.

The incidents of horror grew, through the changing season, through winter and flowery spring, summer then rain and winter again. Roads were closed, there was curfew every night and Kalimpong was trapped in its own madness. The GNLF boys had burnt down government rest houses, circuit house. Men trembled at home for fear of being picked up, being tortured on any kind of flimsy excuse.

Kalimpong was transformed into a ghost town, the wind tumbling around the melancholy streets, garbage flying by unhindered.

What sounded like an ethnic nationalist movement became largely as an opportunity to vent one's rage and frustration "Old hatreds are endlessly retrievable because they are pure because the grief of the past was gone. Just the fury remained distilled librating." The half educated uprooted men like Gyan gravitate to the first available political cause in search for a better way.

He recoils from Sai's obvious privilege and falls in with the ethnic Nepalese insurgent.

At Cho Oye Mutt was kidnapped, and Biju, who had returned from America, was looted—his baggage, his savings, even the dress he was wearing, worst of all his pride.

In the meanwhile in the aftermath of the parade, the police had been reinforced and were hunting down the GNFL boys, combing remote hamlets, trying to weed out Gorkhaland supporter from the Marxist, from the Congress supporters, from those who didn't care either way. They raided tea gardens which were closing down after the attacks by rebels. While the residents were shocked by violence, they were also surprised by the mundaneness of it all. Discovered the extent of perversity that the heart is capable of as they sat at home with nothing to do, and found that it was possible faced with the stench of unimaginable evil, for a human beings to be absorbed by the problem of a missing socks, return, once again to the pressing matter of what to eat. There they were, the most common place of them, these quite mismatched with the larger than life question, caught up in the mythic battles of pasts vs. present, justice vs. injustice—the most ordinary swept up in extraordinary hatred, because extraordinary hatred was after all a commonplace event.

Although the novel is set in 1980s a time of turbulence and change, the judge came from a generation for whom identities are fixed, he is referred through most of the novel as 'the judge,' his cook as 'the cook'. It is only in the judges memories of his painful students years, in a racist colonial England, that he is referred to by his name Jemubhai Patel.

The novel originally was 1,500 pages but in its final shape cut down to 300 pages. Even in its present form there is an overflowing richness in its description—a leak in the toilet, playing hanky tonk, the cook hissing softly to himself as he takes in the soup tureen, the hiccupping back drain at the Queen of Tarts Bakery—as they vividly evoke both the misty mountains atmosphere of Kalimpong and the rat infested underbelly of New York.

Kiran Desai's has not been an inheritance of loss but an inheritance of literary gain. She has been lucky inheriting from V.S. Naipaul and Rushdie especially in her exploration of post-colonial chaos and despair and R.K. Narayana. Her winning on 10th October coincide with the birth centenary of R.K. Narayana. Her first book *Hullabaloo in the Guava*

Orchard set in a small town features a likeable cast of characters who could have wandered down South into Narayana's territory and felt entirely at home. But in her second novel also with ordinary eccentric character muddling along in a small hill station in North Eastern Himalayan town beside a struggling immigrant trying to make his way in the kitchen of New York restaurant that really pays homage to Narayan's traditions of gentle and humane story telling. More than anything there is a common Chekhovian sensibility running through the novel of both writers—delicate stories that unfold in evocative natural setting that are imbued with a gentle concern for ordinary people caught in a changing world.

The greatest literary inheritance came from her mother Anita Desai about whom she writes "was written in her company and in her wisdom and kindness" especially during the writing of *The Inheritance of Loss* "She was not only there to support me, but she was the only one who understood me and my turmoil" and befittingly the book is dedicated "to my mother with so much love."

Anita Desai's novel *Fire on the Mountain* (1977) has a close resemblance to *The Inheritance of Loss*. Anita Desai in her novel dwells into the mind of an embittered old woman who retreats into an ancient house in Kasauli, deliberately disconnected from a world she despises, till a great granddaughter shows up. In Kiran Desai's novel too, a crusty old judge retires to a home in Kalimpong preferring the company of his dog Mutt and his cook to the exclusion of all other till a granddaughter arrives and disturbs this carefully constructed isolation.

Too close for comfort and comparison it must have been delicate and different for Kiran Desai to maintain safe distance from her mother's work, while cherishing security and intimacy it must also have provided her. When asked if Kiran's material were different from hers Anita Desai replied "No, we mostly used the same material." And it is natural given their shared lives, it must be tough for two gifted persons to carve out their own identities and individual voices. It must be terrible—the inevitable comparisons and the avoidable rivalries—seen from Kiran's perspective and her's occupying the same space with a living legend working in silence knowing too that the other is hard at it, right above you. Kiran has been a witness to her mother's creative impulse all her life she has lived and breathed the loneliness that is a writer's fate but now that Kiran's Desai has won, she is bound to be the toast of the literary world and she will have her future carved out in the hullabaloo.

Though Kiran Desai has the fortune of and is aware of her literacy inheritance specially her mother Anita Desai, V.S. Naipaul, Salman Rushdie and the founding father of Indian English fiction R.K. Narayan, she has her original way of taking it forward as Hermione Lee said "she seems to jump on these tradition and create something which is absolutely of its own." The book is movingly strong in its humanity and I think that in the end is why it's own.

There is an accumulation of wisdom in its sweet half stories and fragments, composed of broken paragraph and sighing musical sentences. The novel hints at a lot but never says everything—forcing us to reflect on the aching turns of sub-continental history, the painful, creation and recreation of borders and the endless cycles of oppression endured by the poor and dispossessed, while the future shines brightly for those who are more privileged.

REFERENCE

Kiran Desai: *The Inheritance of Loss*, Penguin Delhi, 2006 (all quotes from the book pertain to this edition).

15

Memory and Nostalgia: The Diasporic Subject in *The Inheritance of Loss*

Nishi Pulugurtha

A major contribution of postcolonial theory has been the reconceptualisation of space and identity. Postcolonial literature is concerned with the important issues of place and displacement. Bill Ashcroft, Gareth Griffiths and Helen Tiffin in *The Empire Writes Back* say that it is in these concerns "that the special post-colonial crisis of identity comes into being; the concern with the development or recovery of an effective identifying relationship between self and place." Differences of culture and place and the question of identity linked with it are important postcolonial concerns. "The dialectic of place and displacement is always a feature of post-colonial societies whether these have been created by a process of settlement, intervention, or a mixture of both."

The Oxford English Dictionary defines diaspora as "the dispersion...the whole body of Jews living dispersed among the Gentiles after their Captivity." The OED locates the first usage of the term in Deuteronomy xxvii, 25—"thou shalt be a diaspora (or dispersion) in all kingdoms of the earth." Diaspora refers not only to geographical dispersal but also brings in the issues of identity, memory and home which such dispersal causes.

Writers of the diaspora often rewrite history, and frame new narratives of family, society and nation with a desire to revisit the past. It is here that memory and nostalgia play a very important role. The diasporic writer occupies a kind of space that is one of exile and cultural solitude. Homi Bhabha in *The Location of Culture* calls this space the third space, a hybrid location. According to Bhabha, the discourse of the wandering people of the diaspora marks a "shifting boundary that alienates the frontiers of the modern nation."

Kiran Desai's *The Inheritance of Loss* won the Man Booker Prize for 2006 as well as the National Book Critics Circle Fiction Award in 2007. Desai's second novel, *The Inheritance of Loss* written over a period of seven years after her first novel, *Hullabaloo in the Guava Orchard*, explores issues of globalization, multiculturalism, economic inequality, and violence. *The Inheritance of Loss* spans two continents and three generations. The story moves between New York and Kalimpong with scenes that contrast the life of illegal immigrants in New York and the growing unrest in Kalimpong. In *Theory of the Novel*, Georg Lukacs says that the novel is the representative form of homelessness. It is a form generated by upheaval and uprootedness, and has evolved from great social, political and economic changes. The protagonists do not belong to the world they find themselves in and must therefore create their own worlds. What Lukacs says about the form of the novel may very well be applied to most postcolonial literature and also to the literature of the diaspora. They are fictions of homelessness. This paper looks at the diasporic subject in *The Inheritance of Loss*. Unlike other diasporic writing which often tends to highlight the evolution of one's identity due to the inheritance of one's culture and the contact and effect of the new space where the subject now lives, Biju, the diasporic subject, who lives in New York, very much remains Indian and what one sees most in his case is his longing for the Himalayan town to which he belongs to.

Set in the 1980s, the novel tells the story of Jemubhai Popatlal Patel, a retired judge in Kalimpong and his relationship with his granddaughter, Sai. An important concern of the novel is Biju, the son of Mr. Patel's cook, an illegal immigrant in New York. Sai falls in love with her mathematics tutor, Gyan, who joins the unrest gathering momentum in Kalimpong. She has been thrust from the sheltered convent boarding school she was attending to the Himalayan town of Kalimpong, since the death of her parents in an accident in Moscow (where her father was studying to become an astronaut). The judge is cold, aloof and despises everyone else. The only creature he truly loves is a dog named Mutt. Fortunately for Sai, however, the cook at Cho Oyu, her grandfather's house, adores her.

In a parallel narrative, the novel reveals the life of Biju, the son of the cook. Biju is an illegal immigrant in New York and spends much of his time dodging the authorities, moving from one ill-paid job to another.

> But Immigration operated independently of Police, the better, perhaps, to bake the morning bread, and Biju fell, again and again, through the cracks in the system.

He ekes out a bare existence waiting tables and sleeping in a basement (even as his father imagines him to be amassing wealth and prestige). Spurred on by his father, Biju came to the United States thinking he could achieve the American dream, but the reality is quite different, he is exploited, poor, lonely and homesick. "The green card the green card"—everyone wanted it, irrespective of whether they were happy or not in the United States. "There was a whole world in the basement kitchens of New York." Biju moves from one low-paid restaurant job to another, living in seedy squalor with groups of other immigrants, "But although Biju's letters traced a string of jobs, they said more or less the same thing each time except for the name of the establishment he was working for." He lives with others like him, some of whom end up leaving for other jobs and towns, some are deported and others return home or change their names. "You live intensely with others, only to have them disappear overnight, since the shadow class was condemned to movement.... The emptiness Biju felt returned to him over and over, eventually he made sure not to let friendships sink deep anymore"

Desai represents the life of the illegal immigrant in New York brilliantly. In New York, Biju catches a television programme on an Indian channel about immigration. The programme depicts a taxi driver who had illegally come to America, to be part of the American dream.

> He was illegal, his taxi was illegal, the yellow paint was illegal, his whole family was here, and all the men in his village were here, perfectly infiltrated and working, within the cab system of the city. But how to get their papers?

These are the sort of people Biju knows in New York and there is yet another set to which he would like to belong—the well-to-do, legal immigrant,—"...he watched the legalized foreigners with envy as they shopped at discount baggage stores for the miraculous, expandable third-world suitcase, accordion pleated, filled with pockets and zippers to unhook further crannies, the whole structure unfolding into a giant space that could fit in enough to set up an entire life in another country." Oblivious of the reality of Biju's life in New York, his father imagines what life would be like with "a sofa, TV and a bank account," and thinks of him as "the luckiest boy in the whole wide world."

Desai's description of Biju's life in America is interspersed with moments of tender and lyrical nostalgic reflections of home back in the mountains of Kalimpong. Lying in his basement bed Biju dreams of home, of his village, of his father, of his grandmother, of the sound that the grass made as the breeze wafted through them, of the way the stream meandered, of the buffaloes in the river. Biju, of course, forgets the harsh life that he had to lead in his small village. When talking to his father over the telephone, Biju is almost able to feel his home.

> The atmosphere of Kalimpong reached Biju all the way in New York; it swelled densely on the line...he could hear the croak trrrr whonk, wee wee butt ock butt ock of frogs in the spinach, the rising note welding imperceptibly with the evening....

Biju epitomizes the plight of the illegal immigrant who has no future in his own country and who must endure deplorable conditions if he is to work illegally in the United States. Always on the run from immigration and often cheated by employers,

Biju suffers furthermore because his father is so proud that his son is doing well in America, and writes to him constantly asking him to help the children of his equally poor friends to find work in the United States. Biju's friend Saeed Saeed, from Zanzibar, faces similar pressures from his family, though in his case these young men arrive at his place of work and apartment demanding help and a place to live. His avoidance of these people provides scenes of dark humour.

Places are important in the novel since each character finds himself or herself displaced. Unfortunate circumstances thrust Sai to Kalimpong, Biju longs for home in New York, Gyan joins the insurgency that promises a new state. Sai takes pains to show the cook New York on a globe that had arrived from the National Geographic.

> They searched out New York, and Sai attempted to explain to the cook why it was night there when it was day here, just as Sister Alice had demonstrated in St. Augustine's with an orange and a flashlight. The cook found it strange that India went first with the day, a funny back-to-front fact that didn't seem mirrored by any other circumstance involving the two nations.

Gyan feels intimidated by the judge's very English and superior ways. He loves Sai but when he joins the movement for a separate statehood, he begins to despise her and her bourgeois ways. He is also fed up with the fact that Nepalese in India are being treated like a minority in a place where they are the majority. As a consequence, he rejects Sai's privileged life. Other finely sketched Kalimpong characters in the novel are two elderly Anglophile Indian sisters who sip tea and read Jane Austen, safe within the confines of the estate they call Mon Ami, and a Swiss priest named Father Booty who keeps a dairy and dreams of teaching Indians to make cheese.

Alternating between Biju's struggle to survive in New York and the steadily gathering insurgency of men and guns in the hills of Kalimpong, Desai's novel portrays a world trying to cope with modernization and the rapid changes it entails. The most disturbing incident is the one in which Biju joins a crowd of Indians scrambling to reach the visa counter at the United States embassy:

> Biggest pusher, first place; how self-contented and smiling he was; he dusted himself off, presenting himself with the exquisite manners of a cat. I'm civilized, sir, ready for the U.S., I'm civilized, mam. Biju noticed that his eyes, so alive to the foreigners, looked back at his own countrymen and women, immediately glazed over, and went dead.

Poor and lonely in New York, Biju eavesdrops on businessmen eating steak and exulting over the wealth to be gained in the new markets of Asia.

> Year by year, his life wasn't amounting to anything at all; in a space that should have included family, friends, he was the only one displacing the air.... Shouldn't he return to a life where he might slice his own importance, to where he might relinquish this overrated control over his destiny and perhaps be subtracted from its determination altogether?

Not surprisingly, he eventually becomes a man with a "wish to live within a narrow purity." For him, the city's endless possibilities for self-invention become a source of pain. Arriving back in India in the climactic scenes of the novel, Biju is immediately engulfed and overtaken by the local eruptions of rage and frustration from which he had been physically distant in New York.

All of the novel's characters eventually come to share Sai's belief that life is more often defined by loss than by fulfillment. Desai explores the pain of the immigrant, and the unfairness of a world in which one side travels to be a servant, and the other side travels to be treated like a king. India is both the place that Biju, an Indian dreams of escaping and where Father Booty, who is not Indian, longs to remain. In New York Biju is not immune from nostalgia. He can "feel the pulse of the forest, smell the humid air, the green black lushness; he could imagine all its different textures, the plumage of banana, the stark spear of the cactus, the delicate gesture of ferns." Longing is perhaps the only thing that the characters in this novel do best—they long for home, love and acceptance, but rarely achieve it. Gyan says it best after he fails to find a sense of purpose in politics—that "happiness has a smaller location." Salman Rushdie says:

> A full migrant suffers, traditionally, a triple disruption: he loses his place, he enters into an alien language, and he finds himself surrounded by beings whose social behaviour and code is very unlike, and sometimes even offensive to, his own. And this is what makes migrants such important figures because roots, language and social norms have been three of the most important parts of the definition of what it is to be a human being. The migrant, denied all three, is obliged to find new ways of describing himself, new ways of being human.

The Inheritance of Loss is at once a novel of class and economic disparity, a love story, and a commentary on postcolonial India. The characters in the novel are insecure and unmoored. Transitions between continents and eras indicate the connections between characters. Biju and his father think constantly of each other, and Biju writes moving letters home. Sai pesters her father for stories of her grandfather's past. She falls in love with her tutor, Gyan, who in turn falls under the spell of an uprising. In the end, the landscape that has engendered great passion and destruction survives both. Sai and Gyan inherit the loss, referred to in the title, as do the cook and Biju. The very mountains suffer: Darjeeling is literally "going downhill," there are landslides everywhere. The rebels protest that it is not their tents but the big house that endangers the hillside. And as Sai feels "Could fulfillment ever be felt as deeply as loss?"

In an interview Kiran Desai says, "Being part of the Indian diaspora gives one a precise emotional location to work from, if not a precise geographical one." Speaking of her art as a novelist, she says that, "The vocabulary of immigration, of exile, of translation, inevitably overlaps with a realization of the multiple options for reinvention, of myriad perspectives, shifting truths, telling of lies—the great big wobbliness of it all. In a world obsessed with national boundaries and belonging, as a novelist working with a form also traditionally obsessed with place, it was a journey to come to this thought, that the less structured, the multiple, may be a possible location for fiction, perhaps a more ethical location in general."

What Desai ultimately highlights is not just individual experiences, but rather the relations of recognition between immigrants, exiles and foreigners who all grapple with the weight of history. Biju does not have a hyphenated identity that is so often the plight of most characters in a diasporic situation. He is completely Indian, the only reason he had come over to the United States was the desire to earn. America was never home to him and he chooses to go back though the homecoming is not the sort that he had ever envisioned. *The Inheritance of Loss* tells the story of two different kinds of diasporas—that of the exploited, illegal immigrants in New York City and an aging, elitist cluster of Indians settled after retirement in a hill town, wonderfully presented in Sai's grandfather, among others. Characters belonging to both these worlds face the challenges of a globalized society that is fraught with increasingly separatist and nationalistic agendas. Desai's novel describes human migration and shows that it has always been part of the human experience. Biju's narrative as an illegal immigrant, all alone, with no future in distant New York, is balanced by that of the other protagonist, seventeen year-old Sai, whose life is ostensibly elitist but shabby nevertheless. Kiran Desai's realistic portrayal of life on two continents, diasporic on multiple levels, demonstrates a deep concern for the human condition.

WORKS CITED

Ahluwalia, Pal. "When Does a Settler Become a Native?—Citizenship and Identity in a Settler Society", *Postcolonialisms*, eds. Gaurav Desai and Supriya Nair, Berg, Oxford, 2005.

Anderson, Benedict. *Imagined Communities: Reflections on the Origin and Spread of Nationalism*. London, Verso, 1983.

Ashcroft, Bill, Gareth Griffiths and Helen Tiffin. *The Empire Writes Back: Theory and Practice in Post-colonial Literatures*. Routledge, London and New York, 1989.

Bhabha, Homi. *The Location of Culture*, Routledge, London, 1994.

Desai, Kiran. *The Inheritance of Loss*. Penguin, New Delhi, 2006.

Grass, Gunter. *On Writing and Politics*, Penguin, London, 1987.

Lukacs, Georg. *Theory of the Novel*, trans. Anna Bostock, London, Merlin Press, 2003.

16

The Colonial Hangover and The Brown Sahib

Madhu Shalini

So for my hacked
heart, veins' mem-
ories, I wear this
past I borrowed:[1]

The Inheritance of Loss which won the Man Booker Prize 2006, shot its author Kiran Desai to fame and placed India, once again, at the literary centrestage. The novel raises important contemporary issues in a powerful and persuasive way. It shows Kiran Desai's deep interest in the complexities of time and history. However, it is the additional layer of the impact of British Colonial culture which shapes the thematic and formal preoccupation of the novel. Desai beautifully exfoliates how the intricate and intriguing ways of the colonial inheritance operate in a specific context. Colonialism does not exist in a formal form anymore but it is difficult to efface colonial attitudes which are entrenched deeply in the psyche of the colonized.

Colonization was a system of institutionalized force. It was a means by which a powerful country controlled the destiny of a weaker one. It is now commonly accepted that the colonizers consciously worked to subdue rebellion on the part of the natives by "educating"[2] them and infusing into them a sense of inferiority and contempt for their indigenous values and culture.[3] This deliberate maiming of the natives' consciousness resulted in his admiration of the white man. To say that the colonized, the world over, carry the burden of their colonial past, like the legendary Sisyphus, would be much too clichéd. However, the intriguing manner in which it etches and shapes the sensibility of the colonized appears to be interesting. The colonized past has a tenacious psychological hold on the subjects of the colonial rule. "The colonized lives for a long time before we see that really new man."[4]

The process of decolonizing the mind is a difficult and complex procedure for the act of colonization moves deeper than mere geographical or surface realities. It involves and is concerned with men and therefore there are deeper complexities involved. In fact one of the reasons accounting for such complexity is the ambevelant and symbiotic relationship which the colonizer and the colonized share. The mutuality of desire which binds them is unique and ironic: and this mutuality hovers around perverseness. There can be no doubt regarding the desire of the colonizer for the colony but the natives who are oppressed nourish an inverse longing for the colonized. How "could the colonized deny himself so cruelly.... How could he hate the colonizers and yet admire them so passionately."[5] This ambiguous love-hate desire, perhaps has its seat in the emotional bedrock.

This self division is psychologically significant but not new. Hegel in his *Lordship and Bondage* had stated that human beings become self-conscious only through the recognition of others.[6] Initially, the master and the slave are involved in a struggle leading to an acceptance by the slave of his subjugation. The important thing in the whole struggle is the phase where the slaves' identity is annihilated. After the initial struggle, his existence is formed by the conquering 'Other.' Sartre too communicates a similar view when he writes "the other holds a secret—the secret of what I am."[7] But colonialism "does not end with the end of colonial occupation."[8] And this view is beautifully reflected in *The Inheritance of Loss*. The novel is set in post-colonial India but the ominous presence of colonial period can be seen and felt casting its shadows on a country which has been given a wakening call to the glorious morn of independence. Kiran Desai focuses on the consequences of colonialisation etched in various walks of a postcolonial Indian life. She also showcases the malaise of a globalized world in the form of conflicts of religion, race and nation.

The story revolves around an Anglophile judge and his granddaughter, Sai who stay in the small town of Kalimpong in Darjeeling. The action of the novel shifts between this small town and America where Biju, another resident of this small town, has gone to try his luck. But unfortunately he is actually "like a fugitive on the run—no papers."[9] The beauty and mystique generally associated with hills as a setting for a story is brutally and purposely destroyed in the very beginning of the novel both by the invasion of the privacy of the judge's house, Cho Oyu, and the newspaper report of the growing "dissatisfaction in the hills, gathering insurgency." This sense of dissatisfaction creates an atmosphere of unrest and hatred which spurs the action of the novel. Also interspersed are snippets from the judge's past life both in India and in England which provide an insight into his past life and hold a key to his present, for an understanding of the present is possible by a grasp of the past.

The judge, Jemubhai Popatlal Patel, was born in a peasant cast family in 1919 "in a tentative structure under a palm roof scuffling with rats at the outskirts of Piphit" (56-57) in Gujarat. So he was a part of a society which was earlier under the reign of the Gaekwad kings and then under the British rule. The small town where time seemed to standstill was jarred from its sleepiness by attempts of the British to modernize it by opening a school and laying rail tracks across it. This move can easily be attributed to the colonizer's intention to create a group of men amongst the natives who would be Indian by birth but English in thoughts, manners and values. Little Jemu received education at the local Bishop Cotton School where he was deeply impressed by the portrait of Queen Victoria. What struck him was the fact that "a woman so plain could have been so powerful" (58). Though the idea seemed odd to him, his respect and admiration for her and English grew stronger.

This quaint oddity is justified in the "Orient's longing for its conquering other."[10] Jemu is the first in his family to receive such an education. His doing well at higher levels of exam spurs his father to send him abroad for studies. Jemu's life during the colonial period is frequently referred to, as also his sojourn in England, with the help of the flashback technique. Jemu boards the ship S.S. Strathnaver, with the natives' aquired love for fanfare from their masters. His father-in-law had hired retired members of a military band to play for him. The journey of Jemu is quite significant as indices of his emotional quotient and helpful in understanding his later behaviour.

The journey which began in a small train compartment, which was taking him to Bombay, made him realize the triviality of his world. The adventurous soul of Jemu is filled with fear for his past, not his future and the "foolish faith" (36) with which he had lived till then disheartened him as he became aware of his lack of self-sufficiency. His luggage containing contradictory items like the choorva and the decorated coconut for tossing into the waves and his new Oxford English Dictionary stand as symbols of the two cultures which are shaping the young boy. In the larger, more open and cosmopolitan atmosphere at the dock in Bombay the vision of his father waving him goodbye mingles Jemu's love for him with pity and shame for he was a picture of a "barely educated man venturing where he should not be" (37). This complexity of emotion which he feels for his father becomes a fixture with Jemu for "Never again would he know love for a human being that was not adulterated by another, contradictory emotion" (37). This show of affection on the part of his mother who had put a banana, along with the typical Indian meal for the journey, which was smashed, infuriates him. For, in the company of the sonnet composing cabinmate, his luggage and his meal had given away his past and his way of life. Humiliation, coupled with anger, engulfs Jemu. He felt angry at his mother for humiliating him, in her attempt to save him from the embarrassment of his inability of using the fork and knife in the dining salon of the ship. (Later, however, he uses a knife and fork to eat his rotis and puris!) Her "undignified love, Indian love" disgusts him and he tosses the food packet overboard. The overt show of affection fills Jemu with an embittered silence.

In England, Jemubhai feels the "dreadful secondariness"[11] of being an Indian. He registers the sight of small grey houses with a sense of amazement for the glorious picture of England which he carried in his heart now seemed colourless. England, for him, was a land of dreams, of glory and beauty and of wealth and happiness. That dream is shattered further when he feels isolated and withdraws into his shell. Without any company he gradually becomes an alien even to himself. This withdrawal goes to such an extreme that he fails to laugh lest others would see his gums—something very private. He is mocked and made fun of and is also discriminated against. When he is wrongly accused of smelling like curry by the young, giggly British girls, he takes to regular washing and covers himself completely. The impact of such experiences is so great that he becomes obsessive for certain things in life like his preference for faded days to sunny lest sunlight reveal his horrifying self. So gradually all these residual traces and memories of subordination play havoc on his senses and restructure his psyche thereby playing a major role in shaping him. The psychic mutations caused due to the colonial impact have been portrayed very convincingly by the author through the judge, Jemubhai Patel.

On his return to India we find a changed Jemu. The fear, insecurity, awkwardness which he flet as a colonized victim in England were now covered with the confidence of the cloak of a foreign degree that too obtained in the very citadels of the colonizers. The judge traverses the genealogy of a Gujarat family "from rural self-sufficiency to colonized civility."[12] Now he virtually has "the conquerer's authoritarian seal."[13] By equipping him with a colonial education the family rewrites its history (the modified version which the cook tells Sai). For them, as for the judge, it is a "faultering generational progress into coloniality."[14] In this endeavour itself is inherent the faultline of "separateness and fear"[15] which prompts the judge to the self-conscious acquisition of Englishness.

The judge is particular, on his return from England, for English manners, rituals, attitude and the general way of life. He has become the Brown Sahib who wants things done with punctuality and precession. Donning the habits of the white masters, following a tight calendar and the "constant exertion of authority" (61) calmed the judge. This authority is inherent in the mechanism of power. For if power is "at once the qualitative difference or gap between those who have it or those who must suffer it, it also designates an imaginative space that can be occupied, a cultural model that might be imitated and replicated."[16] The judge is pleased to keep the Bramhin stenographer waiting or see him occupying a tiny tent next to his own magnificent one. "How he relished his power over the classes that had kept his family pinned under their heels for centuries..." (61). The judge is now equipped with the power of the ruling class endorsed by their educational system. In a similar show of strength, his father-in-law Bomanbhai, who had the power of money, employed a Bramhin cook (being richer than all the Bramhins in town). The feeling of satisfaction they feel is quite natural and can be explained through Foucault' argument:

> Power is employed and exercised through a net-like organization. And not only do indivisuals circulate between its threads; they are always in the position of simultaneously undergoing or exercising the power. They are not only its inert or consenting target; they are also the elements of its articulation.[17]

Once he is posted as a touring official in the civil services he is pleased with the sweetness life has to offer him and "the burning memory of his beginnings" give way to a sense of "relief" (61). Imitating the colonial masters helps him in exercising the phantoms of humiliation he has suffered at their hands.

This penchant of the judge for British affectations is not only limited to the daily activities but is also traced in his grim countenance, expressions and manners, an aloofness which he courts and his dislike for informality. In fact all these help him move up the hierarchial ladder of law and order. During his service tenure, the worse form of contamination which he came across was hearing the cases in Hindi. His face wore a mask-like look, something which he had aquired during his experience in England. This mask hangs on to him now like a real face. His fuss over a fixed English routine began with the bed tea (or Baaad Teee as the cook pronounced) and ended with a hot water bottle, not only in winter but in all seasons in the manner of the colonizers. Even after retirement, the evening tea is more like a ritual—served with fanfare. He wants an accompaniment of pudding with it and serving buiscuits irritated him. This demand of the judge finds an ironic duplication when the insurgents enter the house and demand tea and snacks that too served in a proper manner. They refer to the judge as sahib, sarcastically and order him to prepare the table. The judge, who had never been inside a kitchen, finds himself doing as they desired. They make fun of the judge when only tea is served and the leader says "La! What kind of Sahib?" (6)

To a great extent this behaviourial determinism of the natives to ape the rulers, as exemplified in the character of the judge, is the result of a sense of loss and can be explained through psycho-analytic theories. Psycho-analytical theories have explained the inevitability of loss as a primary field on which the personality, both the individual and social aspects, constructs itself. In the case of men like Jemubhai Patel the loss of self-esteem and dignity prepares the scenario for restructuring the psychic self, ending in their imbibing the same set of cultural values and norms which had caused them humiliation and embarrassment. This is the strange love-hate relation in the encounter with the West—an "implacable enemity between native and invader."[18] This "intimate enemity"[19] between the colonizers and the natives evokes an irresistible temptation to the Masters' way of living and thinking.

In fact, the impact of colonialism is felt and can be traced in the other characters too. Lola and Noni do not want the postcolonial period, which has a hangover of the colonial one, to end. Their fascination for Trollope, BBC, Marks and Spensers' underwear, and joy at Christmas help them to live under the illusion of the colonial period. They are hooked to the band wagon of the colonial era and try to continue it with the help of foreign goods and their way of life. They do not want to give it up. The legacy of the gora-sahibs is there to stay for it has successfully colonized the minds of the natives. Ashis Nandy too explains this view when he makes a blunt distinction between two distinct types of colonialism. The first type of colonialism, according to him, aimed at the conquest of territories while the second was directed towards the conquering of minds, selves and cultures. "This colonialism colonizes minds in addition to bodies and it releases forces within colonized societies to alter their cultural priorities once and for all.... The West is now everywhere, within the West and outside, in structures and in minds."[20]

The judge's dislike for Gyan, the Nepali boy, employed as Sai's tutor, hinges on Gyan's frailty due to his belonging to a lower wrung in the social setup. His presence at the dinner table was "an insolence" (109) for the judge. He discerned an awkwardness and hesitation in Gyan which recalled similar emotions he had felt once. The "recognition of weakness" (109) was very intense—not merely limited to a feeling but extended to a taste. The thought that Gyan had never tasted such food nor in the same manner, flooded the judge with bitterness. He leaves no chance to make Gyan feel uneasy and uncomfortable in his new avatar of a 'sahib.' His initiation into British life and culture had begun long before he left for England. It grew in intensity during the probation period. "He envied the English. He loathed Indians. He worked at being English with the passion of hatred and for what he would become, he would be despised by absolutely everyone, English and Indians both" (119). This ambevelant attraction could not be explained better. The shyness and consciousness at his Indian accent makes him recoil behind a mask of silence. Despite his brave attempts at aquiring the colonisers ways and manners and with the Sahib's pretences, on his return voyage, the judge felt uneasy in the company of the British.

It is not only the rich and the so-called elite but even those who belong to the economically weaker section of society, represented by the cook, who reels under the impact of the syndrome. The cook was disappointed to be working for Jemubhai. The disappointment was rooted in what he considered to be a comedown from his father "who had served white men only" (63). The Indianisation of the I.C.S. displeased him. He would have been happier in serving a white master. The test of a cook to be hired depended on his ability to make good pudding, not any Indian delicacy. The thought of his son, Biju cooking "Angrezi Khana" made him conclude "that since his son was cooking English food, he had a higher position than if were cooking Indian" (17). When Biju writes letters describing the 'angrezi food' and owner for whom he worked, the cook used it as a weapon to impress people back home. "One day his son would accomplish all that Sai's parents had failed to do, all the judge had failed to do" (85).

The fascination of the cook and the likes, for the white skin and their land and their desire to see their sons in the same frame is a perpetuation of the same syndrome. They are gripped by the paralysis of will to imitate. The new generation of Indians as represented by Biju or even the cook are bound by "restrictive confinement of knowledge and value."[21] The America they know and value and aspire for so strongly is always elsewhere. It is the epitome of a fantasy of the British domination. America, carrying within it all the riches and treasures in the world held a passport to their happiness. Behind this fantasy lies the reality of migration, the life as a refugee, being treated as secondary. Biju's humiliation and sense of shame in America reflects the same psychological course which the judge had undergone while in England. He too is gripped with isolation at his realization of being "abandoned with foreigners" (99). An emptiness gripped him. The colonial exploitation, not only of Biju but many like him from Asia and Africa, receives almost a first-hand treatment by Kiran Desai.

The fall-out in the relationship between Sai and Gyan also has colonial overtones. Sai, who has had a convent education, bears a striking resemblance to her grandfather in accent and manner. With her Westernized education, she is a stranger in her own land. Gyan, on the other hand, is a descendant of a Nepali Gurkha family. The initial attraction that blooms between them turns sour as Gyan is caught in the insurgency movement gaining ground, claiming a separate Gurkha land. Any dilemma he faces, regarding the authenticity of the movement and the accompanying march, is wiped out when he sees veracity writ on the face of the marchers instead of cynicism. They had been denied justice—for now power was in the hands of the Brown Sahib who were perpetrating what they had inherited from their colonial masters. Gyan feels ashamed at the tea parties which he has had with Sai. All sense of shame and humiliation gave vent to anger. He feels irritated when Sai and her neighbours celebrate Christmas and blurts out "You are like slaves, that's what you are, running after the West, embarrassing yourself. It's because of people like you we never get anywhere" (163). Gyan later mimics "Sai and her grandfather with the fake English accent and the face powdered pink and white over dark brown" (176). The blind imitation of the British made the judge and Sai, lose their individuality. Gyan is filled with disgust and hatred for Sai who could only speak English and pidgin Hindi. This limited her social circle. Moreover, she could not eat with her hands, had never been to a temple for religious purpose, never chewed a paan nor could she sit through a full Bollywood film.

Gyan's hatred for Sai and the world she represents finds an echo in one of the reminiscences of the judge. His snobbishness makes him look down upon Nimmi, his wife whom he considered uncouth and unfit for himself. "He did not like his wife's face, searched for his hatred, found beauty, dismissed it. Once it had been a terrifying beckoning thing that had made his heart turn to water, but now it seemed beside the point. An Indian girl could never be as beautiful as an English one" (168). His throwing port at Nimmi for chewing disgustedly is reflected in Sai's revulsion at Gyan's "slurps and smacks"

(176) while eating. In fact Sai, Lola, Noni, Uncle Potty and Father Booty stick together for they share similar views. Potty is liked for his Oxford education and his famed lineage and "called his parents Mater and Pater" (197). All of them were "unanimous in the opinion that they didn't like English writers writing about India: ...English writers writing of England was what was nice" (198). Their mind-set betrays that "...certain moves made long ago had produced all of them" (199).

It is however the remark by H. Hardless which Sai finds in The Indian Gentleman's Guide to Etiquette, that conveys the stark reality. "Although you may have aquired the habits and manners of the European, have the courage to show that you are not ashamed of being an Indian, and in all such cases, identify yourself with the race to which you belong" (199). Although Sai is infuriated at reading this, the comment contains the heart of the matter. It is like a pin prick to deflate the dream-balloon of the Indians infatuated by the English mind-set, mannerisms and customs.

The novel thus ropes in the twin polarity associated with colonialism—the aftermath of the colonial domination and anti-colonial resistance in the post-colonial era. Through the characters and their moves, Kiran Desai focuses on a double awareness—of the colonial inheritance as it works within a specific (Indian) culture and of a changing relationship among communities, cultures and countries in the modern world.

NOTES

1. Edward Kamau Brathwaite, *The Arrivants: A New World Trilogy*. London, O.U.P., 1973, p. 148.
2. A.R. Desai, *Social Background of Indian Nationalism*. Bombay: Popular, 1976, pp. 140-41.
3. Franz Fannon, *The Wretched of the Earth*, trans. Constance Farrington. Harmondsworth: Penguin, 1982, p. 32.
4. Albert Memmi, *Dominated Man: Notes towards a Portrait*, London: Orion Press: 1968, p. 88.
5. *Ibid.*
6. G.F.W. Hegel, "Lordship and Bondage", *The Phenomenology of Mind*, Vol. 1, trans. J.B. Baille. London: Macmillan and Co., 1910, pp. 175-88.

7. Jean Paul Sartre, Cited in *Gendizier*, 1973, p. 31.
8. Leela Gandhi, *Postcolonial Theory: A Critical Introduction*. New Delhi: O.U.P., 2006, p. 17.
9. Kiran Desai, *The Inheritance of Loss*. New Delhi: Penguin Books; 2006, p. 3. All further references from the text are from this edition.
10. Gandhi, *op. cit.*, p. 12.
11. Edward Said, "Representing the Colonized: Anthropology's Interlocutors," *Critical Inquiry*, Vol. 15, No. 2, 1989, pp. 205-25.
12. Gandhi, *op. cit.*, p. 13.
13. Vikram Seth, *Mappings*; Penguin Books/Viking, New Delhi, 1994, p. 64.
14. Gandhi, *op. cit.*
15. Seth, *op. cit.*, p. 65.
16. Gandhi, *op. cit.*, p. 14.
17. M. Faucault, *Power/Knowledge: Selected Interviews and Other Writings 1972-1977*, ed. Colin Gordon; Harvester Press, Hertfordshire, 1980, p. 98.
18. Benita Parry, "Problems in Current Theories of Colonial Discourse," *Oxford Literary Review*, 1987, Vol. 9, p. 32.
19. Ashis Nandy, *The Intimate Enemy: Loss and Recovery of Self Under Colonialism*. Delhi, O.U.P., 1983.
20. *Ibid.*, p. xi.
21. Gandhi, *op. cit.*, p. 12.

17

Kiran Desai's *The Inheritance of Loss*: A Parable on the Predicament of Third World Immigrants

Beena Agarwal

Salman Rushdie in his discourse on Diaspora while unveiling the predicament of immigrants came across a very significant conclusion to decode the socio-cultural trauma of the characters that desperately make efforts to seek "wholeness" amid the fractured images of life in alien cultural surroundings. He states:

> Human beings do not perceive things whole; we are not Gods but wounded creatures, cracked lenses, capable only of fractured perceptions. Partial beings in all the senses of that phase. Meaning is a shaky edifice, we built out of scraps, dogmas childish memories, newspaper articles, chance remarks, old films, small victories, people hated people loved.[1]

In the going process of migration, cultural transmission, globalization, expansion of Information Technology, exodus of technical and non-technical labour, the tendency to monopolize economic resources, human civilization is witnessing the absurdity of survival. The onslaught of migration encouraged by professional compulsions and personal choices has dragged society in the twilight of confusions and uncertainty. Expatriates being alienated from their ethnic identities are bound to experience "profound uncertainties" because they find it difficult to reclaim what is "lost." Engrossed in their own plight, they create "fictions not of actual cities and villages but invisible one, Imaginary homelands, Indias of mind."[2]

In the post modern conditions, the literary texts invariably conceal the iceberg of cultural disparities with the prophetic enunciation that the acceptance of the need of diverse cultures to speculate the possibilities of human survival at global level is essential. The vision about the various dimensions of multi-culturalism and cultural variations are closely associated with the creative spectrum of the writers sharing "double consciousness." In the article "Meeting of Streams," Uma Parmeswaran argues that instead of keynote assimilation, the acceptance of diversity is mutually enriching as a necessary tool for cultural synthesis—a direction in which literature can play a significance role,... Literature can not only reflect persistence and change in society but can also lead society into a better appreciation of its multi-cultural and ethno-centered fabric."[3]

Kiran Desai who travels amid three geographical locations inheriting the different cultures from her kinship with Bangladesh, Gujarat and England, infuses in the texture of *The Inheritance of Loss*, a wide and comprehensive perspective on the idea of exile, dislocation and displacement. Still, her sensibility conceives the pattern of life in which she feels 'no alienation or dislocation' but sustains her native Indian heritage. In one of her interview, she accepts, "rediscovering her Indian-ness was vital to her success."[4] She holds on her Indian passport, struggling to get American citizenship but she was hesitant to surrender her Indian citizenship. In one of the interview, she confessed:

> I feel less like doing it every year because I realize that I see everything through the lens of being Indian. It's not something that has gone away—it's something that has become stronger: As I've got older, I have realized that I can't really write without that perspective.[5]

The novel *The Inheritance of Loss* is a representation of the multicultural global society where besides the issues of terrorism, assertion of native identities, the clash of interpersonal relations, isolation of man against religious fundamentalism and all pervasive humiliations of existence against conflicting values, have become the keynote of life. In one of the tribute of the novel, it has been accepted:

> [Kiran Desai's] novel bounces between an insurgency in India and the immigrant experience, Desai sheds light on the tribulations of all Indians abroad and these scenes will resonate with anyone who has felt compelled to compromise their heritage.... Desai details characters hardship head-on and her elegant prose makes their experience hard to forget.[6]

With the increasing passion for McDonalization, the exodus from Third World countries to economically advanced America has led to more complex socio-cultural perspectives. In new cultural and national spaces, immigrants have to redefine their cultural and historical identities, compromising their ethical values and religious faiths. The reflections on social insecurity, socio-ethnic practices, sense of self-respect assume new proportion. The moral considerations are essentially subordinated to the desire to seek spaces in First World countries. Economic opulence is essentially holding the axis of centre. Arjun Appaduri accepts, "the random flow of capital is accompanied by an unprecedented movement of peoples, technologies and information across previously impermeable borders—for one location to another."[7]

The text of the novel *The Inheritance of Loss* is set at Kalimpong, a beauteous mountain range at the outskirt of Nepal border. A retired judge resides there supported by one of his family cook Panna Lal and pet dog, Mutt. The plight of the life of immigrants is projected through the life of cook's son Biju who had gone to America accepting the job of a cook in an English Restaurant. Desai projects a pathetic vision of the growing discontent among the Third World countries and exhibits her concern how growing awareness about ethnic identity, is posing a great hazard in the process of globalization. All through the novel, the cook nurtures the dreams of immigration of Biju through the several letters that he had got from Biju. In one of his letter, he mentions, "No need to worry. Everything is fine. The manager has offered me a full time waiter position. Uniform and food will be given by them. Angrezi Khana only, no Indian food and the owner is not from India. He is from America itself" (140). The self elation expressed in this statement suggests how the migrants from the Third World countries take it a pride to get a job in America and to accept an unconditional surrender for the superiority of the West. In the subsequent narration, the exposition of the excitement of cook and misery of the reality of the life of Biju present the humiliation of the migrants in the Third World countries and also implicit helplessness to retreat their steps. Biju witnesses the racial apathy. Cook has a satisfaction of the fact that his son is cooking English food. He is confident that Biju would make enough money and would secure all luxury and comforts. In contrast of his contentment, Biju had a realization that in America his identity is being acknowledged only as a second citizen and the privileges of legal citizenship will not be accessible to him. He recalls, "all American flags on top, all Guatemalan flag below" (21). Indians in Alkasa, own the last general store in the last town before the North Pole. He was surprised to see that there was a whole world in the basement kitchen of New York. He found, "perfectly first world on top, perfectly Third World twenty steps below" (23). In this way America perpetualizes racial identities. Stuart Hall in his study on multiculturalism confirms that in the process of migration, the idea of "otherness" and the consciousness of ethnicity merely confirms and stabilizes the hegemony of the West. He accepts:

> In these circumstances, ethnicity is always, already named as marginal or peripheral to the mainstream. By contrast, Englishness or Americanness is of course, never represented as ethnicity.[8]

In context of cultural encounter and the plight of immigrants the text of the novel *The Inheritance of Loss* moves at two levels. If on the one hand, cook reconstructs the life of Biju, on the other hand he also records the plight of Lola, Noni and Father Booty who live in Darjeeling as migrants. In spite of their fascination for the exotica of India, they too exhibit their discontent growing in Indian society. Desai affirms that ethnicity and racial prejudice and its dark shadows are seen across the globe, may be inside India or outside India. Noni in spite of her fascination for India advises her daughter Pixie, "India is a sinking ship. Don't want to be pushy, thinking of your happiness only but the door won't stay open forever" (47).

Biju in his exile makes consistent shift in his job. In spite of absurdities and humiliations, the only consolation in his life is that, "in this country people eat like kings." Of course Biju finds it difficult to accommodate in those adverse conditions, in the company of rig rags coming from all the corners of the world. Saeed also finds himself isolated in America. Like a typical postmodern protagonist, Biju finds himself in a state of perpetual 'Exile' and helplessness to accommodate with the social environment. It has been accepted, "The exile is a universal figure—we are made to feel a sense of exile by our inadequacy and our irrelevance of function in a society whose past we can't alter and whose function is always beyond us."[9] Biju during his stay at Tater's Bakery suffers unconscious fear of being inferior. In America he was taught that he should not believe on black people. The derogatory comment, "Be careful of hubshi Ha, Ha.... In their own country they live like monkeys in the tree, they come to India and become man" was enough to give a deep shock to his own sensibility. It is an evidence to the assumption that the hegemony of First World countries is encouraging a greater venom of racial consciousness. Instead of regionalism world view of life regionalism creates an alien sensibility. Bill Ashcroft admits that the crisis of identity in the world view is created by, "Cultural denigration the conscious and unconscious oppression of the indigenous personality and culture by a supposedly superior racial or cultural model."[10] Besides, cultural constructs, the reconstruction of the past and the nostalgia of homeland obstructs their perceptions. Biju in the moments of solitude feels nervous because in New York, innocence never prevails. The terrible sounds of ambulance, fire engine and subway cause convulsions in his heart. Like

Bharati Mukherjee and Chitra Benerjee Divakaruni, Desai also feels that the complexity of technology increases the plight of immigrants.

The Inheritance of Loss justifies that Kiran Desai's approach to the matrix of immigrant experiences is rational and practical than being sentimental. Assimilation and acceptance of diversity is essential but the ideal for making spaces in other cultures is a complex phenomenon and its manifold paradigms can't be estimated within the sympathetic socio-cultural dynamics. She makes an elaborate analysis of the complexity of getting green card in America. Without green cards, immigrants can't be accepted as legal citizens. In the process of legal formalities, they are subjected to humiliations and discriminations. Biju in the moments of restlessness, used to walk to the far where the "homelessment slept in dense chamber of grief." The whole phenomenon of the process of migration is exposed with the undertone of bitter humour echoing the pain of those who have to bear the humiliation of rootless survival without sympathy, without consolation. He calls bakery the "immigration hotline." This hostility of global community gives birth to the psyche of resentment, rebellion gradually culminating in violence. Biju felt a flesh of anger at his father for sending him alone to this far-off country. In contrast of the anxiety and pain of Biju, cook survives in the illusion, "my son is in New York, he is the manager of a restaurant business" (84). He glorifies the emergence of America as the most powerful nation of world with exclusive control on economic resources. With the expansion of the new job probabilities, it has been responsible for new type of imperialism. Cook admires America as, "the best country in the world; all these people who went to England are now feeling sorry" (85). Biju wanted to write on a mail form but he did not know English. Saeed and Biju also find it difficult to make answers on the answering machine. To encounter these oddities, Saeed makes a very pathetic suggestion that it is desirable for immigrants to go back to India to emancipate from the burden of shame and humiliation. He says:

> No jobs here anymore, if I were a youngman, I would go back to India, more opportunities there now, too late for me to make a change, but you should listen to what I'm saying. Everyone says you have to stay, this is where you'll make a good life but much better for you to go back. (98)

Cultural transaction often emerges as a tool for another mode of marginalization. In America, they have no choice of their own, neither of assimilation nor of retreat. They are treated as the burden of Third World countries. For them assimilation in the progressive society of America is not an extension of their 'self.' Kiran Desai shares their anguish in the confession, "then of course, there were those who lived and died illegal in America and never saw their families, not for ten years, twenty, thirty never against" (199). In spite of long stay, they are lacking in belongingness. Biju reminds of his village where he passed his childhood with his grandmother. He reminds his grandmother, 'earthen lamps' of Deepawali, taste of 'roti' and fresh milk. It is not only a romantic nostalgia but an urnest need and passionate desire with these sojourns to relocate the philosophy and vision of the homeland in the midst of alien cultural surroundings. According to William Sofran, "The retention of collective memory, vision or myth about the original homeland—its physical location, history, etc. is one of the six features of diaspora."[11] Kiran Desai no doubt defends American society for its ability to accommodate the people across the world, glorifies its structure and economy but simultaneously she also appreciates the values of the East in contrast of materialistic social structure of the West. People coming from Third World countries are more sensitive to retain their identity but they are expected to redefine it in context of American life. Achootan denies to eat badly cooked meat and Saeed also denies to eat a pig, "they dirty man, they massy. First thing I am a Muslim, then I am a zanzibari, then I will be American" (136). Harish Harry who manages Gandhi Café tries to preserve his Indian identity in the face of American nationality. He does not inspire the American bearings and American habits of her daughter. The anguish of

Harish Harry shows that culture is very much a part of religious faith and digressions from it is a perpetual loss.

Kiran Desai ensures that assimilation may be a compulsion but not the willing choice for Indians staying abroad. Even after the four years of stay in America, he failed to adopt the pattern of life recommended by Americans. At every stage of life, they are humiliated and suspected. In spite of this pathetic situation, even retreat is not possible. She records, "In this room it was a fact accepted by all that Indians were willing to undergo any kind of humiliation to get into States. You could heap rubbish on their heads and yet they would be begging to come crawling in" (184).

Kiran Desai accepts that the legal formalities regarding passport and green card is a threat to the process of vital understanding. It is illustrated in the novel through the suffering of an Indian woman who was willing to come back to India. Subsequently, Biju makes efforts to secure a visa to return to Kalimpong. He finds that retreat is the only solution to escape the trauma of cultural crisis. Tom Ashbrook in context of *The Inheritance of Loss* admits:

> In Desai's new novel, there's a trouble in a global village; unresolved rage and anger from colonial days; stunted, alienated half global citizens, first world-third world power imbalance; and a global economy that crushes as fast as it creates.[12]

The resentment of Biju assumes the proportion of violence. He declares that they should also be given equal rights and respects if they are contributing for the survival of American nationality. He cries out:

> Without us living like pigs. What business would you have? This is how you make your money, paying us nothing, because you know, we can't do anything, making us work day and night because we illegal. Why do you support us for our Green Card. (188)

Kiran Desai accepts that growing violence, discontent and terrorism is a sign of the sickness of the social order. Nandy argues:

> A violent and aggressive society produces in its own special brands of victim hood and privileges and ensures a certain continuity between the victor and defeated, the instrument and target.... As a result none of these categories remain pure. So even when such a culture collapse, the psychology of 'victim hood' and privileges continues and produces second culture which is only manifestly not violent and oppressive.[13]

Kiran Desai establishes the harsh reality that the centre holds a power and marginalized immigrants are in clutches of a situation from where the turning back is not possible. Biju still resolutes to turn back. It was a declaration of freedom against the burden in which he was placed. Biju dreams of the emotional meeting with his father on the other far corner of Atlantic. His Gulf Air Flight arrives at Calcutta Dum Dum Airport. Narrating the psyche of these Indian immigrants, she writes, "Indians who lived abroad, Indians who have traveled abroad, richest and poorest, the back and forth ones, pretending it was nothing, trying to be busy, but every molecule tense and self conscious" (290).

The worst aspect of immigration is that it makes discrimination in the home country also. Biju is disgusted to find that even after coming to India, immigrants coming from America with valid green card are given better and prestigious status. Instead of pleasure and peace, she realizes that 'unbearable arrogance and shame of immigrant" (300). He felt exhilerated by the immensity of wilderness, by lunatic creepers, the shooting and hooting abundance of green. But here too, he was robbed by the terrorists. He got a bitter realization that native is no longer available as the pure unadulterated object of orientalist inquiry. The plight is that Third World countries are losing their purity and making a willing surrender to the hegemony of the West. This situation is responsible for the crisis of existence and the "loss of the ancient non-western civilization."[14] She views that immigration has its own complexity and it is not the access of one in other but an interactive two-way process.

Kiran Desai's vision of immigrant's experience has a comprehensive canvas including the socio-cultural perspective, socio-economic arguments and the awareness of the matrix of home and homelessness. The distortion of oppression is rooted in the psyche of immigrants in which there are little possibilities of escape from politics of dominance and subversion. The romantic quest marked by nostalgia, glorification of native tradition, lingering shadows of lost relationship and an urge for native food, language and habits, are not the ultimate periphery of the immigrant experience reconstructed in the text of *The Inheritance of Loss*. There is also a reassessment of East in the context of West and expansion of the horizon of Western thought that can accommodate the best of the Orient without a reciprocal interaction of the two currents of human thought, the comprehensive, humanistic and pluralistic vision of the world remains a utopia. The upliftment of humanity at large beyond the national cultural codes, can ensure a more stable and progressive community pacing fast in search of global society. Desai's vision has come close to the observation of Edward Said:

> Nativism is not the only alternative. There is the possibility of a more generous and pluralistic vision of the World.[15]

NOTES

1. Salman Rushdie, *Imaginary Homelands*, London, Granta Books 1991, p. 12.
2. *Ibid.*, p. 10.
3. Uma Parmeswaran, *Meeting of Stress*, 1989, p. 80.
4. Interview with Laura Barton *Guardian*. Thursday, Oct. 12, 2006.
5. Wikipedia/Kiran Desai.
6. Tribute Time out Mumbai quoted in the text. *The Inheritance of Loss*. New Delhi, Penguin Books, 2006. (All subsequent references cited in this paper are borrowed from this edition only.)
7. Arjun Appaduri, "Disjuncture and Difference in the Global Cultural Economy," *Public Culture*, Vol. 2, No. 2, p. 17.

8. S. Hall, "New Ethenicities in Black Film, British Cinema," *ICA Documents* 7. Institute of Contemporary Arts, London, 1989, p. 227.
9. George Lamming, *The Pleasures of Exile*, London: Michael Joseph, 1960, p. 35.
10. Bill Ashcroft et al. *Empire Writes Back: Theory and Practice in Post Colonial Literature*, London: Routledge 1989, p. 9.
11. Sofran Williams, "Diasporas in Modern Societies: Myths of Homeland and Return" *Diaspora Spring*, 1991.
12. http://www.onpointradio.org/showes/2006/02/20060217-b main.asp.
13. A. Nandy, "Oppression and Human Liberation: Towards a Post Gandhian Utopia", *Political Thoughts in Modern India* (eds.) Thomas Pantham and Kenneth L. Deutsch. Sage, New Delhi, p. 356.
14. R. Chow, *Writing Diaspora: Tactics of Intervention in Contemporary Cultural Studies*. Indian University Press, Bloomington, p. 8.
15. Edward Said, *Culture and Imperialism*. Chatto and Windus, London, 1993, p. 52.

18

Deviating Ambit and Uprooted Sensibilities in *The Inheritance of Loss*

Vandana Singh

Memory can augment an individual's experience of a place and time, enhancing the richness of the idyllic moments, making it colossal. This memory might not hold the same value if it is incorporated in his life on a daily existence. The reality of the place tends to get distorted in our memories with passing time-expunging the fact that with every second, new events transpire. When the individual returns to the same place after a long time he feels disoriented because the place has changed in reality but not in his memory. This fragmentation is self-imposed because he tends to cling and savour his cultural traditions, which is etched on his mind. He physically moves to another place but feels isolated and nostalgic, his memory anchored in the past. An individual can return as a new persona—having struck a balance between the New and the Old, or he might be stuck somewhere in time, oscillating between the New and the Old. Memory tends to authenticate, contradict or completely alter the actual experience of a place. With globalisation, cross-cultural contact is inevitable, and cross-cultural migration leads to intermingling mixture of multiculturalism. The earliest migration of the Jewish people is epochal but the new immigrants move to different places for the enhancement of socio-economic status. The physical move affects the psyche of the individual. Confronted by the alien culture the individual is faced with psycho-emotional imbalance, as there is a conflict between the real and the idealized, and the real self gets subdued bringing about alienation and loss of identity.

The concept of cultural ethnicities becomes the core study of *The Inheritance of Loss*. The cross-cultural ethnic values and their recognition in their respective worlds would implicitly bulwark the development of imperialistic powers. *The Inheritance of Loss* focuses on the problems of illegal immigration in America and infiltration of insurgency in a small town of Kalimpong in India, due to denial of recognition and identity of Gorkhalis by the residents. The protestors are filled with enraged contempt for the postcolonial attitude of the upper class families residing in the town. The plot in India moves parallel to the plot in America where the focus is on the treacherous journey of illegal immigrants, floating rootlessly in search of identity and recognition. Ironically, in India the insurgents force their ways into the strong cauldron of high class society but the illegal immigrants in America are huddled into dark rooms to avoid the faceless government officials, in case they get caught and deported, without realizing their dreams. Biju leaves India to carve a niche for himself in America and, Gyan, a handsome Nepali and Sai's tutor, joins the insurgency in India. Both of them are alienated to their selves and a constant conflict between heart and mind projects the inner trauma of uprootedness. Caught between the web of finding the finer delights of their respective worlds they tend to lose their identity. Nepalis have always served as gatekeepers and watchmen. The majority population of Nepalese were brought to Kalimpong to work on the British tea plantations. The uprising is not taken seriously by the residents of Kalimpong, even when judge's house is ransacked by two young Gorkhalis and the residents are humiliated. The beginning of agitation does not register on the finer sensibilities of the judge, the cook and Sai. Mutt, the dog wags her tail to the strangers. When a case is filed, the police (already bribed by the head of the agitators) laugh and humiliate the judge with his ICS designation and the judge is unable to protest. The scene projects the pathetic condition of people who still cling to their past colonial sensibilities, refusing to acknowledge the attitudinal shift in the society.

The novel depicts the angst of being tortured as lowly beings, without equal rights in a nation they have served for decades. The schism existent within different stratas of society carries through in America. The novel moves back and forth between New York and Kalimpong, reflecting the life of colonial residuum in form of ICS relic judge, digging for the vestige of past glory, Lola and Noni, who read Jane Austen and grow broccoli on Indian soil from English seeds, safely tucked inside the high walls of the Estate with French name 'Mon Ami,' Father Booty who is Swiss, ironically does not wish to leave India from the Indian Galaxy in the novel. The insurgency awakens them all to the realities outside the safe walls, forcing them to recognize their true identities. Ricocheting between two worlds, Kiran Desai focuses on the trauma and tribulations of hyphenated selves in exile in America, interwoven with the torn sensibilities in the sequestered postcolonial ideologies in India. The novel opens with the atmosphere which posits the future of Kalimpong.

> All day, the colors had been those of dusk, mist moving like a water creature across the great flanks of mountains possessed of ocean shadows and depths. Briefly visible above the vapor, Kanchenjunga was a far peak whittled out of ice, gathering the last of the light, a plume of snow blown high by the storms at its summit. Sai, sitting on the veranda, was reading an article about giant squid in an old National Geographic.[1]

On the other side of the world, in the new imperialistic America, Biju is struggling to realize his father's (the cook's) dreams, trying to stay afloat in the dingy environs of dark alleys, changing jobs to find a better life but to no avail, because wherever he might be he is still an illegal immigrant, sleeping among rats. Biju takes the readers on a rendezvous around America on subway trains. Biju is affronted with the reality that Indians are not liked much. He is acquainted with this fact in other kitchens. He is in awe of white people because he associates them with the white colonial masters who had harmed India beyond reparation. What binds all the characters is their shared legacy (historical) and a common experience of humiliation and impuissance. Gyan is a young, handsome Nepalese who is recruited by the judge to tutor Sai. Sai is the judge's granddaughter, orphaned while studying in a convent. She is been raised in the sanitized environs of a Convent, inculcating taste for the refined sensibilities. Orphaned Sai comes to stay with the judge but it is the cook who looks after her. Sai's early tutor Noni is very friendly with her charge but after a certain period she is unable to deal with her studies and then Gyan steps in. A mutual attraction strikes them and the lessons of physics turns into sessions of cajoling and caressing. Unchaperoned, Sai spends time with Gyan, learning the art of kissing. The experiments of physics and interpretation of physical beauty gets enmeshed, giving new definition to Sai's life.

> Sitting across from Gyan, she had felt so acutely aware of herself, she was certain it was because of his gaze on her, but every time she glanced up, he was looking in another direction. She sometimes thought herself, pretty, but as she began to make a proper investigation, she found it was a changeable thing, beauty. No sooner did she locate it than it slipped from her grasp; instead of disciplining it, she was unable to refrain from exploiting its flexibility. She stuck her tongue out at herself.... She transformed her expression from demon to queen.... This plumpness jiggliness firmness softness, all coupled together in an unlikely manner, must surely give her a certain amount of bartering power?[2]

Gyan does respond and their relationship blossoms, but soon their relationship is shrouded by the protests, as the Nepali populace refuses to take a backseat feeling deprived are forced into demanding their own state and ethnic recognition. Living a life of exile in their own nation they forge forward agitating, becoming aggressive and increasingly militant in their action. Their purpose is to dismantle the colonial imperialistic socio-economic conditions that they are forced to bow down to. Castigated from the society, they retaliate by nabbing their tormentors. Gyan sees his friends marching with the protestors and he no longer sees himself as Sai's lover and protector. He is alienated from Sai as well as himself. The conflict inside confuses Gyan and he does not know where his allegiance lies. He takes out his frustration on Sai as he questions her sensibilities, because she likes to celebrate Christmas and not Diwali (symbolic of Christian and Hindu Festivals respectively). A simple answer could have been that Sai is attracted to the light, joy and happy ambience of Christmas and might hate the sound of crackers. But Gyan takes it as an insult to his Hindu sensibilities where he questions her patriotic sensibilities. Gyan's anger is directed to himself because he had enjoyed the same delicacies that Sai had provided him with insurgency impinges on Gyan's soul and destroys his dreams. He wants to be a man who has to show his allegiance to his motherland alias Gorakhaland. He is burdened by these new developments taking place around him.

> There were those who were provoked by the challenge, but Gyan was finding that he wasn't one of these. He was angry that his family hadn't thought to ban him, keep him home. He hated his tragic father, his mother who looked to him for direction, had always looked to him for direction, even when he was a little boy, simply for being male. He spent the nights awake, worrying hc couldn't live up to his proclamations. But then, how could you have any self-respect knowing that you didn't believe in anything exactly? How did you embrace what was yours if you didn't leave something for it? How did you create a life of meaning and pride? (p. 260)

Sai tries to resurrect her past world, which was full of love and Gyan relents a bit, but Sai finds that he is a weak man, not able to stick to one decision.

The uprising has purloined the couple off their right to transcend class differences and become one. Sai degrades herself by literally begging to get back her love but lunges at Gyan for isolating her.

> The simplicity of what she'd been taught wouldn't hold. Never again could she think there was but one narrative

> and that this narrative belonged only to herself, that she might create her own tiny happiness and live safely within it. (p. 323)

Sai who retreats into herself had opened herself to love, who had overlooked the cook's love for her welfare instigates the cook to tell her the secrets of Jemubhai Patel's (the judge) love story. Jemubhai had gone to London to pursue his higher education. After clearing the ICS, had got married to a girl aged 14. Bela was exotic for him and Jemubhai refused to subjugate the girl without her will. Jemubhai, who had cajoled his bride for a bicycle ride full of romantic essence, had turned into an embittered individual when subjected to racialist segregation in England. He is a weak man, a escapist who runs away instead of saving the life of an Indian being beaten by a white. His existence as an exile in London forces him to retreat and he returns as an embittered and humiliated man. In India, he is welcomed as a king and his wife ransacks his belongings taking away the powder-puff. This simple act of sensuality on the part of Bela, his wife, enrages him and an enraged Jemubhai forcefully rapes his wife. He abhors his wife's rustic ways and subjugates her physically and mentally. He detests his Indianized circumstances and subjects his wife to inhuman treatment, beating her out of her senses when he finds out that she had unknowingly attended a lunch with Pt. Nehru and had shaked hands with the Indian leader. Jemubhai's character is weak and broken. He refuses to change. The circumstances can be blamed to a certain extent but with his academic hopes crushed, his failed marriage and his pathetic attachment to his dog, is resultant of Jemubhai's inner conflict. He refuses to reconcile with his circumstances and it proves fatal for him. He is one of those individuals who could not get rid of what he had broken his soul to learn and whose Anglophilia turns into self-hatred. His stoic attitude towards his surroundings stops him from accepting change. He is thoroughly ruined man, who is given into his inner flaws and conflicts. He retreats and give up, reacting only when his dog is stolen. Stealing of his dog seems to be his final humiliation and he turns to God to resurrect his lost inheritance. Every problem has its solution in its womb and an individual has to resolve it, but when inner self is dislocated, the solution seems impossible. The judge's house is the first one to be attacked but he sits in his chair pokerfaced. He has erected the wall around him so that no one can reach him. He goes looking for his dog, lowering himself from his perch to converse with locals who ridicule him, people who have nothing to eat refuse to look out for a dog. The uprighteous judge gets irritated and angry when the dog is referred to as 'Kutti.' The loss is discussed with Father Booty, Uncle Potty, Noni and Lola who symbolise the difference in society. The Anglophile sensibilities clash with the native sensibilities.

> The world had failed Mutt. It had failed beauty; it had failed grace. But by having forsaken this world, for having held himself apart, Mutt would suffer. The judge had lost his clout.... He remembered all of a sudden why he had gone to England and joined the ICS; it was clearer than ever why—but now that position of power was gone, frittered away in years of misanthropy and cynicism. (p. 292)

The world seems to be lost for the elite in Kalimpong. Lola and Noni feel the bite, as their estate is being encroached by the Nepalese insurgents. Their requests to be left alone are sniggered off. Protected inside the high walls of estate with French name Mon Ami is no longer a safe haven. Lola is humiliated by the leader of the protestors who passes derogatory remarks about her physical appearance and lonely existence. He offers to appease her physical needs. Lola returns ashamed and crest-fallen, shuts herself inside the bathroom unable to face the world. Noni and Lola who get Marks and Spencer under-garments to satiate their delicate sensibilities are forced to retreat and awaken to their identity in India. Noni and Lola replicate the English environ and ambience in their lives, living a life with their heads undercover in order to elude the storm, refusing to accept the changing times. They indulge themselves in pretence of being.

> The real place had evaded them. The two of them had been fools feeling they were doing something exciting

> just by occupying this picturesque cottage, by seducing themselves with those old travel books in the library, searching for a certain angled light with which to romance themselves, to locate what had been conjured only as a tale to tell before the Royal Geographic Society.... It was the center for the sisters, but they had never treated it as such.... (p. 247)

The experience of the post colonial elite is bicultural and, biculturalism is an experience full of irony and detachment. Even the cook has his own ghosts to fight with. He is accused of not looking after the dog, Mutt. He is hounded by this fact, transiting into a state of delirium. Loss of Mutt seems to be loss of son. He has been expecting his son to call but the possibility is nullified as the town is under control of the New Power—the protestors. Suddenly the cook is gripped by the universal truth—his son had existed only in his mind. The thought pushes him off the brim, he gets drunk and returns to the judge's house, wakes him and requests him up to beat him. He confesses to the judge about his dealings with the poor fellow souls and how due to his fault Mutt is lost. This Christian-Hindu way of penance reflects how people from lower class get influenced by the ways of elite sensibilities. The cook's poverty is the stimulant in him cheating his master. His son in the New World would bring him the respect and success that he himself could not achieve. Loss of contact with his son in the crucial period proves cataclysmic and he loses touch with reality, feeling lost in the whole Universe.

> The cook didn't mention his son...he had none...he'd never had one...it was just his hope writing to him...Biju was nonexistent.... (p. 321)

Biju, who's been struggling as an undocumented immigrant in America, assuages his homesickness by taking a job in Gandhi Café and sleeps in the rat infested kitchen. He is paid a wage below the minimum and exploited to the maximum. Feeling distraught and homesick he fights back, refusing to work. His contact with Saeed Saeed, an African immigrant, has exposed him to the nuances of his identity and self-respect. His identity as the cook's son in India is submerged under the burden of being an illegal immigrant in America and Biju feels burdened by expansion of his self-consciousness and dilemma about his real identity. Saeed Saeed, who floats rootlessly in the New World is unable to penetrate Biju's psyche, because Biju clings to his memory and his mind is conditioned to the past culture. Biju does not enjoy his undocumented identity and feels humiliated. He also acknowledges the gulf that exists between the green card holders and undocumented immigrants, the elite and the lower class, racism, white and black and Indians and other nationals. Drunken cook asking to be beaten for his wrong doings starkly brings about the difference of class and mentality in India. When Sai visits the cook's quarters both feel ill at ease. Though Sai is close to the cook yet she is different due to her convent education and the cook's semi-literate status—the difference lies in her being an English-speaker and him a Hindi-speaker. The society in India and America is full of dissimilitudes and the characters of Kiran Desai depict the disparity existent in the socio-cultural-economic environs of both the worlds. Biju is closest to Saeed Saeed because when they meet at Queen of Tarts Bakery, Saeed Saeed tells him that he hails from Zanzibar and Zanzibar is full of Indians. He reveals the fact that even his grandmother is an Indian. This creates a special bond between the two and emphatically points out to the melting peripheries of multiculturalism.

> Don't you know?? Zanzibar full of Indians, man! My grand mother—She is Indian! (p. 53)

The disparity in class and attitude is again focused on as Sai visits Gyan's house and looks around the neighborhood. Still she wants to bring Gyan back because she loves him. Both of them fight and loathe each other for the difference of class between them—Sai's attempt to bridge the gap goes in vain because Sai is a foreigner for Gyan, who feels disgusted at his own inferior existence. Gyan decides to return to his roots and fight for a separate Gorkhaland, while Biju frustrated and uprooted in America, returns to India in order to find semblance in the discordant notes that had been tearing him apart in America. He has to smuggle back on a plane that takes a long detour. On his way back he observes the people standing in line to get their tickets and how Indians are left stranded on the airport while Air France caters to French nationale and other people. Couped up is the plane, back to home he realizes his plight but is unaware of the calamity that would befall him on his own homeland. Biju, who had refused to befriend a Pakistani on the ground of preconceived attitudinal problem, is robbed off his rights to live a decent life in Kalimpong. He is forced to escape through the cadaverous forest after being robbed off by the protestors. Everything that he had got from America for his father is taken away and to camouflage his identity as an American immigrant is taken away from him. The dollars earned had been hiding in the sole of his shoes is taken away. Left in an undergarment he is ordered to run to safety. A women's robe is offered to him, which he dons to escape further humiliation. Biju goes to the Land of Dreams with 'Nothing' and returns home with 'Nothing.' He is forced to acknowledge that he had taken a wrong decision to come back home. The dream to use his earning to buy a decent life for himself and his father, crashes as he runs uphill to save himself. Nothing has changed for the hills nor for Biju, Sai, the cook, judge, Noni and Lola. Gyan is lost and Sai awaits his return. Life goes on as it did earlier, except people around have lost their inheritance to live with dignity.

> All night it would rain. It would continue, off and on, on and off, with a savagery matched only by a ferocity with which the earth responded to the onslaught. Uncivilized voluptuous green would be unleashed; the town would slide down the hill. Slowly, painstakingly, like ants, men would make their paths and civilization and their wars once again, only to have it wash away again.... (p. 323)

Kiran Desai deals with themes of globalization modernization, terrorism, multiculturalism, immigrant sensibilities, life's ironies and brutalities—its harshness and humour, human emotions and turmoils, interlinking the intricacies of life with aplomb. The novel ends on a positive note where Sai decides to recreate a new life for herself, taking her own decisions. Biju who had hoped to regain his identity in

India is embraced by an exuberant father. All the characters like the judge, Noni and Lola seem to be stranded in past time, living the life as it used to be. Its another ironical aspect in the novel that Biju (an Indian) wishes to go away from India to realize his dreams and Father Booty (not an Indian) prays to be in India and serve the Indians. Judge's adherence to hatreds learned in England collates to his love for British sensibilities in India. Gyan's allegiance to the Nepalese insurgency is antithetical to his family's allegiance and contribution to British army in India. The two Anglophilic Indian women discuss V.S. Naipaul's *A Bend in the River* criticizing him for not unburdening his past legacy, they talk about Naipaul's ignorance of a New England emerging, a completely different cosmopolitan society, where Chicken Masala Tikka had replaced Chips and Fish, but are unable to adjust to the new boundaries being erected inside their safe compound. Modern world which changes every second, peripheries change and cultures merge and submerge to create the New World—Sai resolves to be free of past and stay afloat in the present to engrave her future.

> Time past and time future
> Allow but a little consciousness
> To be conscious is not to be in time
> But only in time can the moment in the rose garden,
> Be remembered; involved with past and future.
> Only through time time is conquered.
> (Four Quartets 16)

NOTES

1. Kiran Desai: *The Inheritance of Loss*, p. 1.
2. *Ibid.*, p. 74.

19

An Eco-critical Reading of Kiran Desai's *The Inheritance of Loss*

Neeta Kulshrestha

Besides being an era of progress in science and technology, ours is also an age of environmental destruction which is the result of man's disconnection from natural world. It is not only the consequence of increasing use of technology in human life but also an imperceptible change in man's mentality that fails to recognize the inter-relationship of all things existing in the universe. All the developments of science, technology and commerce, in the name of progress, are mainly anthropocentric (human centred) and definitely neglect the claims of our natural environment. Such a disbalanced view of progress in due course of time compelled man to make his approach bio-centric (earth centred) so that the natural environment may be protected and its balance with human life may be maintained. Eco-criticism, a relatively new branch of literary criticism is obviously the result of the new consciousness that very soon, "there will be nothing beautiful (or safe) in nature to discourse about, unless we are very careful."[1] The term 'eco-criticism' was first used by William Rueckert in his essay *Literature and Ecology: An Experiment in Ecocriticism*, published in 1978. Here he defined it as "the application of ecology and ecological concept of the study of literature."[2] The extensive use of the term started with WLA Conference in USA in 1989, when Cheryll Glotfelty, an Associate Professor of Literature and the Environment at the University of Nevada, Reno, revived the term and made an appeal to its adoption to refer the dispersed critical field, previously known as 'the study of nature writing.' Later, with the publication of two seminal works *The Ecocriticism Reader*, edited by Cheryll Glottetty and Harold Fromm, and *The Environmental Imagination* by Lawrence Buell, in 1996, the term heralded with a boom.

Since the 60s, the main emphasis of academic and research studies has been on class, gender race and post-colonial perspective, but during the last twenty years, attempts are also made by a few thinkers to critically analyse post modernity linked dangers for the natural world. They stressed the need of expanding the notion of 'the world,' not limited to human beings but including the entire ecosphere:

> A new paradigm has to emerge to assert the original, greater and all important reality of life, destiny and mankind. An emergent civilization has to find its clue in a unified flow of cosmic power in making up a single verse of the Universe: Life.[3]

Jonathan Bate, Professor of English Literature at the University of Liverpool, published his famous book *Romantic Ecology, Wordsworth and the Environmental Tradition* in 1991 where he read the writings of the romantic poets to seek a balance of culture and nature debate. He calls Wordsworth to be an example of eco-critical thinker who views nature not as an outward entity but an integral part of human sensibility. His appeal to human beings to "see into the life of things" clearly indicates his anxiety about the growing indifferent attitude of man towards nature. Brain Clarke's award winning novel *Stream* is also an eco-consciously written text, revealing a section of river, which during the period of five years transforms from a flourishing stream of clear water to a stinking ditch of contaminated water, causing destruction to whole of the ecosystem, that remains effective in water. Bate's *The Song of the Earth* (Picador, 2000) is the latest contribution to the field of eco-criticsm. Here he makes a plea for "an imaginative re-unification of mind and nature." He argues that if ecology is the "language about our earthly dwelling place" (an idea he has taken from Heideggar) a place from which we have become divorced, then literature can return us to it. "There is a need to recover a more visceral response to what literature can do," he explains.[4]

Compelled by the idea of saving the environment from total chaos, a number of creative writers of last two decades, made it a point to deal with nature as an important entity in their literary texts. When these texts are studied from eco-critical perspective, the reader finds the inter-relatedness of all factors within the ecosystem like social, political and phenomenon of natural world. Even the physical setting in the plot of the literary text plays an important role in the total understanding of its meaning. The novel *Inheritance of Loss* by Kiran Desai is undoubtedly a saga of the modern society at global level. The securing images of the distortion of natural environment and its impact on the survival of man has become an integral life spirit of the text. The eco-critical insight undertaken in this paper would contribute to a new dimension of thought, communicated through the text of the novel.

The novel appeals the reader at the very first reading, for its eco-centred approach:

> (Kiran's) description of mountains and the people of Kalimpong, the changing seasons and the inner mindscape of her characters are mesmerizing.[5]

It opens with reader's encounter with the description of natural beauty of Mount Kanchenjunga with its 'wizard phosphorescence.' The house in which a retired judge with his orphaned granddaughter Sai, a servant and a dog, Mutt, lives is situated at a place from where the beautiful treasure of nature can be easily enjoyed. "The rooms were spacious in the old manner of wealth, windows placed for snow views."[6] It is an old house and stands in true testimony of contemporary eco-friendly architect where one can receive maximum of nature's blessings. Though it is winter season and the surroundings are very cool, nature proves to be a source of energy to Sai, the judge and even to Mutt. They are involved in their activities and simultaneously enjoying the pleasures of natural beauty. They prefer to sit in veranda because "inside the house, it was still colder, the dark, the freeze, contained by stone walls several feet deep (p. 1). The approaching evening and misty environment could not hamper the spirit of Sai rather she gets motivated by them and begins to walk into the garden. She feels human like existence of nature:

> The caress of the mist through her hair seemed human and when she held her fingers out, the vapours took them gently into its mouth. (p. 2)

The mist covers everything, it indicates cessation of activities and finally Sai also stopped to further wait for Gyan, her mathematics teacher. In a way, it may be asserted that nature is a source of energy for those who look at it in an eco-friendly manner like Sai. It guides them to act and react in the existing circumstances and in a way inter-related to human life. The portrayal of characters who act according to the will of nature definitely hints at novelist's purpose to present a text which not only revolves round their mechanical action but also portrays them as active entities in the total planning of nature.

The point is, human consciousness cannot be separated from the consciousness in Nature, even Nature that is still to us a supernature.[7]

In contrast to the peaceful and serene atmosphere, the novelist has also portrayed the efforts of those who intentionally wish to break the lovable bonds which unite man and nature. Their only wish is to establish their supremacy by disturbing its peace. "They had come through the forest on foot in leather jackets from Kathmandu black market..." (p. 4). They are the young boys who have been demanding for a separate Gorkhaland. They used to disturb the silence of nature by firing the bullets. Their job is to terrorize people and rob their wealth, specially their guns. Here the novelist has tried to show how a changed mentality of a few persons may easily disturb the balanced, eco-friendly lifestyle of a larger population. Terrorist activities, motivated by political reasons, easily turn heaven-like nature into a hellish experience. Kiran Desai like an eco-critic maintains here:

> Nature really exists out there beyond ourselves, not needing to be ironised as a concept by enclosure within knowing inverted commas but actually present as an

> entity which affects us, and which we can affect, perhaps fatally, if we mistreat it.[8]

Otherwise, most of the population of the area lives, maintaining a harmony with nature. Even in the special hatts of Kalimpong, the products those are sold, do not have any chemical treatment, rather they are in natural form—"...muddy mushrooms, covered with brackish leaves or greenery, already half-cooked in the sun. Powders, oils and ganglions of roots were proffered by Lepcha medicine men" (p. 83). When the cook looks at the dried azalea and juniper in the hatt, he remembers the day when "they had burnt this incense all along the path" (p. 84) on the arrival of Dalai and Panchen Lamas in Kalimpong and the whole of the atmosphere was full of refreshing smell. But today's "greasy bus station with its chocking smell of exhaust" (p. 84) appears to be in complete contrast of that day. Hostile treatment of nature in the hands of human being definitely affects human life adversely and gives rise to various problems.

> Like Goethe's sorcerer's apprentice, we have turned the tap on of technology without being able to control the flow. When mechanization takes over, the laws of life are bound to be trampled upon.[9]

The growing discontent, anxiety, persistent insecurity and faithlessness are the natural consequences of the ravishing scenario of nature. Besides mental imbalance, physical health is in continuous peril at the face of increasing anti-human and anti-ecological activities.

Sometimes, our ecosystem gets disturbed in the name of national security and protection of cultural heritage. Those who used to live the place in complete harmony with nature are turned off in the name of big political jargons, especially in "areas of high sensibility" (p. 221) like Kalimpong. Father Booty who used to live here for more than forty years, all of a sudden is asked about his nationality and the decision is taken by the government authorities to turn him off from his fine and beautiful shelter:

> Father Booty felt his heart fail at the thought of his cows being turned out in favour of army tanks, looked about

> at his craggy but of mountain side—violet bamboos, orchids and pale ginger lilies.... Such wilderness could not incite a gentle love—he loved it fiercely intensely. (p. 220)

He is a man who "had done much more for development in the hills than any of the locals" (p. 223) but he becomes the easy victim of political prejudices and has to sacrifice his love for nature's creation silently. The district like Darjeeling which used to be famous for three Ts 'Tea,' 'Timber' and 'Tourism' gradually loses its attraction under the army operation and whole of the natural set-up gets disturbed. Increasing militant activities against Gorkha Movement (GNLF) disturb whole of the life cycle of local inhabitants: "Nobody came to Himalayan Hotel," "The Company guests houses closed" (p. 237). The novelist has portrayed realistically the pathetic conversion of a beautiful place from its dignified state to a place of terrorist and militant activities. It is not only the increasing use of science and technology that is disturbing our balanced ecosystem but the increasing terrorist activities are also responsible for it. Man is not satisfied merely by living with nature rather he wants to establish his supremacy by conquering it. The name of Tenzing is mentioned with pride as he for the first time stuck his flag on the highest peak of Himalayas but:

> Sai had wondered, should human conquer the mountains or should they wish for the mountains to possess them? (p. 155)

Through the reaction of Sai, the novelist has tried to point out that man's will to conquer nature definitely hints at his sense of superiority and pride over nature.

Perfect symbiosis of man and nature is possible only through the feeling of love. Man's intense desire to be independent gradually lessens his love for nature, though nature has always been congenial to the feelings of love. Kiran Desai has proved it through a number of instances in the novel. Not only love between Sai and Gyan but also love between her parents initiated and bloomed, getting sustenance from nature. Her parents met for the first time in a "public park" in Delhi. Her mother, then a student, used to go to dry her hair in the "shade and quiet of a neem tree" and her father, Mr. Mistry used to go there for jogging.

They became acquainted in this grassy acre, cows tethered to enormous rusty lawn mowers slowly grinding back and forth before a crumbling Mughal tomb (p. 26).

Thus, nature promotes that sensibility which is the foundation for human love and can invoke passions that can perpetualize human relationship. The love story of Sai and Gyan, her mathematics teacher gets refreshed time to time by the tender touches of nature. Both of them love to enjoy the beauties of nature and feel enlightened in its lap. Gyan "enjoyed the walk to Cho Oyu and experienced a refreshing and simple happiness, although it took him two hours uphill" (p. 72). Similarly, Sai's happiness knows no bounds in the monsoon months. Throughout the time she remains calm and cheerful. Concerning the seasons, Kiran Desai, employ 'rain' as a central metaphor to reveal the love relationship. Sai and Gyan also could not save themselves from its spell bound charm. Their emotions get uncontrollable midst the gusty winds of monsoon.

> A fine drizzle spelled an ellipsis on the tin roof....
>
> Moments clocked by precisely and finally she couldn't bear it—she closed her eyes and felt the terrified measures of his lips on hers, trying to match one shape with the other. (p. 125)

Even the nick names they selected for each other were taken from the beautiful objects of nature—Sai called Gyan "Kaju" and he called her "Kishmish." Though the novel establishes the fact that the relationship between the judge and his wife was not cordial and he never gave her the status equal to him, he remembers, even after thirty or forty years, the time when he offered her a ride on his father's Hercules Cycle, first time after his marriage:

> They went faster and faster, between the trees and cows, whizzing through the cow pats and ultimately...the ground sloped, and as they flew down the incline, their hearts were left behind for an instant, levitating amid green leaves, blue sky. (p. 92)

The impressions of this first experience of love are the integral part of the subconscious of judge because it is inevitably associated with the beauty of nature. It signifies that man's association with nature has a deeper and profound relationship corresponding with his relationship with external variables.

Nature is the source of enormous energy, provided we aspire to use it. In the world of today, man suffers from the permanent fatigue syndrome and to overcome it, the easiest way is the lap of nature, where nature would heal our impaired faculties and rejuvenate us for further efforts. The judge in the novel has a past which he does not wish to revive at least before others. When his granddaughter asks him about her grandmother, he intentionally avoids her but simultaneously gets disturbed by this reference and abruptly leaves his moves on the chess board.

> ...then he got up and walked into the garden. Flying squirrels chased one another through the circination of fern and mist, the mountains were like ibex horns piercing through. He returned to his chessboard and made his move.... (p. 89)

Thus, nature provides him with the impetus with which he can fight with himself and may overcome his weaknesses. Disturbed mental state and feeling of irritation check him from making a move on chess but the refreshing scene of nature boosts him up to overcome this negative feeling and ultimately he makes the right move on the chessboard. Fresh air, which is gradually becoming a dream in the metropolitans, heals us not only physically but also mentally. When Sai, feels nausea and begins to vomit, Noni advises her "Take some deep breaths, dear, that food was very greasy, they've really gone downhill—dirty kitchen—Oh, just the sight of that waiter should have been enough to warn us" (p. 215). Even Father Booty stretches himself in the lap of nature after his exhaustive journey in car and gets back his lost vitality:

> Father Booty got out himself, walked up and down, stretching his limbs, glad of the rest of his aching behind, when he spotted a remarkable butterfly. (p. 216)

Our relationship with nature is a matter of faith. The more we rely on it, the better is our realization of its blessings. It also becomes synonymous to God, provided we try to understand its mystery. When the SDO looks at the beautiful flowering creeper in the garden of the judge, he says:

> Beautiful Blossoms, Justice Sahib. If you see such a sight, you will know there is a God.

Though a man of police, he loves such a beautiful creation of nature and looks after his plants exactly "as if they were babies" (p. 226). The observation of SDO justifies that in order to avoid the growing chaos in the life of modern man, it is necessary that man must make efforts to revive and re-establish the bonds of kinship with the spectacle of nature.

Judge's love for Mutt, the female dog, in the novel also hints at the fact that nature through her creation definitely supplies to us whatever we miss in our life. The hollowness which he faces at emotional level gets compensated in his love for Mutt. Her presence in the home is more important than any other member of the family. She responds positively to his feelings and sincerely understands his love:

> Mutt followed him to his room. As he sat brooding, she leaned against him with the ease that children have when leaning against their parents. (p. 113)

A sense of loss that haunts judge's mind, he wants to mitigate in his possession of such a fine creature as Mutt. He calls her by sweet names like 'my darling,' 'my darling mutton chop,' etc. Such an affinity with animal species too indicates man's dependence on nature's creation which definitely has an embalming and healing influence on injured psyche of man.

Kiran Desai's *The Inheritance of Loss* is a text with new alertness to the present day need of ecological holiness. Nature has been interwoven with text in such an artistic manner that it has become a persistent presence guiding, motivating, inspiring and enlightening those who read it. The novel deals not only with the lifestyle of the inhabitants of Kanchenjunga but also its landscape. It reminds us of non-human perspectives like trees, rivers, mountains and animals and their relevance in the total understanding of environment. Nature is rapidly being gobbled up by culture nowadays, so ecological balance is the foremost need of today and the novelist has tried to intensify this need through the text. Negation of the idea of interconnectedness of all things, existing in the world, gives rise to a disbalanced human life having various social, emotional, psychological and health problems. The socio-political scenario of the present world also works as a catalyst to enhance the gravity of the problem. The ecocentric texts can at least sensitize people to think seriously about these problems and to find out a solution for it. Kiran Desai's efforts in this direction are praise worthy as through his novel Inheritance of Loss, she affirms that the plight of modern man is integrated not only in socio-political concerns but also in a manifestation of man's growing insensibility towards inherited environment.

NOTES

1. Pramod K. Nayar, *Literary Theory Today* (Asia Book Club, New Delhi, 2006), p. 291.
2. Reprinted in Cheryl Glotfelty and Harold Fromm, ed. *The Ecoriticism Reader: Landmarks in Literary Ecology* (University of Georgia Press, Athens and London, 1996), p. 107.
3. Lokesh Chandra, "Creativity and Environment" in Vidhya Niwas Misra, ed. *Creativity and Environment* (Sahitya Academy, New Delhi, 1992), p. 55.
4. James Hopkins, "In the Green Team", *Archive*, May 12, 2001. http://www.guardian.co.uk/Archive/Article/0,4273,485023.00.html
5. Quoted from "The Praise for the Book" published on the very first page of the novel itself, from *The Sunday Express*.
6. Kiran Desai, *The Inheritance of Loss* (Penguine Books India Pvt. Ltd., New Delhi), 2006, pp. 6-7. (The subsequent references are from the same publication and are mentioned with page numbers in brackets.)
7. Sisir Kumar Ghose, "Creativity: The Ecological Challenge", Vidhya Niwas Misra (Ed.) *Creativity and Environment* (Sahitya Academy, New Delhi, 1992), p. 114.
8. Peter Barry, *Beginning Theory: A Introduction to Literary and Cultural Theory* (Viva Publication, 2007), p. 252.
9. Sisir Kumar Ghose, *op. cit.*, p. 111.

20

Portrayal of Relations in Kiran Desai's *The Inheritance of Loss*

Anju Bala Agrawal

The Inheritance of Loss tells parallel stories set in post-colonial India and the United States simultaneously. The range of Kiran Desai is not narrow, limited to the family life of middle class families. Though many successful writers have dealt with typical middle class housewives and have been successful, Kiran has tried to raise several angles of relations in human life. "Human Relationship is what a writer is involved with. Person to person and person to society relationships—these are the two primary concerns of a certain writer."[1] *The Inheritance of Loss* is a saga of parallel stories of relations. The judge Jemu Patel is the center of almost all relationships delineated in the novel.

The novel is set in Kalimpong, a small city at the foot of the Himalayas and a part of the novel shows the United States. All relations revolve round these two places along with descriptions of some other places. The main character in the novel is the retired judge Jemubhai who lives alone in a house in Kalimpong. Originally, he belonged to a small place called Piphit. His father was a poor man but had an ambition of sending his son to England for higher studies. He had not money enough to send Jemu to England, so he goes to several moneylenders but in vain. An idea comes to his mind that money can be got if Jemu gets married. The dowry will be used to send Jemu England. He was so passionate to send his son

England that he was ready to compromise with any girl only if he gets a huge amount of money. A dark and ugly daughter of a rich man seemed their best bet."[2] Jemu was lucky that the offer comes from a rich merchant of Piphit. The merchant thought if Jemu succeeded, he would be the father-in-law of the most powerful man in India, perhaps a bargain to enhance his business. So the merchant, Boman Bhai Patel goes to Jemu's house with the offer of his most beautiful daughter, Bela. The offer is accepted and the bride brings a huge amount of dowry with her.

> The dowry included cash, gold, emeralds from Venezuela, rubies from Burma, uncut kundan diamonds, a watch on watch chain, lengths of woolen cloth for her new husband to make into suits in which to travel to England, and in a crisp envelope, a ticket for passage on the SS Strathnavar from Bombay to Liverpool. (p. 91)

The family sells the jewels to get money to send Jemu to England. At the time of marriage, Jemu was twenty years old. When he returned after five years, he was a totally changed person, thinking himself as a foreigner in his own home. When everyone was curious and excited at his returning home, he behaved in a strange manner shouting wildly and making fuss for his smallest possession. The relatives, with whom he had a rapport, became strangers to him. He couldn't tolerate any one. His wife, who attracted him at the time of marriage, did not attract him. In fact, he forgot that he was a married man.

> He did not like his wife's face, searched for his hatred, found beauty, dismissed it. Once it had been a terrifying beckoning thing that had made his heart turn to water, but now it seemed beside the point. An Indian girl could never be as beautiful as an English one. (p. 168)

He takes his wife to Bonda, the place of his first posting in India, but now she is only a means for satisfaction of sexual desires. She is a simple, illiterate girl born and brought up behind curtains. He wants his wife to be English speaking and well to do lady, so he arranges a tutor for her. Nimi is too simple to learn English and other worldly ways. She can't stand on equal terms with her husband. These things irritate him so much that he behaves brutally with her. He beats her mercilessly and never allows her to go out of the house. Living alone in the house, she is at the verge of losing mental control. Suddenly, he gets a chance to send her to her parental home and thus gets rid of her. Perhaps he does not know that she was pregnant at that time. She gives birth to a girl child. After childbirth, she is expelled even from her parental home by her uncle. After the birth of a child, Jemu's father comes to him and requests him to keep Nimi with him. Jemu was too rigid to be persuaded. In fact, his behaviour with his father was like a stranger. The money, power and education had suppressed the emotions and feelings in his heart. He does not have a contact with his family also. The judge no doubt was an Indian and lived in India but his habits and his demeanour was more of a foreign nature because of his sojourn in the foreign land. He had been rude and extremely cruel towards his Indian docile wife who suffered mutely and perished miserably in the end.

As regards to the relationship between husband and wife which is considered to a primary type of relationship and a life long devotion of each partner to other, the judge fails in this affair. In Indian society, especially in Hindus, marriage is considered a sacred institution. "Marriage denotes those unequivocally sanctioned union which persist beyond sexual satisfaction and thus come to understand family life."[3]

Atrocities committed by the judge to his wife Nimi have been shown in a parallel way by the loving life of Joydeep and Lola. Joydeep had a romantic notion of living in countryside, so he sells his property of Calcutta and settles in Kalimpong. He leads a happy life with his wife Lola but death deprives Lola of this happiness. After the death of Joydeep, she lives with her sister Noni. Both sisters lived together on his pension but the insufficiency was to be met out someway for which Noni took up the tutor's job offered by the judge. The tumult that arises in Kalimpong leaves a lasting impression on Lola. The GNLF have made illegal huts on her Mon Ami property. In order to get rid of this encroachment, she pays a visit to Pradhan, the flambuoyant head of the Kalimpong Wing of the GNLF. She complains against his men but he does not accept this encroachment. He along with his men insults her so much that one may commit suicide out of shame and anger. She feels the loss of her husband and yearns for her husband. First, she blames him but later she consoles herself recollecting the happy days she had spent with him.

> Your eyes are lovely, dark and deep.
> He used to kiss those glistening orbs when he departed to work on his files.
> But I have promises to keep
> first one eye then the other—
> And miles to go before I sleep—
> And miles to go before I sleep?
> she would make a duet—
> And miles to go before I sleep—
> He would echo.
> To the end, and even beyond, he could resurrect the wit that had fired her love when they were not much more than children. (p. 246)

Thus, Desai has portrayed different aspects of husband-wife relationship. People like the judge are still a part of Indian society. Even in twenty-first century we can get several examples when an illiterate and simple wife is renounced for the sake of modernity as she proves misfit in social status of a high-posted man.

Next, we can see a detailed description of parental roles. Desai shows a clear and parallel description of a parent-child relationship. The judge as a father is a total failure. He did not even see the face of her daughter. Often fathers are very curious and feel ecstatic at the birth of the first child. His condition was different. His daughter had a loveless childhood due to her mother's untimely death and father's pernicious influence. This led his daughter, marry a young man, whom she loved and who in return satiated her parched life. But as fate would have it, the judge's granddaughter who was an absolute stranger to him and vice-versa came to stay with him forever as a result of the demise of her parents at a road accident. The judge's feeling, towards his granddaughter was no more than he had for his wife or daughter. Rather, he loved and cherished his dog Mutt much more than them. His attitude likes him more to the Britishers who valued the pets more than the Indians, who were human beings and precious creations of God. When Sai comes to live with him, he keeps her in his house with the reason that "It would be good to have an unpaid somebody in the house to help with things as the years went by" (p. 210). He does not hate her as he hates his other family members after returning from England but we do not find a single incident where he spends a happy time or showers parental affection on the orphaned girl. Both feel uneasy in each other's company. In India, it is said that interest is dearer than the principal money, i.e. grand children are more darlings than own kids. The judge as a grandparent is a feelingless figure. Whatever may be the cause, but he is totally devoid of all emotions. Kiran Desai seems to have a good understanding of relations that she has been able to portray such a stonyhearted egoist figure.

As contrasted to the judge, the cook is "a powerless man, barely learning to read and write, had worked like a donkey all his life, hoped only to avoid trouble, lived only to see his son" (p. 11). With preparing tea for the judge and milk for his pet at 4.30 a.m., his day begins and he works till late in the night. The rigors that he ceaselessly undergoes tell upon his health. To quote him: "Terrible! My bones ache so badly, my joints hurt? may as well be dead. If not for Biju" (p. 3).

The novel contains a suggestive reference to the life of poverty the cook is doomed to live with a few cheap domestic items at his disposal.

> It pained Sai's heart to see how little he had: a few clothes hung over a string, a single razor blade and a sliver of cheap brown soap, a Kulu blanket that had once been hers, a cardboard case with metal clasps that had belonged to the judge and now contained the cook's papers, the recommendations that had helped him procure his job with the judge, Biju's letters, papers from a court case fought in his village all the way in Uttar Pradesh over the matter of five mango trees that he had lost to his brother. And, in the sateen elastic pocket

> inside the case, there was a broken watch that would cost too much to mend, but was still too precious to throwaway? he might be able to pawn the parts. (p. 13)

Already deprived of money, the cook got deprived of his wife at a crucial time of his life. His son Biju was just five when destiny took her away from this world—making cook's life more miserable:

> She had died seventeen years ago, when Biju was five, slipping from a tree while gathering leaves to feed the goat. An accident, they said, and there was nobody to blame—it was just fate in the way fate has of providing the destitute with a greater quota of accidents for which nobody can be blamed. (p. 14)

The judge is insensitive to the hardships that his cook's life is beset with. Whenever the cook prays for an increase in salary, he is rebuked in harsh words to which he has become accustomed. Judge's insensitivity to cook's pathetic condition fills the heart of his granddaughter Sai with annoyance at her grandfather and sympathy for the cook. Expressing her sympathetic attitude towards the cook's family she says:

> They are the poorest family in the village. Their house is still made of mud with a thatch roof. (p. 67)

Villagers tell Biju that his wife's ghost is threatening to take Biju with her. The village priest asks him to sacrifice a chicken to pacify the soul. He wants to do it for the sake of his son. When the judge refuses to let the cook go for this superstitious work, he makes a false story of the roof of his village, having blown off again in the latest storm. This act of Biju may be superstitious but it shows the intensity of love how a father is concerned for the welfare of his son. Such things happen even today in all parts of India. Here kids are not allowed to earn at an adolscent stage. Parents try to look after them even at the cost of their health, wealth and comfort. It also presents a strong contrast of the judge's behaviour towards his daughter.

The cook is very curious to send his son to America. When he sees an advertisement of recruitment for cooks in abroad, he tries his best to take the advantage of this chance. He arranges several recommendations for his son's selection like a typical Indian father. Along with a medical certificate, he deposits his hard-earned eight thousand rupees as a processing fee and the cost of training camp. His efforts prove useless as the recruiting company proves to be a fake one. He is not disheartened. He has courage enough to take a second chance and luckily Biju is successful in going to America. His happiness knows no bound when his son is selected as a waiter in an American restaurant. To whomsoever he meets after getting the news of his son's selection he reveals his happiness and boastfully says, "My son works for the Americans" (p. 14). Having been victimized by the judge, the cook and his son repose greater trust in foreigners than in Indians. Biju is very happy to know that the manager of the restaurant is American and not Indian. In his letter addressed to his father he writes:

> Respected pitaji, no need to worry. Everything is fine. The manager has offered me a full-time waiter position. Uniform and food will be given by them. Angrezi Khana only, no Indian food, and the owner is not from India. He is from America itself. (p. 14)

The cook believes in earning and saving money, but doing it at the cost of health is not his cup of tea. It was for Biju that he ignored his health. His following advice to his son is of great relevance in the modern time of gross materialism and consumerism:

> Make sure you are saving money. Don't lend to anyone and be careful who you talk to. There are many people out there who will say one thing and do another. Liars and cheats. Remember also to take rest. Make sure you eat enough. Health is wealth. (p. 18)

Biju does not get proper job in America. He leads a very hard life. Often he has to change his job. His visa has expired and he does not have enough money to purchase a return ticket but he does not let his father know about his condition, as it would disturb him. This shows that the concern is not from father's side but the son is equally concerned. When Biju comes to know about the turmoil arising in Kalimpong, he is worried about his father. Somehow he gets money to make a phone call to his father and asks about his welfare. Later, he prepares himself fully to return to India. Biju feels a kind of emptiness, as he can't talk to his father in detail. He feels a deep anguish in his heart and a vague yearning hovers in him that "if he continued his life in New York, he might never see his pitaji." He thereby makes a strenuous effort to return and manages to fulfill his desire. He somehow gets a return ticket and returns to India. The cook finally gets his son Biju back. But his journey was so miserable due to Biju being fleeced at every step back to Cho Oyu that a compassionate reader is in tears. The poor chap reaches his dear old father in a tattered and mud smeared night-gown as all his belongings along with his clothes had been snatched away on the way back. Nevertheless, the weak old eyes did not fail to recognize his son and the reunion was remarkable for the reason that love is yet not lost and where there is will, there is a way. Despite all hardships, the father and son meet and the wide distance between them has not lessened their love for each other.

Thus, we can see how powerful is the bond between father and son. The judge is devoid of this bond. He does not shower love on his granddaughter and in return he does not find the concern of Sai towards him as Biju and the cook are concerned of each other in spite of their poverty.

Desai has also depicted the adolscent love affair. She has given the minute shades of love between Sai and Gyan, her maths tutor. Sai got proper guidance from Noni to move ahead in life disregarding the strenuous circumstances. Sai would have to break the shackles of adult restrictions and go ahead with her dreams and aspirations to materialize them and make her life successful by serving a remarkable niche for her in society. Absence of love, affection and craving for attachment takes her nearer to Gyan and made her cling on to him for support. Gyan came to her life when Sai was sixteen and Noni suddenly discovered that she was unable to teach physics to Sai. Gyan was then appointed her physics teacher. Ever since Sai had come to Kalimpong, elderly crowd consisting of Lola, Noni, Uncle Potty and Father Booty, the judge and the cook had surrounded her. Gyan was a pleasant change for Sai being nearer to her age. His pleasant demeanor made her believe that there was brighter side of life and other things worthy to live for.

After Gyan's arrival in her life, she feels about herself for the first time. All the emotions, feelings and imaginations of adolscent stage suddenly attack at her. Suddenly she 'had felt so acutely aware of herself.' "That night Sai sat and stared into the mirror" (p. 74) like a teenager, she becomes conscious of her appearance with a vague yearning to attract Gyan towards her. Till now she had been living in the company of two handy legged men over the days. "Over the days, she found herself continually obsessed with her own face" (p. 74). She suddenly begins to understand love and is curious to know about the love affairs of others. She inquires the cook about the judge and his wife. She presents herself in all her glory before Gyan. Gyan, a young man of twenty, is also attracted towards her. Their romance flourishes even when the trouble has started in Kalimpong. They are so much engrossed in love that they use nicknames for each other.

> Gyan said: "you are my momo"
>
> Sai said: "No, you're mine."
>
> "kismish," he called her to cover it up and "kaju," she called him. (p. 140)

Sai goes on excursions with Gyan and visits almost each and every place of Darjeeling and other picnic spots. Gyan's feelings towards Sai are volatile whereas Sai considered her feelings towards Gyan with substantial seriousness. Somehow, the upsurge in Kalimpong takes Gyan in its grip. Gyan sees a procession in the market demanding Gorkhaland. He sees his friends as a part of this procession. Out of curiosity, he also joins the procession. The procession ends with the speech of a leader. The speech of the leader affects him so much that he becomes aware of the deficiencies in his life and begins to compare his poverty with the luxuries that Sai enjoys.

Thus, when Neps revolted against the glowing impact of the outsiders, the Bongs with clear animosity, Gyan shifted his loyalties from Sai to the revolution. Neps considered themselves strangers in their own homeland and for this they held Bongs responsible who took away the key posts from them and subsequently they were forced to lead the life of an underdog. The sudden change of nature from a docile boy into a raging young man ready to hurt Sai to soothe his seething heart hurt Sai to a great extent for she had been getting gradually serious about her relationship with Gyan. Kiran Desai has admirably shuffled with the fluctuating graph of feelings in her novel. This fluctuation has been successful in keeping our curiosity to know the outcome, alive throughout the novel.

Next, we can see the relationship between the master and the servant that is between the judge and the cook. The cook is a permanent servant. He looks after the household work as a wife looks after in Indian middle class families but the judge's attitude towards the cook is like an authoritative master. He does not understand his poverty and helplessness. His opinion about the poor is like a typical moneylender.

> Give these people a bit and one could find oneself supporting the whole family forever after, a constantly multiplying family, no doubt, because they might have no food, the husband might be blind and with broken legs, and the woman might be anemic and bent, but they'd still pop out an infant every nine months. If you let such peopled get an inch, they'd take everything you had. (p. 264)

As is evident from the above passages, the general perception of the poor is marked with contempt for all that they do. The cook is treated badly by the judge only because he is poor. His devotion to his master goes unrewarded. All that he gets in lieu of his twenty-four hours of service is the little money that he spends on himself and his son Biju. For the low payment that he gets monthly he performs all kinds of domestic chores including preparing and serving of tea and food, polishing of shoes, washing and ironing of clothes, cleaning of utensils, taking care of the dog and so on and so forth. In spite of doing all these things sincerely and diligently he is often abused and even sometimes beaten by the judge. In fact, "It was his habit to be a master and the cook's to be a servant" (p. 209). The disappearance of judge's pet adds to his plight. The judge holds him responsible for the loss of his pet and threatens to kill him if the dog is not retrieved. Unable to find the dog despite all the possible efforts, the cook one day drinks heavily and in a state of intoxication requests the judge to punish him for his negligence in looking after the dog. This infuriates the judge to the extent that he beats the cook with his slipper. The judge repeatedly kicks and hits with "all the force of his sagging, puckering flesh" (p. 321). The cook bears all this mutely only because he is without money. Once he had rightly said "Terrible to be a poverty stricken man, terrible, terrible, terrible..." (34).

Desai has presented a parallel picture of relationship while dealing with other relations, but the relationship of a master and a servant is the same everywhere. She has shown this aspect how Biju suffers in America while working in different restaurants. An example is noteworthy. Biju, while working in Harish-Harry's kitchen, slips on some rotten spinach and gets his knee hurt. He was unable to get up so he asks Harish-Harry to get a doctor. The master, who used to shed tears in the lap of Biju, suddenly changes and denies his responsibility of arranging a doctor. "I take you in. I hire you with no papers, treats you like my own son and now this what you repays me! Living here rent-free.... YOU should have to pay ME for not cleaning, living like a pig. Am I telling YOU to live like a pig?" (p. 188). This shows that there may be changes in other relations and their values and norms but there is no change in master-servant relationship. It appears to be a universal relationship.

Desai has also given some nuances of friendship also. We see the friendship of Uncle Potty and Father Booty. Both of them are persons of different nature yet, it is the friendship that's why Father Booty began to think himself as an inhabitant of this place. He purchases a plot of land in the name of his friend and made a house. He used to call his house 'Sukhtara.' When he has to leave India, Uncle Potty consoles him to look after his assets. On the other hand, the judge's friendship with Bose is a feigned one. When Bose comes to Darjeeling to meet the judge, the meeting was not a pleasant one and the judge swears not to meet him again in future.

Apart from these relations, Desai has also given several pictures of relations that Sai enjoys in the company of Lola and Noni, Uncle Potty and Father Booty and the cook. Her relation with these persons is quite different from the relation she has with the judge. The cook looks after Sai as an elderly grandmother and takes care of her. Sai is also dependent on him. Similarly, Uncle Potty and Father Booty also showers their selfless love on Sai. She often goes to Darjeeling and other places with them. She can open her heart to Lola and Noni. When Gyan avoids Sai and she is mentally disturbed, she goes to Uncle Potty and gets some relief to her aching heart. Lola and Noni are curious to know about Sai's love affair:

> "Who is the lucky boy? Tall and fair and handsome?"
>
> "And rich?" Noni
>
> Sai. "Let's hope he's rich?" (p. 251)

To conclude, Desai has given a vivid and clear description of various relations that are found in society. She has given a parallel picture of these relations which is in fact, a picture of Indian and western version. In Indian society, people are very careful about relations but the impact of westernization is weakening the roots of these relations. Joint families are converting to nuclear families. Relations are distorting, as people are self-centred still there are people who are careful for their relatives. Desai has given a psychological and authentic picture of different shades of life and relations people enjoy in changing Indian society. She has tried to explore the deep recesses of the human soul. In an interview, Kiran says that *The Inheritance of Loss* is a book that tries to capture what it means to live between East and West and what it means to be an immigrant. On a deeper level, it explores what happens when a Western element is introduced into a country that is not of the West, which is what happened, of course, during colonial times and is happening again with India's new relationship with the States.

I also wanted to write about what happens when you take people from a poor country and place them in a wealthy one. How does the imbalance between these two worlds change a person's thinking and feeling? How do these changes manifest themselves in a personal sphere, a political sphere, over time?[4]

Living between two worlds and portraying parallel relations is not an easy task. It was a challenge for her but her range is not a limited one restricted to only home affair. With a wide range of relations, she has presented the tense, chaotic, antagonistic and shifting locations and also the precarious, disgraced and displaced lives, existence and identities of the Diaspora.

NOTES

1. Shashi Deshpande to an interviewer in *Indian Communicator*, 20 November 1994, p. II.
2. Kiran Desai, *The Inheritance of Loss*. New Delhi: Penguin Books, 2006, p. 89. All the subsequent references given parenthetically are from this work.
3. R.H. Lowie, *Marriage in Encyclopaedia of the Social Sciences*, Vol. V, p. 146.
4. 'Human warmth is such an innate part of India' The Rediff Interview/Novelist Kiran Desai...trips. www.rediff.com/news/2006/jan/30inter1a.htm

21

Postmodern/Postcolonial Spatiality in Kiran Desai's *The Inheritance of Loss*

Arpita Chattaraj (Mukhopadhyay)

The postmodern and the postcolonial conditions manifest certain commonalities of attitudes and perspectives, since both the discourses subsume the reconfiguration of the self-other, man-society dichotomy and thereby rejecting certitudes which determine self-identity. A significant preoccupation of both the discourses is the demystification of spatiality, underscoring the link that the idea of space has with contemporary cultural, political and theoretical structures. The postcolonial dialectics of local/global is contiguous to the patterning of the postmodern world. Therefore, the postmodern and the postcolonial attitudes towards spatiality overlap to provide a critical vantage and insight into the processes of ideological redefinition of identity, culture and nationalism. Foucault had insisted that, "the anxiety of our era has to do fundamentally with space, no doubt a great deal more than with time" (23). Decolonization and neo-imperialism, which coincide with the periodicity of postmodernism, have witnessed mass movements of bodies across the globe, demographic shifts out of all proportion, which lends urban sphere with a diversity of culture. The postmodern space is thus a product of the negotiation of multiple spaces, which is continually decentering and reconstituting boundaries thereby subverting any attempt to fix a singular autonomous meaning—these multiple inflections working upon the postmodern space pertain to race, class, and gender. Fredric Jameson captures the spatial specifity underlying this blurring of borderlines and the comparability of the contemporary neo-imperialism (globalization) and post-Enlightenment European imperialist enterprise in his *Postmodernism or The Cultural Logic of Late Capitalism* thus:

> Postmodern (or multinational) space is not merely a cultural ideology or fantasy, but has genuine historical (and socio-economic) reality as a third great original expansion of Capitalism around the globe (after the earlier expansions of the national market and the older imperialist system, which each had their own cultural specifity and generated new types of space appropriate to their dynamics). (88)

Epistemological inquiry in the 20th century is directed towards understanding the relation between the mental space and the social space. In Foucault's discourse on 'heterotopias' and its instrumental association of space, knowledge and power the concept of space is decentred from the geographical context as well as psychological context and focussed on spatiality of another kind, which is the 'external space,' the actually lived and socially produced space:

> The space in which we live, which draws us out of ourselves, in which the erosion of our lives, our time and our history occurs, the space that claws and gnaws at us, is also in itself, a heterogeneous space. (23)

This heterogeneous space of sites and relations represent real society without their perfected utopian form. These 'heterotopias' functions according to Foucault, not as substanceless void, not just a physical form that can be plotted and mapped but a lived space, a socially constructed space. Lefebvre had claimed, "Space is not a scientific object removed from ideology and politics. It has always been political and strategic.... Space is political and ideological. It is a product literally filled with ideologies" (31). Edward W. Soja extends Lefebvre's arguments further when he summarizes his spatialized ontology as "...substantiated and recognizable product, part of a second nature, which incorporates as it socializes and transforms both physical and psychological spaces" (129). Soja's trialectics of spatiality contest the binary notions of spatiality that has been at the centre of traditional discourse. He challenges the oppositions of objectivity versus subjectivity, material versus mental, real versus imagined and space versus place and initiates an argument in favour of 'Third Space.' 'Third Space' in Soja's framework is a lived space of social practices. 'First Space' or perceived space is empirically measurable and mappable; 'Second Space' is conceived space, imagined and a domain of representations. Soja's 'third Space' is the immediate material world of experience and realization. This is the inhabited space that includes the perceived and the conceived space and extends beyond their scope.

The postmodern concept of 'Third Space' is also nuanced in postcolonial discourse. Colonial culture like the contemporary culture is hybrid. Colonial/Postcolonial discourse does not simply signify the East/West, Self/Other dichotomy but also conflates the "points of conflict or crisis" (Bhabha, 82) of these binaries. In the confrontation/interaction of dissimilar cultures, by the historicity of power imbalance that colonialism enforces, the autonomy or discreteness of the categories in the binaries is impossible to retain. What results is in Bhabha's term the *liminal space*, the borderline, the threshold or the in-betweenness of cultures. The resulting cultural hybridity suggests a spatiality, which marks a continuous flux in the process of identity formation. The 'location of culture' in Bhabha's postcolonial discourse is focused less on physical locations (borders between nations) and more on the spatiality of cultural hybridization. This duplicates the postmodern tendency of erasing boundaries. This hybridization is thus an interface, consequent upon the ideological dialectics of Self and Other, Master and Slave, Colonizer and Colonized debates, which extends into socio-political structures. Bhabha clarifies this emergence of 'Third Space' in postcolonial discourse in an interview titled "Third Space":

> For me the importance of hybridity is not to be able to trace two original moments from which the third emerges, rather hybridity from the 'third space' which enables other positions to emerge. The third space displaces the histories that constitute it, and sets up new structures of authority, new political initiative. (211)

This paper attempts to explore the confluence of postmodernist (Soja's) 'Third Space,' which is a spatial manifestation of social structures in polyethnic, multicultural, globalised world, and postcolonial (Bhabha's) 'Third Space,' which is a spatial manifestation of cultural conflicts and crises in a specific historical and political context, in Kiran Desai's Booker awarded novel *The Inheritance of Loss*.

II

The Inheritance of Loss has been hailed as "the best kind of post 9/11 novel" (Mishra) despite the fact that it has been set in the mid-1980s. This overlapping of sequential historicity in seeking the meaning of the text perhaps indicates its perplexing spatiality. Desai's elegant exploration of the lives of few "powerless individuals" leads on to far more serious perspectives on issues that straddles our narratives, both 'grand' and 'petit'—issues of globalization, multiculturalism, separatism, insurgency, diaspora, immigration, exile, alienation, identity and more. The narrative meandering between past and present, India, England, USA, lives of judge Jemubhai Patel, Sai, cook, Biju, Gyan, Father Booty, Uncle Potty, Lola, Noni, is actually a palimpsest of spaces—spaces that swarm with movements, differences, colours and polyphony. As Desai herself asserts in an interview:

> I think I was fighting to create a sense of place while also undoing anyone's claim upon it as being sole, firm or integral. Working on this book, I became aware of the novelistic momentum that come from many stories overlapping, of realising that one's place in the world is incidental, it is just perspectives, the location isn't really firm at all. Past, present, or future.

The novel seeks to unravel the lives, past and present, of characters living in Kalimpong but existing as traces or residues of spaces they have inhabited evaded or yearned for. The crumbling decrepit cottage Cho Oyu, occupied by the cantankerous retired judge Jemubhai Patel, his orphan granddaughter Sai and their cook, is emblamatic of a site of intersection of diverse lived spaces. The judge is an anachronism, with his quaint ways and strange accent, a relic of a colonial past, resembling in this respect the house he occupies. The history of the house is also resonant with the exploitation of the colonial masters. Built by a Scotsman who is sucked in by the exotica of the East, a passionate consumer of The Indian Alps and How We Crossed Them, Land of Lama, The Phantom Rickshaw, and Black Panther of Singrauli, the house is a space for impinging his adventurous spirit. The irony lies in the fact that his appetite for excitement necessitated the labour of the porters who "...carried boulders from the riverbed—the legs growing bandy, ribs curving into caves, backs into U's, faces being bent slowly to look always at the ground" (12). It is fitting that the judge, a retired ICS officer, a cultural hybrid, 'inherit' this colonial legacy and seek to perpetuate the same pattern of domination-subordination on the cook (his only subject) of which he had been both a victim and an instrument. Judge Jemubhai Popatlal Patel, born to peasant caste in obscure Piphit, in Gujarat, had in his boyhood great promise as student, so that his father, whose livelihood depended on procuring false witnesses for the court, had pinned all his hopes on him. To materialize those hopes, Jemubhai Patel had travelled to London with an ambition to join the ICS, and in this switching, he felt it imperative to leave behind a past he was ashamed and terrified of, the past that seemed to throttle him in the form of mother's thick love, the mundaneness of his father, the unreality of a 14 years old bride. He refuses to throw the coconut in the waves as an offering to bless his journey, thus negating/denying a past that occupied a psychological space. Significantly, he has a new Oxford English Dictionary with him in his journey to London, perhaps the second 'great book' in English after Bible, indicating another kind of space that he seeks to cleave towards. He is however caught in an inexplicable struggle in London, he is filled with such a sense on inadequacy that can only lead to self-loathing: "he forgot how to laugh, could barely lift his lips in a smile, and if he ever did, he held his hand over his mouth, because he couldn't bear anyone to see his gums, his teeth" (40). The confrontation of cultures instills in him a sense of ineffectuality, he is haunted by a feeling of worthlessness that issued from his belief in his racial inferiority. His obsessive cleaning could not mitigate the stench of curry that he feared he carried around him. Jemubhai's response to this deeply entrenched ineptness is a deliberate withdrawal, of a kind Fanon speaks of in his *Black Skin, White Masks*:

> On that day, completely dislocated, unable to be abroad with the other, the white man, who unmercifully imprisoned me, I took myself far off from my own presence, far indeed, and made myself an object. (112)

Jemubhai buries himself in the library where he is reacquainted with his own country but viewed from a different lens, that of imperialist agency. He reads about Gujarat in Expedition to Goozerat, about the transfer of land and power to East India Company, about the French, Dutch, and Portugese colonizers but all from a distance, from an objective space because "He had learned to take refuge in the third person and to keep everyone at bay, to keep even himself away from himself" (111). The reversal of perspectives also produces a difference in Jemubhai's strategies of surviving in the midst of an alien culture, filled with shame about his own past and fear of the alienness that surrounded him. Along with Bose, Jemubhai engaged in the enterprise of being Anglicised—"he corrected his pronunciation, listened to Caruoso and Gigli, read A Brief History of Western Art, A Brief History of Philosophy, A Brief History of France." This was his way of taking "...revenge on his early confusions, his embarrassments gloved in something called 'keeping up standards': his accent behind a mask of a quiet" (119). Jemubhai survives his English experiences by becoming a cultural hybrid, what Bhabha identified as 'mimicry' with its attendant ambivalence. Jemubhai returns to India, with intensified hatred for Indians and an insatiable yearning to inculcate Englishness. The space that he inhabits is a space of mimicry and hybridity that cannot essentially incorporate or take up the life he had left behind. So his family seems insufferable and his wife Nimi repulsive. His impotent anger at not being able to measure up to the standards of Englishness, since Anglicized is not English, and his inability to adjust to the space (both physical and psychological) around him is routed in the tortures that he inflicts in Nimi.

Judge Jemubhai had chosen Cho Oyu as his space for isolation and segregation. Born in Gujarat, trained in England, worked in Northern India, is ironically caught in yet another struggle for space. The insurgency in the hills which intrudes his life is ideologically the struggle for local control of and respect of 'place' or 'space.' It is this event that forces Jemubhai to confront the loss of a dear one (Mutty) and revisits his past guilt that he had driven to the deepest recess of his psychological space. The crumbling of the edifice can be studied in parallel with the crumbling of the order in the quotidian pattern in the household: "For the first time, they in Cho Oyu were eating the real food of the hillside. Dalda Saag... Bhutiya Dhania...Ninjo fiddleheads...churbi chees" (281). A shift is hinted at but not of a conclusive or determinate kind. His merciless thrashing of the cook is a desperate attempt to cling on to the remnants of the identity and the space that he had constructed for himself.

Kiran Desai had revealed in an interview that "This book is made up of many little bits and pieces, of half stories, and immigrants in a basement you just see briefly as you pass by." The narrative presents a quilt/patchwork of 'lived spaces;' there is a criss-crossing and intertwining of journeys by different individuals of diverse spatial significance. Judge Jemubhai Patel's spatial shifts (not only physical, but psychological and 'lived') can be seen in close parallel to the spatial dislocations experienced by Biju, his cook's son. The circumstances may be apparently unconnected, but both their spatial switches/transpositions are pervaded with a similar kind of alienation, isolation and ineffectuality. Biju, encouraged by his father undertakes a journey to the United States only to drift from one ill-paid job to another, pursuing the ever-elusive green card. Jemubhai's passage to another country, culture and existence was fraught with anxieties of a colonized psyche. Biju's efforts to switch to a life of affluence and security are percolated with issues of a more complex nature. Jemubhai's journey was to an overtly hierarchized society, where his anguish was nonetheless intense, but his choices and attitudes could follow a definite pattern. For Biju, an illegal immigrant to a country that is confusion between the melting pot and nosaic of multiculturalism, the choices and attitudes are further problematic. Underlying the facade of polyethnicity of the space he inhabits, augmented by effects of globalisation, the hierarchies and divisions are kept intact and further modified:

> Biju at the Baby Bistro
>
> Above the restaurant was French, but below in the kitchen it was Mexican and Indian....
>
> Biju at Le colonial for the authentic colonial experience
>
> On top, rich colonial, and down below, poor native. Colombian, Tunisian, Ecuadorian, Gambian. (21)

The superficially cosmopolitan nature of Biju's occupied space is in reality fragmented and polycentric—the spatial structuration of 'above' and 'below' provides an interpretative framework of the deeply embedded internal colonization. This spatial configuration also inheres contradictions and paradoxes, which are legacies of the space that are culturally and psychologically carried within. Thus, Biju is always on the border, threshold, an observer to the ambiguities and in-betweens of identities set aside and those constructed by expediencies. The young Indian women to whom he delivers food from Freddy's work adeptly balancing their 'Indianness' and cosmopolitan foreignness in their condescension that "he might comprehend their friendliness completely in this meeting between Indians abroad of different classes and languages, rich and poor, North and South, top caste bottom cast" (50) fills him with contradictory emotions of hunger, respect and loathing. Biju, despite harbouring prejudices about Muslims and hubshis, strikes a strong friendship with Saeed Saeed who emphasizes that he is from Zanzibar and not Tanzania. This assertion of spatial specifity is anomalous considering his single-minded determination to get hold of a green card. The socio-spatial dialectic is manifest in his marriage of convenience to procure the green card and simultaneously marrying another girl of his own country, biding his time to be free from the legal entanglement of permanent residency in US, get rid of his first wife and settle into the homeliness and familiarity that his second wife brings into his space. The hyphenated existence of the diaspora is explicit in Harish-Harry, the Ugandan Indian who had a flourishing chain of Gandhi Cafés with his brothers Gaurish-Garry and Dhansukh-Danny in New York, New Jersey and Connecticut. The split in their identities is explicated by the split in their names, so that Harish-Harry refuses a discount offer on a trip to India but readily sends a donation to Cow Shelter in New Jersey. He refuses to pay for Biju's treatment when he damages his leg in the Café kitchen but brings in prasad for him from the temple in Queens. Desai, subtly, focalizes the spatial problematic in post-industrial capitalist society where the class struggles between master-serf is deeply embedded in the configurative contradictions of socially organized space:

> ...in that prasad Biju knew not to expect anything else. It was a decoy, an old Indian trick of master to servant, the benevolent patriarch garnering the loyalty of staff; offering slave wages, but now nad than a box of sweets, a lavish gift. (189)

Biju refuses to live a fake version of life in another country, the unreality and emptiness of his existence compel him to realign his perspective. Realization dawns in him that "...in a space that should have included family, friends, he was the only one displacing the air..." (268). The unheimlich had produced in him space for self-loathing and self-pity.

The spatiality of rootlessness and displacement cannot be determined by its geographical implications. The psychocartography of alienation is manifest in the 'lived space' or the 'third space.' Lola and Noni, the Bengali sisters who live in a Bunglow with a French name and reads Mahasweta Devi's works in translation by Spivak, the Afghan princesses who had lost their homeland and settled with their slaves and dogs in Kalimpong, Uncle Potty, living off old money from his family in Lucknow, Father Booty, a Swiss missionary who had lost the urge to renew his visa, making an alien land his home, Mrs. Sen who tries hard to keep up with the elitist circle that surrounds her, all manifest doubleness of consciousness. They inhabit a space that is made up of unreal fantasies of a way of life that has ceased to be, and are rendered caricatures contrasted to the more substantial space that surrounds them. The encroachment of the hostile space around them is most severely felt by the sisters—they are reduced to ridiculous and irrelevant presences in their pretentious cottage, their property and identity invaded, their life led in a simulucrum world of Trollope, Bronte, Whitman, CNN, BBC, Christmas revelries, cheese toasts obviate the estrangement and rift in their identities.

Sai is a legatee of a love that sought to cross ethnic divides; her father, a Zoroastrians and her mother, a Hindu, had in their secular romance "felt free and brave, part of a modern nation in a modern world" (26). Space in its scientific connotation is curiously inserted by Desai in Mr. and Mrs. Mistry's narrative. He is a space pilot who dreamt of becoming "the very first Indian beyond the control of gravity" (27) but lost his life along with his wife in an inglorious manner under the wheels of a local bus in Russia. Instead of "blasting through the stratosphere" (27) with a 'bang' he exits with a 'whimper,' metaphorically underscoring the fate of Indo-Russian relations and that of Soviet Republic as well. The intervention of the political-spatial dialectic in Sai's parents' lives is continued even in her associations and 'lived space.' Educated initially in a convent, later continuing her learning under the aegis of Lola and Noni in Kalimpong, she is a typical bleached, distorted, image of a colonial aftermath "a westernized Indian brought up by English nuns, an estranged Indian being in India" (210). Sai's love for Gyan cannot reconcile to the reality of his genteel poverty, his 'otherness' as construed in cultural and social terms. Gyan, the Nepalese math tutor, desperately seeks adulthood in a militant quest for homeland without either understanding or being emotionally and ideologically involved in the struggle. They are both trapped, enmeshed and hedged in their own spatial confines.

The spatial structurations that comprise of social practices, cultural exclusivities are deeply imbued with ambivalences, which stem from hegemonic influences. The territorialities of experiences that contribute to identity formation impose segmentation in order to totalize, closure in order to homogenize, and individualization in order to obliterate differences and otherness. These homogenizing tendencies of post-industrial capitalist society need to be viewed in consonance with the tendency of the colonizers to stereotype the subject. The developing and iterative metaphor of the newspaper in the novel is the site which underlines this tendency to totalize in the randomness with which unrelated, discordant clips of news from different spatial significance jostle to fit in the space that has been carved out for them:

> In Bombay a band named Hell No was going to perform at the Hyatt International
> In Delhi, a technology fair on cow dung gas stoves was being attended by delegates from all over the world
> In Kalimpong...there was a report of new dissatisfaction in the hills, gathering insurgency, men and guns. (9)

The novel traces the journeys in the lives of the characters across space and time—some are journeys of resolution from incoherence to the familiar, known, heimlich (Biju's) while some are journeys back and forth, past and present, across the hyphenated existence of the imagined and real identities (judge's, Lola's). The multiplicity of these journeys hint at the possibility and necessity of exploring further into other spatial sphere:

> Sai stood there—
>
> She thought of her father and the space program. She thought of all national geographics and books she had read. Of the judge's journey, of the cook's journey, of Biju's. Of the globe twirling on its axis.
>
> And she felt a glimmer of strength. Of resolve. She must leave. (323)

The novelist too in the process of writing the book undergoes a spatial shift of her own kind. In an interview she acknowledges that:

> The book was a return journey to the fact of being Indian, to realizing the perspective was too important to give up. America might give me half a narrative, but I had to return to India for the other half of the story, for emotional depth, historical depth.... The vocabulary of immigration, of exile, of translation, inevitably overlaps with a realization of the multiple options for reinvention, of myriad perspectives, shifting truths, telling of lies—the great big wobbliness of all. In a world obsessed with national boundaries, as a novelist working with a form also traditionally obsessed with place, it was a journey to come to this thought, that the less structured, multiple may be a possible location for fiction, perhaps a more valid ethical location in general.

WORKS CITED

Bhabha, Homi K. *The Location of Culture*. London: Routledge, 1994.

——. "The Third Space: Interview with Homi K. Bhabha," Jonathan Rutherford (ed.) *Identity, Community, Culture, Difference*, London: Lawrence & Wishart, 1991.

Desai, Kiran. *The Inheritance of Loss*, Penguin: New Delhi, 2006.

Fanon, Frantz. *Black Skin, White Masks*, trans. Charles Lam Markman Pluto, 1986.

Foucault, Michel. *Of Other Spaces*, Diacritics 16, 1986.

Jameson, Fredric. "Postmodernism, or the Cultural Logic of late Capitalism," *New Left Review*, 1984.

Lefebvre, Henri. *The Survival of Capitalism*, London: Allison and Busby, 1976.

——. *Reflections on the Politics of Space*, trans. by M. Enders, Antipode 8, 1976.

Mishra, Pankaj. "Wounded by the West," *NY Times*, Feb. 12, 2006, http:/ www.nytimes.com/2006/02

Soja, Edward W. *Postmodern Geographies*, Rawat, New Delhi, 1997.

http/www.themanbookerprize.com/perspective/40 on 15.05.08

hhhp/booksgaurdian.co.uk/manbookers 2006/story/html on 15.05.08

22

Reflective Moods in *The Inheritance of Loss*

Shaleen Kumar Singh

The Inheritance of Loss by Kiran Desai which won the Man Booker Prize 2006 is a story of Sai and her grandfather. Sai is a young girl who takes refuge at Jemubhai Patel, the grandfather, a retired judge residing at the foot of Mt. Kanchenjenga in his home Cho-Oyu,—which at present shows the little sign of its former glory. The judge wishes to lead the remaining days of his life in seclusion and stoicism obliterating the past and even the existing today but as the ill-luck would have it or say fortunately, his sedition is shattered completely by the sudden intrusion of his granddaughter Sai. The relation between Sai and grandfather is very typical for both of them do not know anything about each other. As the judge or the grandfather was leading life full of isolation and seclusion, he has to accept the girl after the tragic accident of his son and bride. In a crumbling isolated house at the foot of Mt. Kunchunjanga where the judge is residing in a disciplined and tight-scheduled life, the girl Sai tries to adjust her frequencies. Sai is a westernized Indian girl brought up by English nun and so she is well-acquainted with the discipline of encroaching others personal zones.

Kiran Desai remains meditative from the beginning, the delineation of situation, the weaving of the plot and the infusion of 'thought' make her exquisite. Sai is the key-figure of the novel who narrates the reflective mode of the novelist.

> No human had ever seen as big as apples to scope the dark of the ocean, theirs was a solitude so profound they might never encounter another of their tribe. The melancholy of this situation washed over Sai. (20)

And he continues:

> Could fulfillment ever be felt as deeply as loss? Romantically she decided that love must surely reside in the gap between decisive and fulfillment in the lack, not the contentment. Love mars the ache, the anticipation, the retreat, everything around it but the emotion itself. (20)

Like Hardy's novels, fate plays a dominant role in the Desai's novel. Sai's father becomes the victim of fate, though he was one of the candidates and the first Indian to be chosen beyond the gravity. Here, we can again see the author musing:

> ...the fates decided otherwise, and instead of blasting through the stratosphere, in his life, in this skin, to see the world as gods might, he was delivered to another vision of the beyond when he and his wife were crushed by local bus wheels,...
>
> Thus they had died under the wheels of foreigners, amid crates of babushka nesting dolls. If their thoughts were of their daughter in St. Augustine's, she would never know. (27)

A close affinity gets developed between Sai and the cook of the house who is associated in the company of Jemubhai Patel, the grandfather for quite a long period, so she (Sai) tries to enquire much about her grandfather's past life. Sai comes to know about cook's personal life and love also his only son. The cook says at first:

> I may be as well be dead. If not for Biju....

The author introduces Biju adding:

> Biju was his son in America. He worked at Don-Pollo or was it the, The Hot Tomatos? Or Alibaba's fried chicken? His father could not remember or understand to pronounce the names and Biju changed jobs so often, like a fugitive on the run—no papers. (35)

Biju, the only son of the cook who somehow manages to send him to unknown land for better future, reflects the shadow of long line in him and the hard life of the foreign country is experienced by the one among the many whose parents and their sums for the foreign country and pine for the love of motherland. Kiran Desai's portrayal of Biju reflects the loveliness of such persons, who runs to and fro in his struggles for existence on account of undocumented immigrant and stumbles from one low paid job to another. His fantasies about the life full of facilities and luxuries that each man aspires to have and he frantically wishes to purchase everything for the same.

Life, in reality, is full of strife and dreams can do nothing except shielding contemplation. Contrary to this the arrival of Sai in the life of the retired judge makes him forcibly to ruminate about the past when he left his house at Pilphit to commence his journey overseas. After a bright career of joining the Indian Civil Services, he flew to England and returned home to a pampered survival, banishing a kind of royal verdict over his country. He is unfortunately one of those 'ridiculous Indians' who is incapable to come out of the strong clutches of foreign exposure. He leads a busy life totally devoted to work and work only, thus ignoring his family and children. His wife becomes the target of his frustration and anger. Kiran Desai presents him before as an introvert personality who is more at ease in the company of his pet dog Mutt than his family and his children. The portrayal of judge is done by Kiran Desai as an eccentric character totally disciplined man doing everything at sharp time. For example, 'At 6:30 he would bath in water,' 'at 8:30 he'd rode into the fields, with local officials and everyone else in the village,' 'at 2:00 after lunch the judge sat at his desk under a tree to try cases usually in a cross mood,' 'at 4:30 he had to be perfect, at 5:30 out he went into the country side with his fishing rod and gun, at 8:00 saved his reputation, cooked a chicken and at:

> 9:00 sipping ovaltine, he filled out the registers with the days gleanings. The patromax lantern would be lit—what a noise is made—insects fording the black to dive-

> bomb him with soft flowers (moths) with iridescence (beetles) lines, columns and squares. He realized truth was best looked at in tiny aggregates, for many baby truths could yet add up to one big size unsavory lie. Last, in his diary also to be submitted to his superiors, he recorded the random observations of a cultured man, someone who was observant, schooled in literature as well as economics: and he made up hunting triumphs: two partridge...one deer with thirty inch horns.... (63)

Sai falls in love with Nepali boy Gyan who is appointed as the tutor of her. Gyan gets involved in the Gorkha Separatist Movement with a obscure motive behind him as Gyan is portrayed as the victim of circumstances who cannot but join the liberation army forcibly:

> as he floated through the market, Gyan had a feeling of history being wrought, its wheats churning under him, for the men were behaving as if they were being featured in a documentary of war, and Gyan could not help but look on the scene already from the angle of Nostalgia, the position of a revolutionary. But then he was pulled out of the feeling by the mansoon—stained grottos. Then he shouted alone with the crowd and to create a relevancy, an affirmation he had never felt before, and he was pulled back into the making of history. (157)

Gyan is pain-stricken because of his unrequited love for Sai on one hand and his hatred for everything that Sai mirrors in Indian society. When the Kalimpong was burning under the fire of separation, the GNLF fighting for the separatist state, the police were hiding their own identity rather than protecting the common mass. Kiran Desai broods over the whole traumatic situation and portrays all in the novel. She makes affine balance between the portrayal of the grand and saintly Kanchenjenga and the state of fear, terror and death. Both the plot and the thought are clearly portrayed by the novelist. Jemubhai Patel is also panic-stricken and grief-stricken but he is sullen for his dog Mutt who goes missing. The situation makes us think the cold temperament of the high class society towards the ongoing situation. Nandoo, the cook admits his guilt that he committed in his life and holds himself responsible for Mutt's disappearance. In the meantime Biju, his son gets non-existent. Here Kiran Desai makes us again think about the philosophy of life and death. She writes as:

> The cook didn't mention his son.... He had none...he'd never had one...it was just his hope writing to him.... Biju was non-existent. (321)

Off and on the author makes us realize the truth of terrestrial life and the satiric situations. Even the judge who tortures the cook for a dog remains silent at a critical crisis hovering over the nation. Sai watches everything and makes us think about the negligent attitude of the judge even who can keep the calm at the wrong happening in the society but cannot pardon his cook for a petty mistake.

Sai remains a thoughtful character throughout the novel. She desires love from Gyan but in vain. Desai portrays their relations vividly and compares and contrasts the both. Finally she writes:

> As she saw her recast her eyes and mouth remembered that he abandoned her, not the other way around and she was bitterly angry.
>
> Dirty hypocrite.
>
> Pretending one thing, living another. Nothing but lies through and through. (257)

The absurdity of Gyan and pure feelings of Sai makes us think again the traumatic result of true love and Sai's renouncement makes us again to ruminate when Sai feels a vacuum all around and finds herself unable to overcome the situation. Sai thinks:

> She thought of her father and the space program. She thought of all the National Geographics and books she had read. Of judge's journey, of the cook's journey, of Biju's. Of the globe twirling on its axis. And she felt a glimmer of strength. Of resolve, she must leave. (323)

Again Biju comes back alone and stands at the gate of Cho Oye. Father and son meet and embrace each other and the son feels comfortable in father's shelter. Desai here again makes us realize the truth of blood relations can never be a lie or blood is thicker than water. Situations, places or incidents may vary, complexities may crop up and overpower man's mentality but the relations can never be changed. Sai, on the other hand, realizes:

> Life was not single in its purpose...or even in its direction. The simplicity of what she'd have been taught would'nt hold. Never again could she think, there was but one narrative and that this narrative belonged only to herself, that she might create her own tiny happiness and live safely within it. (232)

Love is the strongest thing in life and the golden peaks of Kanchenjenga can only be overcome by firm determination, faith and zeal:

> The five peaks of Kanchenjenga turned golden with the kind of luminous light that made you feel, if briefly, that truth was apparent. All you needed to do was reach out and pluck it. (324)

Thus, Kiran Desai in her novel muses over the various aspects of life as well as make the readers think over the eccentricities and paradoxes of life. She continues her reflective mood from beginning to the end. With instruments of humour and irony, Desai explores the inexplicable and mysterious world. Dr. Shubha Mukherjee observes:

> With a touch of humour and irony, Kiran Desai explores into the inexplicable and mysterious world their beauty and truth lie within reach but invisible.

Dr. A.K. Chaturvedi raises the issue of tribal marginalization in the seventeenth chapter of the novel in which the young boy of town Saeed who is a worker at the Queen at Tart's Bakery in America. He is landed into an unexpected trouble by the presence of some poor boys (the very tribal of his native town who having no source of livelihood in their own country visit America for finding employment) at the gate of Bakery. Nobody in America is ready to help the tribal in realizing the aim for which they left their country. They are neither helped nor even sympathized.

The gates of Queen of Tort's Bakery are close to them, so is the gate of fates to him. Desai raising the issue of tribal's marginalization presents the picture of globalization and urbanization in modern India. The tribals are desperate and hapless. Dr. Chaturvedi observes:

> Thus, like in Kamla Markandaya's *The Coffer Dam.* The tribal in *The Inheritance of Loss* represents a marginalized community facing the challenges and problems that have no easy solutions. In the present age of globalization and urbanization the tribal are desperately trying to break out of their traditional boundaries so as to search for the opportunities to ameliorate their hopeless condition. (9)

WORKS CITED

Chaturvedi, A.K., 'Kiran Desai's *The Inheritance of Loss*: The Issue of Tribal's Marginalization,' *Indian Book Chronicle*. Ed. P.C. Mathur, Feb. 2007, Jaipur.

Desai, Anita, *The Inheritance of Loss*. New Delhi: Penguin Books, 2006. (All the quotations are culled out from this edition.)

Mukherjee, Shubha, "*The Inheritance of Loss*: Comedy Blended with Contemplation," *Hindustani Innovator*. Kullur Nagappa Vol. III, No. 1, 2007.

23

'Imagi-nation': A Reading of Kiran Desai's *The Inheritance of Loss*

Jati Sankar Mondal

The idea of 'nation' as it is prevalent in our times is itself a result of evolution from philological point of view. When I use the word 'nation' I do not imply what the ancient Greeks wanted to mean by it or the audience of Shakespeare understood when they came across the word. To generalize widely and wildly, they tried to mean 'state' by the word 'nation.' It is only in late 18th century that the term along with its political sense took some ethnical and philosophical dimension which very soon became one of the most influential doctrines in Western Europe. Let me briefly consider the evolving perceptions of the idea enshrined in at least in three idealist schools based on elitist rationalistic views. First, primordialist school, which coined the term to refer to a number of different views whose only common element is that they tend to regard nations as intrinsic to the human condition. This gave rise to organic nationalism that the nation resembles an organism in nature. Next, Pierre van den Berghe, an anthropologist gave birth to its socio-biological meaning that holds ethnic groups and races and describes nation as the ultimate product of individual genetic reproductive drives. In third phase, Clifford Greertz argues that the idea of nation must, in the process of nation building, account for efficiency and 'civic ties' in one hand and retention of 'primordial ties' and certain 'cultural givens' (cited in Smith) in another.

However, he felt that the drive was undermined by the overriding importance attributed by the people to basic identity cleavages like race, ethnicity, region, religion, custom, etc. Eric J. Hobsbawm also made significant contribution to form the present meaning of the term. He opines that nations are not only recent but also 'invented.' Social constructs engineered by ruling states through judicious selection of 'invented traditions' (cited in Smith) of national community, history, mythology and language. In the 1870s, while Hobsbawm has been writing this, nation becomes a form of social control and nationalism comes to be encouraged in order to manipulate the masses in rapidly industrializing and democratizing societies.

Much later, in 1983, Benedict Anderson in his book *Imagined Community*, almost echoing Hobsbawm, argues that nation is a community which is not tied by religion or kin, but by its imagined status as "the members of even the smallest nation will never know most of their fellow members, meet them, or even hear of them, yet in the mind of each lives the image of their communion" (Anderson, 15). I want to focus two words here, 'invented' as used by Hobsbawm and 'imagined' as coined by Anderson. This will show the shifting terrains of ideas ranging from rationalistic view to constructionalist view. Taking cue from Anderson, Homi K. Bhabha proceeds further and raises objection to the view. But he differs from Anderson that while Anderson celebrates only a kind of imaginary monoculture, Bhabha includes other factors and identifies the space of hybridity, "a difficult, agonistic process of negotiation" (Huddart, 113). He bisects the word 'imagination' as 'imagi-nation' and describes it in terms of its narration. He argues that although nation-state is historically specific and a recent trend, but it has an ahistorical performance of time immemorial. "Nation, like narratives, lose their origin in the myths of time and only fully realize their horizons in the minds eye" (Bhabha, 1). He points out that nations have their own narratives, but very often a dominant or official narrative overpowers all other narratives, including those of minority groups and thereby he opens a new space for rethinking of identity or national identities. Instead of taking a monocular or monologic view, he described nation and national identity as well as history in a palimpsestic design of discourses. Originally palimpsest is heavily annotated manuscript where every writing is visible underneath newer writings. Rushdie in his book *The Moor's Last Sigh* very clearly shows how the idea of palimpsest is applied upon a place: "Place where worlds collided, in and out of one another...one universe, one dimension, one country, one dream bumpo'ing into another, or being under, or on top of. Call it palimpstine" (Rushdie, 226). Such palimpsestic or palimsestine design creates a new space or third space which is the space of hybridity where several narratives, sometimes opposite to each other, can co-exist competing for their own space. In such a space, every narrative is influenced by other narratives and every writing presents an in-between state of the conceptual and the practical which Bhabha described with two terms—'pedagogical' and 'performative.' In this respect Bhabha argues in his book *Location of Culture* that every artist, either consciously or unconsciously, is using "repetitious, recursive strategy of the performative" (Bhabha, 142) to resist the easy temptation of the static and the self-sameness of community, "the continuist, accumulative temporality of the pedagogical" (Bhabha, 145).

When I read *The Inheritance of Loss* by Kiran Desai, I am struck by the proliferation of such discursive formations. There, as I found, that several narratives are competing for their space and yearning to be heard. Like a palimpsest every narrative can be found under or on the top of some other narratives and as a whole the novel enjoys a hybrid space, an in-betweenness of the pedagogical and the performative. Desai placed her characters of the novel in the foothill of Himalayas, in Kalimpong. The place is famous for three Ts—tea, timber and tourism. In North Eastern India, far away from city or even district town, tossed with Gorkhaland Movement, her characters represent a nation in miniature and the palimpsestic design is created by various groups of people who are mainly differentiated by means of class which is further sub-divided by ethnicity, religion, education and language.

Desai mainly presents two classes: Anglicized upper middle class, consisting of retired old judge Jemubhai Patel, his orphaned granddaughter Sai, Mrs. Sen whose daughter Munmun is now a green card holder in America, Lola and Noni. Lola's daughter Piyali or Pixie is the newsreader of BBC and later, of CNN. They are contrasted by the cook of Patel's bungalow whose son Biju is an illegal immigrant in America, struggling for green card, Gyan, the maths tutor of Sai, Budhoo, the watchman of Lola and Noni's residence Mon-ami, Keshang, another watchman and characters like them who form the lower strata of the society. The lower class is divided by caste and ethnicity—there are Nepali, Lepcha, Bhutia, Sherpa, Rai, Pradhan, Gurung and several other. The main language used by them is Nepali which differentiates them from the upper middle class which speaks in Bengali, Hindi or English. Father Booty and Uncle Potty, two other characters of the novel who have their origin in some western country, are curiously enough described by Desai as "foreigner...but an Indian foreigner" (Desai, 220). That particular description when twisted a little can serve as a description for all the upper class people living in Kalimpong with their souls in Kolkata, Mumbai, New York or elsewhere. While Father Booty and Uncle Potty try to appropriate them, consciously trying to be a part of the land retaining their own individual culture, Jemubhai and Mrs. Sen and Lola and Noni try to cut themselves off from the mainstream as they consider themselves more sophisticated than the rest of the people. Noni observes, "it was important to draw the lines properly between classes or it harmed everyone on both sides of the great divide" (Desai, 67). They do not even trust their local Nepali servant, as Lola comments after the robbery at Cho-oyu: "Budhoo? But he's a Nepali. Who can trust him now? It is always the watchman in a case of robbery" (Desai, 43). On the other hand, the hatred of lower class towards the upper class is evident in the speech of a Gorkhaland movement leader: "We are labourers on the tea plantations, coolies dragging heavy loads, soldiers. And are we allowed to become doctor and government workers, owners of the tea plantations? No! We are kept at the level of servants" (Desai, 158).

In order to upgrade themselves from the level of servants, they either want a separate Gorkhaland that will give them a distinct identity and some of them, like Biju, want to fly to America where they will do some odd jobs but get paid in dollars. Desai describes the young masses and the effect of globalization on them that they are "unleased Bruce Lee fans in their American T-shirts made-in-China coming-in via Katmandu" (Desai, 157). They also form a new class without a name.

The unfruitful, almost a one year stint of love between Sai and her maths tutor Gyan is probably an escape and an effort from confinement to dissolve the boundaries of caste and class. Initially, a boy of 20 and a girl of 16 have not paid much attention to the events on the hillside, the disturbance and the difference between them and continued their pursuit of love. But when they become conscious of the questions of social scale, they locate the wide differences and ultimately their love collapses. Gorkhaland movement appears to Gyan as a pursuit of his identity formation and he joins in the movement. He constantly questions his identity and the identity of Sai. He questions why she or the upper class is going to celebrate Christmas, and observes: "You are like slaves, that's what you are, running after west, embarrassing yourself. It's because of people like you we never get somewhere" (Desai, 163). Only for being a poor Nepali, he is belittled by the retired judge almost in the same manner he was once harassed by the examiners of Open Competitive Examination, 1942. The examiners were British, the colonial masters of the empire, now he takes his revenge sadistically upon his fellow countrymen who are not the member of his class. Gyan, on his part tries to assault the judge and passes out the information of his haunting rifle to his fellow activists who rob it and psychologically harass the retired judge. As the Gorkhaland movement becomes violent day-by-day and turns almost into a form of terrorism, Gyan being an activist is merged day-by-day in it and his feeling for Sai just evaporates. What remains is his hatred for her as she is the member of the upper middle class. Desai also portrays the other side of the dream of Gorkhaland where the GNLF leaders are like kings in their state or robbers guiding their band,—fiery, ambitious and unpredictable. When Biju, though a son of the soil, returns from America he is robbed of everything and that is probably a hint about the chaos after revolution that is trying to overturn and discard hierarchy. Setting the movement as a backdrop the old judge, Jemubhai also revisits his past, his service life and the freedom movement of India that he had experienced from the side of the colonial masters. The intertwining of history is interesting.

Another aspect of the novel, the diasporic nature of it, also demands a close reading and analysis. There are at least two diasporas. First one is the upper class and upper middle class who came to Kalimpong from various parts of the country, always thinking of their own city or town and contrasted themselves with Kalimpong, not feeling at home here, considering themselves as outsiders. Next one is represented by Biju, an illegal immigrant of America, constantly shifting himself from one restaurant from another in New York as a waiter or engages himself in some odd jobs. He is struggling to find his way to green card there and his experiences there opens a new world in front of us, the untold behind-the-curtain story of the land. In India, Biju is a Nepali but in America he is an Indian where it means, at large, cheap unskilled labour and illegal immigration.

From other kitchens, he was learning what the world thought of Indians:

> In Tanzania, if they could, they would throw them out like they did in Uganda.
> In Madagascar, if they could, they would throw them out.
> In Nigeria, if they could, they would throw them out.
> In Fiji, if they could, they would throw them out.
> In China, they hate them.
> In Hong Kong.
> In Germany.
> In Italy.
> In Japan.
> In Guan.

In Singapore.
Burma.
South Africa.
They don't like them.
In Guadeloupe—they love us there?
No. (Desai, 77)

Desai observes the crisis of identity in diasporic society and narrates it in terms of self and place.

So what Desai actually does is that she presents, through her intertwined narrative, the inner mindscape of her every character which is a darker territory. In her novel every space collides with each other where every space is competing with others. It illumines the reader regarding the problem of local which becomes global and places the reader in front of the unresolved question of identity, both individual and national.

WORKS CITED

Anderson, Benedict. *Imagined Community: Reflections on the Origin and Spread on Nationalism* (London, Verso, 1983 p. 15).

Bhabha, Homi K. *Nation and Narration* (London and New York, Routledge, 1990, p. 1).

Bhabha, Homi K. *Location of Culture* (London and New York, Routledge, 1994, pp. 45, 124.

Desai, Kiran. *The Inheritance of Loss* (London, Penguine, 2006).

Huddart, David. *Homi K. Bhabha* (Abingdon, Routledge, 2006, p. 113).

Rushdie, Salman. *The Moor's Last Sigh* (London, Vintage, 1996, p. 226).

Smith, Anthony David. "Nation," Microsoft® Encarta® 2007 [DVD]. Microsoft Corporation, 2006.

List of Contributors

Melissa Dennihy. Department of English, General Literature, and Rhetoric, Binghamton University, State University of New York. United States of America.

Ana Cristina Mendes. University of Lisbon Centre for English Studies, currently a Fundacao para a Ciencia e Tecnologia fellow in Portugal.

Devika. Assistant Professor, Languages Group BITS, Pilani.

Krishna Singh. Assistant Professor, Department of English, Government P.G. College, Shahdol, Madhya Pradesh.

Jackie Haque. Senior Lecturer, Tarunnessa Memorial Medical College, Gazipur, Bangladesh.

Elisa Armellino. University of Turin, Italy.

Reena Mitra. Senior Reader, Department of English, Christ Church P.G. College, Kanpur, Uttar Pradesh.

Sanghita Sen. Senior Lecturer, Department of English, Presidency College, Kolkata.

Anita Singh. Professor, Department of English, BHU, Varanasi.

Gulrez Roshan Rehman. Senior Lecturer, Department of English, Marwari College, Kisanganj, Bihar.

Kripanath Mishra. Reader in English, Sonarpur Mahavidyalaya, University of Calcutta.

Srutimala Duara. Senior Lecturer, Department of English, Handique Girls College, Guwahati, Assam

Purnendu Chatterjee. Research Scholar, Rabindra Bharati University, Kolkata.

Sharada Iyer. Head Department of English, Vasanta College for Women, Rajghat, Varanasi.

Nishi Pulugurtha. Senior Lecturer, Department of English, Brahmananda Keshab Chandra College, Kolkata.

Madhu Shalini. Senior Lecturer, Department of English, B.R.A. Bihar University, Muzaffarpur.

Beena Agrawal. Reader, Department of English, D.S. College, Aligarh.

Vandana Singh. Department of English, Patna Women's College, Patna, Bihar.

Neeta Kulshreshtha. Reader, Department of English, S.V. College, Aligarh, Agra University, Agra.

Anju Bala Agrawal. Reader, Department of English, R.C.A. Girls' P.G. College Mathura.

Arpita Chattaraj (Mukhopadhyay). Lecturer in English Presidency College, Kolkata.

Shaleen Kumar Singh. Department of English, Kisan Degree College, Uttar Pradesh.

Jati Sankar Mondal. Lecturer in English, Triveni Devi Bhalotia College Raniganj, Burdwan.